Bernard Clark began his career as an investigative TV journalist, newsreader and director for the BBC. He went on to direct several acclaimed documentaries and originated *Watchdog*, the BBC's long-running investigative series, as well as the series *Timewatch* and *Bookmark*. He then set up Clark Television, one of the first major independent production companies in the UK, producing worldwide current affairs and documentary programmes. He continues to make television series, combining this with writing. He lives in London and North Carolina.

Alex Bell is currently the adoptive mother of seven children, the foster mother of an eighth child and the guardian of a ninth. Seven of the children have Down's syndrome, one has a life-limiting condition and another is autistic, and she cares for all of them at her home in Salford, near Manchester. In 1984, at the age of 28, Alex Bell became one of the first women in the UK to adopt as a single mother. She has since created a flourishing, happy family of nine children with disabilities. Bernard Clark has spent several years with Alex and her family to turn her unique, groundbreaking story into a book.

A Mother Like Alex

One defiant woman
Nine special children

BERNARD CLARK

harper
true

harper
true

An Imprint of HarperCollins*Publishers*
77–85 Fulham Palace Road,
Hammersmith, London W6 8JB

The website address is: www.harpercollins.co.uk

First published by HarperTrue 2008

1 3 5 7 9 10 8 6 4 2

A catalogue record of this book is
available from the British Library

ISBN 978-0-00-727167-2

Printed and bound in Great Britain by
Clays Ltd, St Ives plc

Page 203 photograph by Alice White

Mixed Sources
Product group from well-managed
forests and other controlled sources
www.fsc.org Cert no. SW-COC-1806
© 1996 Forest Stewardship Council

FSC is a non-profit international organisation established to promote the
responsible management of the world's forests. Products carrying the FSC
label are independently certified to assure consumers that they come
from forests that are managed to meet the social, economic and
ecological needs of present and future generations.

Find out more about HarperCollins and the environment at
www.harpercollins.co.uk/green

Contents

'To Billy, who touched my soul'

Alex Bell

List of plates

Original portraits by Norman Long of Preston. Norman visited the Bell family on numerous occasions, went horse-riding with them, and went to Emily's adoption ceremony. His painting of Matthew has been exhibited at the National Portrait Gallery in London.

Preface

I first heard about Alex Bell in 1996 when a work colleague and his wife discovered that their new baby had Down's syndrome. The odds of that happening were 1,000 to one, it was shocking and seemed so unfair, and we all wondered how they would ever get through it.

In most families the birth of a baby with Down's syndrome changes everything, putting enormous pressure on the parents, especially the mother. Apart from the emotional traumas, there are time-consuming practical problems, including longer stays in hospital and endless discussions with social workers. And hanging over every feed and every nappy change is one harrowing question: Will the couple take their baby home? And as that question nags away, they receive little help in coming to a decision, so the discussion goes round and round – to keep or to have him or her adopted?

Then I heard that my colleague's wife had discovered a remarkable single woman near Manchester called Alex Bell, who had already adopted five children with Down's syndrome, and who might want to adopt their daughter, Chloe.

* * *

Some time later Chloe became Alex's sixth adopted child with Down's syndrome – she was to be her first daughter. As time passed it became apparent to me that this was a tragic story with an uplifting ending – as Chloe settled down happily with her new family, and continued to see her birth parents, with the encouragement of Alex. To me this was so intriguing and confounding that I kept tracks on Alex over the years that followed, eventually deciding to travel up to Manchester to talk to her about writing a book.

On greeting me at the front door, Alex played that northern conjuring trick of being bossy and friendly at the same time. 'Don't you let the cats in,' she said, without offering a hand to shake or a cheek to kiss. 'I'm at the kitchen table with a social worker. Listen in if you want, doubt if you'll learn anything.'

But I did; I learnt that Alex knew more about special needs children than the 'experts'.

To give just one example: Alex was actually talking to a postgraduate PhD researcher who was meant to be helping out with one of her adopted children, Nathan. At that time, Nathan was having terrible tantrums.

'*Bitch! Bitch!*' he would shout and swear at everyone, even at me, without knowing what it meant. He would throw chairs, slam doors.

Although working for a consultant psychologist, the researcher seemed to have little idea what was going on and wondered if Nathan might have Tourette's syndrome.

But Alex knew that wasn't the case. Nathan *chose* when to swear – and Alex knew this meant it was not Tourette's. In fact, it quickly became apparent that the researcher was writing down everything *Alex* said, rather than the other way round.

'I would let you take me for lunch,' she said when the social worker had gone, 'but Louise is coming back with the older boys

– Tom and Adrian, and Matthew's on half day off – so I promised to go to the chippy.' With that, she picked up her battered purse and headed out. 'Well, are you coming?'

I followed her out.

Louise is Alex's full-time helper, who was setting the kitchen table when we returned. She is mid-twenties, larger than life in every respect, and no less direct than Alex.

'I still remember my first day here, my first moment,' she said. 'There were seven then, watching *Bedknobs and Broomsticks* on TV. Alex took me in, and Nathan stood there in his little pyjamas with sailboats on, looked at me and went, "You. Watch this!" He pulled his pyjamas off, literally, just put them under his chin, and started Irish dancing, because that's what they were doing on the telly, and I just sort of thought, "Oh dear." So I hope you know what you're letting yourself in for.'

Adrian and Tom walked in, stood there, offered their hands, unsure about whether to shake mine. Tom was clean-shaven, good-looking, but with unfocused, rolling eyes; Adrian was shorter, definitely Down's in an old man way, mumbling, 'Nathan birthday today.' I took their hands, shook both together.

They stepped back politely, still unsure, but Alex was calling them. 'Now go and wash for dinner,' as Matthew appeared, stooping, fleshy-faced, smiling, forming a phrase.

'You want to write about me. I'm an actor.'

Matthew did know how to shake hands – with a little bow, Japanese style – looking past me at the meat pies and curry sauce.

In the afternoon I sat with Alex. She was at once open and yet wary. 'You can write what you want, but I wouldn't like anyone to get hurt. This is a big family, far bigger than you expect, birth parents, foster parents, brothers and sisters, and there are people still very raw, I suppose they always will be …'

As ever, she was hovering around the wooden kitchen table, a fashionable contrast to the cluttered units and the crayon drawings on the refrigerator that seemed to mark her off as just a housewife and cook.

I could imagine how many visitors had misjudged Alex over the years. She was fifty, looked like a college student's mum, in that netherworld between motherhood and grandmotherhood, still attractive yet anonymous, a few wrinkles but no frown lines, with round cheeks and short hair, all dominated by mischievous arched eyebrows. The face of an experienced but sardonic angel, or a senior nun who was too playful to be mother superior, she was almost deliberately disarming. So my guard was down when she asked the difficult, the delicate question.

'Why do you want to write a book about us?'

'Why?'

'Yes, why?'

Louise had walked in and I already knew better than to soft-soap the two of them.

'I just think it's a great story,' I tried.

They glanced at each other. Not good enough.

'Well, nine Down's kids, I mean that is pretty special—'

'Only seven are Down's,' corrected Louise.

'And you've only met three – the most polite ones …' Alex was filling the kettle.

My initial reaction when I first heard of Alex's family had been instinctive: a single woman taking on nine very difficult, disabled children, that's got to be a 'triumph-over-the-odds' tale, an epic saga of resolution and courage. I felt intrigued but now couldn't work out why.

I looked out of the kitchen window at a grey afternoon; a 14-year-old boy with a rubbery, grinning face had arrived back from school in a white minibus; a thin man was unloading a wheelchair containing what appeared to be small mop of fluffy blonde hair; a girl in a yellow dress was waltzing down the path from a taxi, followed by a very pretty Down's girl in jeans, scowling and trying to pull her hand away from the driver …

'That's Chloe,' said Alex, waving hello through the window.

Chloe poked out her tongue, screwed up her face – and then I did know why I wanted to write the book.

It was about facing demons.

I remembered the first time I heard about Alex. My sense of fascination concerned her being drawn to children most people shied away from, if not fled from, that she would eagerly go where we fear to tread. How could this be? Though I knew very little about Down's syndrome, I assumed 'disfigurement, ugliness, revulsion' – why did she not feel the same? And there was more. This single woman looked after all these seemingly hopeless ogres as a self-supporting family – what could that actually look like? I was mystified. But also captivated.

That afternoon when I saw 8-year old Chloe through the window – bright-eyed, bad-tempered, gorgeous – I finally realised what had attracted me to the story. Alex Bell had no fear. She was like one of those battlefield commanders who lead from the front, almost willing the bullets to strike them. Indeed she sought after the very thing we ran from, and I wanted to understand. And anyway, as if to ridicule my miserable preconceptions, it turned out that the disfigured beast I expected was, instead, beautiful. As were Tom and Adrian and Matthew – not necessarily physically beautiful like Chloe, but beautiful from the inside.

Alex read my thoughts. 'I think they're beautiful, you know.' And I did know.

* * *

When I look back on that moment, two years ago, I realise that my focus began to shift from admiration for Alex to fascination with her children, many of them now grown up. Because of that, I was gradually, and happily, drawn into the innocent, open-hearted world of people with Down's, far richer and more engaging than the usual self-conscious interactions of everyday life. I got to know Alex's family through an emotional dimension, and they became my family as well.

Take Simon, for instance, who can neither walk nor talk. How is it that every time we meet I feel a special joy in his presence? All he ever says is 'Apple pie, apple pie,' but he seems to relish all that goes on around him, and dispense love as his own exclusive gift.

And what about Adrian? No one could invent him. Last August, when we met at a special needs fun park near Bristol, as he shook my hand he mumbled, 'Fifty-seven today, Bernard, fifty-seven ...' That was true. It *was* my 57th birthday. But how could he know? Granted, he may have overheard me mention my date of birth to Louise a year or so earlier during a random conversation, but this is a guy who can hardly think, let alone remember and then calculate my age. How does he do it? Indeed, how?

Then there's Andrew, the ultimate deaf-dumb-blind pinball wizard – except that he's not deaf. The size of a 5-year-old at 17, with a mental age of 12 months, but happy as a sandboy listening to loud music on his headphones, with more emotional nerve-ends than a symphony orchestra.

'Hiya,' he says. 'Hiya,' knowing that you're there only by some kind of sixth sense.

In the next two years I was to embark on a voyage of discovery that took me into the heart of an extraordinary family.

During that time I've learnt a lot. I've learnt, especially, that Down's people are still people. Some of them may have flatter faces, wider necks or shorter legs than the rest of us, some of them may babble and need forever to wear nappies, but they connect soul-to-soul, which is the hallmark of being part of humankind. At least, they connect with me, because I learnt to let it happen. I learnt you don't have to use words to communicate; you can touch or smile, grimace or groan, or just feel. Especially feel. And it's fun, pure fun. That's probably the loveliest discovery of writing this book. These people are fun. Pretty well always.

In the early days of research I thought of Alex as an angel, dealing on a daily basis with tragedy, but gradually the penny dropped. She's lucky. And I have also been lucky. To meet nine of the nicest, weirdest, toughest, funniest, most generous, open, honest, wackiest, happiest people on the planet. Yes, happiest, because tragedy's a state of mind, our minds, not theirs.

So that was the final thing I learnt: They're lucky, too.

Chapter One

The Bell family kitchen table

The Bell family home is a brick-built modern house at the end of a pot-holed lane, between a fast commuter road and the steep Irwell valley in Clifton Park, a windswept suburb of Manchester. From the front it seems to be single storey, perhaps four bedrooms, but with an element of Alice in Wonderland because at the back there's another whole floor hidden down the hillside, adding up to a total of ten bedrooms.

Most families have a gathering area, a focal point, a coming-and-going 'central station', and the Bell family are no exception. The kitchen table – big, wooden, beaten every day, but indestructible – is the heart of their universe. Each evening it groans under the Bell family tea – disjointed, chaotic, messy and noisy. Very noisy. But to Alex, it's the sound of music.

'How was school, today?'

'Another sausage, Tom …?'

'Mummy, who was Shakespeare …?'

'Callum, slow down, slow down …'

'James Bond on tonight …'

'Can I have a drink, please?'

'I'm Captain Hook, me …'

'Apple pie! Apple pie! Apple—'

'Stop shouting, Simon.'

'Did you know that Sir Matt Busby almost died in an air crash?'

That last question comes from Matthew, Alex's first adopted son, now 25, who has taken a whole minute to remove the top from a strawberry yoghurt carton. Matthew talks to no one in particular. Just as well, because no one has the slightest idea what he means, except for 9-year-old Emily, and she doesn't care. Emily has neurofibromatosis, a life-threatening genetic disorder of the nervous system, the only one of Alex's nine children who is not Down's syndrome or autistic, and she can't see Matthew because he's on her left, the side of her 'poorly eye'.

Every fragmented, guttural half-sentence, every nod and grunt, even the bolting down of food at breakneck speed, is a fairy-tale miracle, as Alex knows. This is her family, chosen one by one, from pictures in adoption magazines thumbed through at this very table.

'Yah-yah-yah-yah-yah-yah!' Simon wants a hug. Nathan rams a fork into his Winnie-the-Pooh mat and shouts 'You're joking.' Chloe gets up for the tenth time for no reason – 'Chloe, if you want ice cream, sit down ...'

The Bell family are like every other family in the land – and absolutely unlike any family anywhere, nine extraordinary human characters, rushing through a tea of macaroni while talking or bawling across each other. The youngest is 8, the eldest 29, two little girls, seven males, except one is missing – Andrew, who can't feed himself, and who is flopped in his cot, listening to his CDs, in a world of his own.

As usual, tea is at five o'clock. Alex wanders around behind each chunky chair, putting down plastic bowls, fulfilled, content, in charge, at one with her family. '*In*, Tom, *in*.'

Thomas, 23 this year, with his own paper round, has let his tongue protrude. He slips it back in. The table goes quiet as pudding takes over. Alex steps back, calculating logistics for the evening.

'It's Tuesday, Down's night at the Pool. Debbie can take Chloe and Emily to Swinton Baths, but Nathan's got an ear infection. Callum's key worker, Angie, is coming at 6.30 – must tell her he's been at the curtains again. Matthew has theatre practice in Bolton. [Bolton's about five miles from Clifton Park.] I could take Adrian with me, but he'll want to be back for the James Bond film – it's *For Your Eyes Only* – at eight. What about the advertising leaflets Tom will need to hand out during his paper round …?'

While Alex ponders, Chloe gets up again, as Emily says, 'Need toilet, Mum.'

'No you don't,' replies Alex, 'and sit down, Chloe.' She carries on making her plans. 'If Louise drops Matthew off on her way home, I can feed Andrew, sort out Tom's papers, and still have time to get started on the ironing – all six foot of it …'

The phone rings, a heavy old BT handpiece anchored to the wall by the front door. Matthew plays receptionist, chatting about his day, but in walking the ten feet from the cluttered lobby back to the kitchen he forgets who is calling.

It's Nathan's birth mother, Sue. Nathan is 18 years old, mercurial, and still struggling through adolescence in his own inimitable, often tempestuous way.

'How is his ear infection?' Sue asks. 'Are the antibiotics working?'

'The ear's better, only wish it could do something for his temper,' Alex tells her, while reaching up for the key to let Angie in – it's already 6.30. For obvious reasons any keys need to be kept in a safe place and out of reach – on a top shelf.

The main problem is Chloe. She's 'a runner'. If the keys were left in the door, she'd be out and off. (Tom used to be even worse, but has settled down now.) The keys are actually at eye-level, to the right of the front door, next to an A3-sized chocolate-box-style studio photo of Alex's parents, and all their grandchildren including Alex's nephews and nieces, and her own adopted children – Matthew, Simon, Adrian and Nathan. But not Alex – she doesn't like being photographed.

As she opens the door for Angie, Alex remembers something else. 'The cats, the cats,' she gasps, but it's too late: Max and Milly race past from the dark and rain outside and dart under the kitchen table.

'Callum's been chewing at the curtains,' Alex mentions to Angie, then continues down the phone to Sue, 'Yeah, the green ones that matched the sofa.'

Back in the kitchen, Adrian is clearing up – sort of. Short, stocky, self-contained, he's 29 years old. He's putting the polka-dotted beakers and plates in neat rows by the side of the sink, but then loses his way, so he pushes Simon in his wheelchair, past the lifesize mural of Elvis by the shiny black fridge, off to watch TV in the playroom that's painted from floor to ceiling as a wild animal jungle.

Abruptly, the kitchen is empty. All that remains are the multicoloured place-mats: Piglet, Eeyore, Tigger, Winnie-the-Pooh with Nathan's fork marks, and the cats refusing to be caught under the table. The Bell family have dispersed around their huge, rambling house. Alex puts the kettle on.

After the unremitting in-your-face noise of the last half-hour, the quiet, the calm, is astonishing. Where is everyone?

'Looking after each other,' Alex replies, and leans back against the work-surface, waiting for the kettle to boil.

There are piles everywhere. In the far corner, behind the microwave, a spreading pile of files and letters, many in official brown envelopes. Along the work-surface, a pile of children's CDs and videos, scattered around a bright pink player; and then, over by the door from which a menacing black plastic spider hangs, a pile of photos and a couple of albums: a magazine wants to publish a story and Alex must play picture editor.

'This kitchen table sees a lot of life. It's my office, where I meet social workers, and where I fill in forms, write letters. I have boxes of them – you can't take on kids like these without paper-work.'

At these moments, when everyone is elsewhere, Alex has an introverted, almost guilty, serenity – as if a snatched minute of peace is sinful. Then Simon screeches for an unknown reason, joyful but loud, and any guilt is gone.

'A lot of the social workers I've dealt with are brave, they have to be to take on such difficult cases, but they can't understand, can't "get it". They don't ask me "why?" It's too big a word, it would be impolite, but I know they're wondering. Why? Why does she want these kids? But if they did ask, I couldn't help them, not in social-worker-ese, even if they came to tea, saw what you've seen. They'd see turmoil, hardship, trauma, not a big happy fam-ily who are simply the most fascinating, satisfying kids – people – anyone could ever find.'

The kettle boils. Nathan drifts in from talking to his birth mother, sits down, says, 'I'm Captain Hook – arrrgh!'

Alex takes no notice. And when Emily puts her tousled head over the half door that keeps her in the playroom to say, 'Mummy, my foot hurts …' Alex fills the teapot – and still takes no notice. She's a past master at pacing herself and preserving her energy. Otherwise she would have worn herself out years ago.

'I always say to social workers that I don't do easy. Yes, all of these kids have had hard times, dreadful times, having-me-in-tears times, all of them, because they're difficult little beings. But I don't take them on for "oh isn't it a shame", because "isn't it a shame" doesn't last for long.

'No. I take them on because they need permanence, because they need a family, and the children I take on are very complex children who might otherwise stay in the care system. And it fascinates me to work out how they are who they are – because they're all so different.'

The tea is ready and she pours us both a cup. I've quickly come to realise that Alex combines confidence with reticence. She's happier doing things than talking about them. She talks best while ironing, driving, making sandwiches, tidying the kitchen, but when the tea is made, and she sits down at her kitchen table, a diffidence, a shyness, creeps in. Then she notices the leaflets for Tom's paper round beside the cooker.

'The kitchen table is our assembly line, too.' She licks her fingers to separate the thin sheets, and begins dealing them into piles, ready to be inserted into tomorrow's *Salford Advertiser*.

'My doctor is lovely, but he probably thinks that I should be sectioned. Every time I go for an adoption medical he'll say, "Oh my God, Alex, why? Why are you taking another child?" And the last time I said to him, "Martin, do you remember when you were a young man and you had a burn inside you to be a doctor – that you wanted it so much that it burnt you?" And he said, "Yeah I do remember that." I said, "Well, yours has gone, but I've still got my burn." And he laughed.'

Nathan shouts to himself, 'You must be joking,' as Debbie, the calm-faced, diminutive lady-who-cleans (not the Cleaner – 'she'd feel insulted,' says Alex) arrives to take the girls swimming.

Louise comes upstairs with Matthew – they're off to the theatre. Debbie will pick him up on the way back from the baths.

The phone rings – they ignore it, but Simon shrieks, until Alex says, 'It's all right, Simon, we can hear it ringing.'

Humanity ebbs and flows, then suddenly, with the cars gone, Simon in bed and Adrian in front of James Bond on ITV, the house is quiet again. Alex's day of spinning plates and juggling schedules is coming to an end. It's seven o'clock; in two hours the swimming party will be back to go to bed, but until then there's a luxurious peace. Along the corridor, a pair of tiny trainers are upturned on the patterned carpet, a tracksuit top hangs from the banister, all the lights are on.

Alex stops dealing the leaflets and wanders through to pick up Andrew, lifting him from his cot, cuddling him close as she carries him back to the kitchen for feeding. It's his one-to-one moment, the special time of his day when he can know the contact of another person, warm human softness through his skin.

Andrew is almost impossibly small and delicate, with fluffy blond hair and ruddy red lips and cheeks. He can't see, can't walk or really talk, probably can't think. But he can feel, he can sense that he's secure, loved, that he's part of a family who are committed to him for the rest of his too-short life.

The odds of his living to be 17 were millions-to-one. Apart from cerebral palsy, Andrew's digestive system does not properly digest, so he can't 'thrive', hence he's terribly fragile. Some of his organs are in the wrong place – for instance his bladder is back to front. Each and every day is a miracle, every breath a bonus.

And if the family of which he is a part may be strange – a single mother and eight other boisterous people with every disability in the spectrum – Andrew doesn't care. The world he knows is far better than could ever have been expected.

'Stop it, Andrew.'

As she feeds him with a spoon, Alex uses her free arm to push back his hand that has been pinching her leg. It's the only movement he can control, the only way he can express himself, but he does pinch hard. Andrew giggles, he's got a reaction, now he can concentrate on swallowing.

Alex shrugs. 'You should see the bruises.' But they're a small price to pay for being the centre of a young man's world. That's her commitment, that's her purpose, that's the reason for the Bell family, for any family – being there for each other.

The house is hushed now. Only the sound of Andrew gulping, and gunfire on a distant TV; even cats Max and Milly have gone to sleep outside in the shed.

Alex folds Andrew back in his cot with a soft 'goodnight', then picks up some of the six-foot pile of ironing and drops it on the kitchen table. In her practised hand the iron caresses a set of Jungle Book pyjamas, smoothing out the wrinkles from a day of bumps and scrapes.

Alex smiles slightly at a fleeting memory, before reaching for a pair of children's jeans. She's managed to iron two inches of the pile. Only five foot ten inches to go before bedtime.

So much ironing for so many children. And so many memories.

Chapter Two

A lad called Billy

Alex Bell was born ten years after the end of the Second World War on 31 May 1955 to Donald and Doris Bell. Her birthday should have been in June, she jokes, but her mother had a cough.

In Swinton, the suburb of Manchester where she was brought up, everything seemed to be closing in the 1950s and 60s. The pits were closing; the mills and factories closing; and Swinton town centre was being bulldozed to make way for a concrete centre, with grey car parks and a supermarket. The town wasn't down-trodden, it was more passed by – Swinton is divided by motorways, providing good commuter roads for the jobs and clubs in Manchester. It was and still is old-fashioned, neither working class nor middle class. In a class of its own, the people of Swinton would say.

Alex always thought Donald was a horrible name – 'Don … old' – and says her father had a terrible childhood.

'His mum died in childbirth – that's pretty sad, isn't it – he was handed around between all these relatives, and brought up by his dad and his grandma, so he was a spoilt only child. He was from Salford, one of the worst parts, down Langworthy Road, the

Coronation Street part – Seedley. It was a real slum at the time but going very upmarket now – even the BBC are going there.

'Dad was a grammar school boy who got way above his station in life. My granddad, who brought him up, was a master cobbler and one of my earliest memories is going in my granddad's shop. He had those wooden feet they used to have all over the shop, so you never went in for a pair of shoes. He just made the shoes to fit your foot, because he had a wooden model of your foot. I can remember his shop smelt of leather. He was called Frank Bell, a lovely old fellow. He died when I was tiny.

'I never liked my dad. He was never satisfied with what he had and he always wanted everyone else to improve themselves and be better. He had a well-paid job at Littlewoods Pools and ended up a Tory councillor, but it was like he had this arrogant air that he was better than everyone else, and I never liked him because of that. He was a magistrate as well – very hard on anyone that hurt children or animals, wicked on them, which is right.

'But I used to say to him, "Why do you think you should be a magistrate? Why do you feel superior?"

'We lived in an ordinary three-bedroom semi, and we were very lucky because we always had a car, as long as I can remember – and not many people did have cars. And we had a dog for me fifth birthday – Prince, a bull mastiff. I used to ride him, great big thing.

'Dad used to shout a lot and he was always at work, or doing his TA. He would wear a uniform, playing at soldiers in the Territorials, it was one-upmanship on everybody else, and I never liked that, me. Because I'm dead down and basic.

'He was 70, I think, when he died – 1994 – I was about 38, and I remember Mum saying, "I've got a bit of freedom now." He was very hard work, he was one of those people who came in, expected his food on the table, expected his children in bed before he got home, and I don't think that's particularly nice for a father, do you? I remember him as a person you just saw on a Sunday that you had to be quiet for.

'I think my mum probably loved him at one time but that later it was very much habit. A lot of marriages are habit and I think my mum used to think, "Well, he brings in the money," and she never did, and it was his house. I don't think they were happy, I don't think they were happily married.

'So I decided when I was 8 years old that I was never getting married. Because I didn't think much of it, if that's all it was about, and I've still not changed my mind. I watched me parents and thought, there's nothing that appeals to me about marriage. I'm sure you do see some happy marriages but it doesn't appeal to me and it never has done. It was a definite decision, and I don't usually waver.'

At the age of 10, Alex went to see *The Sound of Music* and was captivated. She went to see it again the next week – and after that thirty or forty times – and wanted to be Julie Andrews – or at least she wanted to be Maria, the novice nun who becomes the adoptive mother of the seven Von Trapp children, to inherit a ready-made family without necessarily having to get married and give birth. To this day, she will gesture to her family, all nine of them sitting around the kitchen table and affectionately say, 'I blame the NUN.'

If Alex's father was autocratic and dictatorial – one of the generation who habitually dismissed or undermined women, especially freethinking daughters – her mother was very different, a formidable woman. Statuesque, though not tall, she commanded affection and respect, because she 'got on with people, and things, in her own way'. While, like Alex later, she had a no-nonsense approach to life, she was a bulwark of help and support to Alex as she grew up.

'My mother was called Doris – another horrible name. She was also born in 1924 – in fact there was only nine days between them. She was a care home manager for old people, and when I was 11 I lived in the old people's home with her. We had a flat there. We all used to go home to where me dad was at weekends, but she used to live in the old people's home from Monday to Friday.

'It was called the Limes. It's still there in Swinton. It put me right off old people. I don't dislike them, but they were always dying, as soon as you got friendly with one of them. I used to work there and get up in the morning, lay the table for breakfast, help the old people come down and have breakfast with them. I'd go off to school, come back, talk to them and play games with them. They were lovely.

'There was one old lady – I loved her to bits – called Mrs Jones, who taught me to knit. Then one night she died. I do remember them dying in the night, because the night nurse used to get me mum up, but I didn't know who until the next morning, when they didn't come down to breakfast.

'Mum used to do a lot of WVS work, and was forever doing meals on wheels – you used to burn your thumbs on the gravy because in those days it was really hot – they used to feed them properly.

'I went to an ordinary primary school, then to a private school, Ash Lea. I loved it there. It was three-quarters Jewish and I was among the quarter that wasn't. It was just right for me, but my mum and dad never went on holiday while I was there. They really struggled to pay the fees, and then all I wanted to do was look after kids. For me dad that must have been very sad, because I had already made my major decision when I was 13.

'I saw other families and thought, this isn't what I'm going to do, but I *did* want kids. I'd never, never, never, ever *not* want to have kids. And one day when I was 13 it became clear.'

The day her life changed.

Her 'Billy Moment'.

It happened on a grey ward, on a visit to the forbidding Victorian monolith that was Swinton Hospital in 1968, as she wandered with her mother through the forever-stay hospital ward, past the Down's patients and long-term disabled, in short socks and school uniform. The sounds of that ward – the grunts, whoops and murmurs – and the stale hospital smells still haunt her today.

'They were in a wide, grey, square day room – the big boys. And they were wandering around, with bibs on, dribbling all over the place, nappies hanging out. It was like hell …'

And it was in this hell that she met a lad called Billy.

'Billy was the lad that changed my life. I shall be eternally grateful. He must have been in his thirties, and he was built like a wall. He was huge, he was fat, he was slobbery, he had this plastic bib on – I can smell the plastic even now when I think about it, I can smell the plastic and I can see the dribble dribbling down this disgusting plastic bib.'

Alex's mother took sweets to the inmates one afternoon a week, touring the ward-cum-dayroom-cum-secure unit that was the lock-away place of the adult imbeciles, chatting as she went.

Alex never asked her mother the purpose of her visits. She just went. Which was, and sometimes still is, the special down-to-earthness of drizzly Manchester – where normal folk still find space in their hearts for the neighbours, and the neighbour's neighbour, not out of duty but because of 'involvement'. Mrs Bell was definitely like that.

The 1960s sub-normality wards held 118 men, women and a few children, segregated by 'sex and temper', slumped on daybeds, or sat to attention, vacant, watching but not seeing, with bowl-shaped hair, Mongoloid. Banished. Into this scene – the nightmare underbelly of draconian Health Service Acts, kept out of sight to be out of mind – strolled the imposing figure of Mrs Bell, with Alex tagging along in uniform, mildly curious, on just another boring Swinton after-school.

'Of course me mum, "the toffee lady", took it all in her stride, because she did this every week and it was nothing new to her; she was like, "Here you are, Billy, here's your sweets." And then he found me, and lunged towards me, and I'm stood behind me mum thinking, "Oh my God, what is this?"'

'And this Billy just grabbed me, because he assumed I had sweets for him, he grabbed me, this adult man, who was about four times my size, and the plastic bib was all round me, and it was horrendous, and he got me in this bear-hug, because it was affection to him, and I was being squeezed to death, until the nurses got Billy off me.

'After that I ran out of the building, I was physically sick, because I was repulsed by what I'd seen and what had happened to me. I remember me mum coming out saying, "Oh you're here, are you?"'

'And I said, "Yeah, don't ever, ever, ever take me anywhere like that again. Why didn't you tell me what it was?"'

'And she only said one thing – it was all she ever said to me. "They're just babies in big bodies, they don't hurt you." She said, "Come on, we'll go home," and nothing was said about that experience again. For her it was finished.'

But not for Alex.

The transformation in her psyche that followed is a mystery, a pure somersault in all her feelings and attitudes. She spent the next week thinking about what she'd seen, worrying about it, uneasy with her reactions, appalled at her revulsion.

She had already sensed that there was something very different about Billy and people like him – as if they were strange but wonderful beings from another planet. And without even realising it, her initial fear was quickly turning to fascination.

'When the nurses said, "Come on, Billy, leave her alone," you realised that he must have bounded at lots of people and loved them in his way. But I was physically sick because of this affection and it was horrendous. How can you forget something like that? I considered it for the whole week and eventually I came round to thinking like my mum; thinking that this wasn't anything to be worried about, these people weren't there to hurt you.'

Thirty-five years later, the sub-normality ward is no more, Swinton Hospital has gone, demolished in the 1980s, and Billy has slipped unceremoniously into oblivion, perhaps cremated by efficient administrators and scattered anonymously in the sharp Pennine winds. But his being lingers, beyond a memory, as an unwitting but ever-changing presence in Alex's life.

'If I'd been prepared it might never have affected me so much. It was totally unexpected, that's why it caused such an impression upon me. I couldn't believe that society had locked these people away, so totally that I didn't even know about them. And I thought it's ridiculous, and I'd been ridiculous. Billy didn't mean me any harm, he wasn't dangerous, he didn't hurt me – it's my reaction that was the problem.'

So why *had* society locked them away? Why hadn't she seen them before? What was the big secret? Who were they? How do they work?

This isn't merely remembering the trauma of meeting Billy. Alex relives it, and has been reliving it for thirty-five years, because it's her way of never forgetting how people still react, deep inside, to encountering Down's syndrome. The shock of that face-to-flat-fleshy-face first encounter – astonishment, confusion, fear, horror, disgust, alienation – still occurs thousands of times a day somewhere in the world, as a new generation of children, supposedly enlightened, draw their hands back and gasp. But there is also a minority in whom horror and shock turns to wonderment and fascination, the minority who are drawn in, attracted, infatuated. People like Alex.

She went back to the hospital and spoke to the Matron – they still had matrons in those days – and asked to work there. It was hardly surprising that the Matron's response was firm – and negative.

'You're a 13-year-old little girl,' she replied. 'Go away.'

But this simply made Alex more determined. 'No, this is where I've got to come and work,' she insisted.

Again she received a sharp rebuke and a one-way escort to the front door. But Alex would not be put off.

'I pestered that woman to death,' Alex remembers. 'I'd knock on her door and say, "I do want to work here, this is where I want to be."'

Eventually the Matron capitulated and gave her a supervised shift on the baby ward, once a week after school – 'probably just to get rid of me'.

The 13-year-old Alex bustled around the wards, precocious and practical, but self-consciously hiding a growing commitment to severely disabled people. A churchgoing Christian might say she had a 'revelation', or 'a calling' from God, but the truth is simpler: Alex was awestruck by her first violent reaction, fascinated by what had occurred within. She had a hunger to understand why people were like this, she couldn't stop reading – she borrowed every book on disability in the Swinton Library, and then sent off for more, always questioning.

'Seeing their faces, the way they smiled, the way they laughed, waved their arms and shook their heads was like seeing a roomful of friendly aliens. If I'd met a group of green men, the fascination would have been less. Like being burnt, but not being able to get away from the fire, I went from one extreme of the spectrum to the other – from "yuk" to an enthralling new world.'

Alex wasn't being voyeuristic, she was seeing each person as an individual, looking past the deformities, the grunts and institutionalised anonymity, to a human being with feelings. Which was almost subversive at the time.

Until then, many children born with Down's syndrome never left hospital. The authorities took charge, persuading parents that it would be best for all concerned, including 'the unfortunate child', if the hospital got on with the job – 'Have another baby, sorry this one didn't work out'. And so the mother would leave hospital numb and empty-handed, and gradually the pain would ebb away, until the memory was contained in a place marked 'don't go there'. Such children had no legal rights. The law did not recognise them – dogs were better protected than 'Mongols'.*

* * *

*The term Mongol was originally coined as a racial category to describe the distinctive appearance of the Mongolian people of East Asia, but from Victorian times until the 1960s and even 1970s it was also still being used as a synonym for people with Down's syndrome, and also as a generic insult meaning 'idiot'. The association with Down's was largely to do with their 'different' facial appearance which superfically has some resemblance to Mongolian facial characteristics (for example, almond-shaped eyes caused by a skin fold of the upper eyelid, and upslanting palpebral fissures – the separation between the upper and lower eyelids).

Swinton Home – only later was it called Swinton Hospital – became an institution for 'mental defectives' in the 1930s, and was considered advanced by the standards of the time. Originally the building had been part of the Industrial School, a magnificent Victorian manorial house for orphans and 'the children of help-less penury'. In 1850 Charles Dickens christened it the Paupers' Palace – 'an easy distance of five miles from the great Cotton Capital (Manchester), on the road to the great Cotton Port (Liverpool), a splendid brick edifice that is generally mistaken for a wealthy nobleman's residence'.

In 1927, in a stunning act of municipal vandalism, the Industrial School was demolished, along with many of the enlightened social attitudes of the North West of England during Victoria's reign. Swinton Hospital remained, now charged to detain in legal custody 'mental defectives and incapable patients neglected by persons naturally able to act for them'.

Examination of the meticulously documented Register of Mechanical Restraints from the 1950s gives a flavour of the place: methods used include 'splints on both arms, to be tied in a sheet'. Staff were instructed that some patients should be 'netted in bed at night' fastened to a chain, 'gently and loosely, like a baby'. Others were to be 'restrained to a chair using a pinafore', a method that became known as 'restraint jacketing', and later a strait jacket.

So it was that the patients/inmates/imbeciles, many of them 'bedfast', sat in hospital for years, were fed, watered, washed, given rudimentary medical treatment, while everyone waited for them to die and the hospital could write a sad but cursory letter implying that nature had run its course. 'Bronco Pneumonia' was the standard entry on the death certificate.

This wasn't seen as cruel, because it wasn't seen at all. Family and friends were essentially prohibited – the only entry in the visitor's book was by the official guardians, known as the Visitors of Institutions for Mental Defectives for the County of Lancaster, who came twice a year, invariably stating, 'We the undersigned certify that everything is satisfactory.'

Into this world 'at the dark end of the furthest corridor' came Alex, at first one afternoon a week straight from school into the baby ward.

'I used to take them for walks and bath them and feed them and put them to bed and all those kind of things. I read to them, played games, just sat with them. I used to go every day at one time, weekends, every weekend, I spent every spare moment there.'

Attitudes were softening at that time, the late 1960s. Although the hospital administrators continued with their 'lock 'em away' policy, the staff, in particular the nurses, were stirring, and welcomed Alex – up to a point.

Individuals who had been called cretins, imbeciles, Mongols, inmates, now became 'long-stay patients', but were still not officially recognised as autonomous human beings or accorded legal rights. Alex was allowed to entertain them, but education, however cursory, would be wasted, and might even be disruptive. And Alex was discouraged from emotional attachments.

'You were warned they can die at any minute, so don't get involved. But I *was* involved. I can remember certain kids, who I know now as adults, and they were smashing kids, I can remember smiles, the smiles are the things that you remember about kids that don't speak, their smiles.'

It was thought that they could die at any minute because half of them were born with holes in the heart. In the 1960s, before such heart operations on Down's babies became routine and safe, heart defects took a terrible toll of Down's teenagers – so they did, indeed, literally drop dead. Now, of course, with the holes being patched up soon after birth, that's definitely no longer the case.

As for children with cerebral palsy and encephalitis, they were simply left to die, even in the late 1960s. For instance, the techniques for draining fluid from the brain were not that good. Alex has stories of kids with heads that grew so big they could not lift them off the pillow. This wasn't because the nurses were heartless – it was simply the way medicine was.

Down's kids were considered 'uneducable', unable to learn, so they sat in rows of seats 'like pieces of meat'. Some would be like this literally for years. Those who 'wandered' were ordered back to their beds. A select few might be allowed to clean dishes in the hospital kitchen, or set the table in the dining room, but even the brightest never went out. They would ask Alex what it was like to travel on a bus, go shopping, or about the animals she had at home.

And all the while Alex couldn't get enough: she would go every night after school, and for the whole weekend, bustling round the wards in her blue and silver school frock, a sight that remains etched into the ward nurses' memories.

'I met one of the nurses recently, in a restaurant, and I was with five of my kids. The nurses weren't "Nurse whatever" then – it was Jones or Smith, that's how they called each other, by surnames, and I think her name was Robinson. She was in the restaurant looking at me and I was in the restaurant looking at her, and eventually I went over and she said, "Yeah, I remember you, you're Alex."

'And I said, "Yeah, look what I've got now," pointing to my five kids. And she said, "I'm not bloody surprised."

'They were nice, they were lovely caring nurses, but I never once, in all the time I was there, saw a parent visit.'

*   *   *

During the 1960s, investigative television and independent, more robust journalism began lifting the veil. A series of scandals nagged at the nation's conscience.* In that single decade, ignorance became disbelief, became disquiet, became impotence, became shame. Followed by anger and, at last, action.

Just like the transformation Alex experienced, there was a transformation of attitudes to 'Mongolism' that was occurring in the wider society at that time, to the public and the government, where revulsion was being recognised, reconsidered, dealt with – and one day would be turned into enlightened care.

Crucially, under the 1971 Education (Handicapped Children) Act, responsibility for 'handicapped' children would be transferred from the Ministry of Health to the Department of Education. This seemingly bureaucratic nicety changed everything. Mongolism would be called Down's syndrome, after scientist John Langdon Down, who identified the condition 100 years earlier. Special schools were to be established, not just to contain but to educate, and Down's patients would have rights, albeit limited, but in the eyes of the law they would now be treated as people whose 'special needs' should be catered for and respected.

A revolution had begun and Alex Bell was ready to reap the whirlwind.

---

* Similar scandals have been exposed more recently, such as children with serious mental or physical deformities in Romania or Albania being treated like animals or worse, locked in cells and left to rot.

Chapter Three

'Von Trapped, but happy'

In 1972 at the age of 17 Alex left school, wondering about a career – with only one consideration: She wanted to continue the hospital work full-time, to work with special needs children, and her choice was to go into nursing, the social services or teaching.

'I'd got my O levels, went on to sixth-form college, which was part of a grammar school, then left there to study social work.

'But the reason why I didn't become a social worker was that I did this two-year course and had a placement in Preston. One day we had to clear a house out that an old lady had lived in and died, and all they did, the social services, was to get a skip in front of her house and throw all her stuff in the skip. And I'm picking things up out of the skip like her wedding photos and saying, "You can't throw this away – this is this lady's life," and all the social workers said, "Just put 'em in skip."

'I thought, I can't do this, I can't, I can't disown a person like this and throw them in a skip, and that's what made me think I can't do social work. If that's what it was all about, I couldn't do it.

'At the end of this two-year course you had to make a decision – what next?

'I was still living at home and my dad wouldn't let me go into nursing. He said nursing was "all bums and noses, there's no future in nursing". But he was quite happy when I said, "Right, I'll go into teaching."

'"Yeah," he said, "yeah. I can tell people that you're a teacher – I don't mind that." So I went into teaching. But for special needs only. I went to Preston Poly for three years and it was teacher training where the main course was "mental handicap", as it was known then. Other people did biology and art, I did mental handicap. Then I just applied to Salford Education Committee, and they took me on to their pool of teachers.

'But after about a year, when I was about 22, I went to Elmstead School for Special Needs as a class teacher. I loved that, the headmistress was all right – she could eat three Cadbury's Creme Eggs in one go, she could put them all in her mouth together, that's all I can remember about her really.

'Elmstead was where I learnt everything I had to learn about the kids. I was there for eleven years. I only ever wanted to be a class teacher. I had no ambition to go into paperwork, because that's what it is if you get promoted. You aren't with the kids, are you?'

For Alex it was the perfect job. She taught a class of nine wriggling, impossible, fascinating, frustrating, surprising, wonderful special-needs children, no longer 'uneducable', now just 'pupils'.

There was, however, a problem.

'I needed them with me all the time. I hated to see them go home at night. It was like, "Oh they've gone and left me, I'm all on my own in this classroom and that's not what I want" – it wasn't enough.'

She loved them, she adored having them at home with her, they gave her purpose – otherwise weekends stretched out. The company of real live laughing, needy, fascinating human souls was way better than sewing curtains or watching ITV. And when you're young, and everything is possible, you don't want to wait until next weekend, or tomorrow night. The children were Alex's entire world. She had a social life, there were a few boyfriends, holidays, but her thoughts were always the same: when could she get back to the school, to the kids?

Alex already knew that she didn't want to follow the conventional route of marriage with children.

'I've never had this deep urge to pass on my genes, which is what most people have children for, but I don't think bad eyes and bad veins, which I got from my mum and dad, are worth passing on to anybody.'

Gradually, Alex realised that she could satisfy two needs at once: the children's need to be supervised after school and at weekends, if only to relieve parents, and her need to be with children more of the time. Alex was now 21, a qualified teacher, but she couldn't look after such profoundly disabled children at her parents' home, not while living with her sceptical father. So she moved into her own house.

'That's when I started to take kids back home at night and for weekends. Parents were coming to me and saying, "There's nowhere for our kids, we can't have a night off, we're going away for the weekend, will you have them?"

'I'd say, "Of course, no problem." I used to have four, five kids at weekends and never think twice about it. It wouldn't be possible now – what with risk assessments – my God, now they'd be going mad at the things I did with the kids.'

The 'things' Alex was doing included: taking the children home without having a personal criminal check; having more than two in the car at once; allowing them to sleep three in a bed;

or not writing up dozens of forms – were perfectly normal then, but things that wouldn't, of course, be allowed nowadays.

Parents in the Swinton area tell colourful stories of Alex Bell's determination – some call it near madness – to give the special needs children more exciting, normal lives. She was pushing at the boundaries, taking the new rules further than her head-mistress, and the traditional authorities, considered sensible. But Alex had a vital group of allies – the parents. The law now put them in charge and they supported Alex's rebellious energy, mainly because the kids had such a great time.

Alex was in her element, playing a role from her youth: at long last she could be Maria Von Trapp for real. She was also learning how far it was possible to go with profoundly disabled children, and what the limits were on them being out in society safely.

'We did have a few major disasters,' she says, remembering taking four kids on her own to Blackpool seafront for the week-end. Two were severely autistic children, another was a girl who walked round with her eyes closed – nothing wrong with her eye-sight, she just wouldn't open her eyes.

This was illumination week, the busiest week in Blackpool's calendar, and the whole city was heaving with hundreds of thou-sands of holidaymakers thronging the most famous mile in Britain. Alex was clutching the hands of the two younger chil-dren and the two older children were holding on behind.

She looked round, they were there behind her; two steps later, she turned round again – and they'd gone.

Two severely disabled children lost on illumination night, when it was so crowded that Alex couldn't even see the pavement.

'It was like panic. *Panic.* What the *hell* am I going to do now?'

She went to the police station at the back of the tower and said, 'I've lost these two disabled kids.'

'What are they like?' they asked.

'Well, one is a very hyperactive young little lad, and one's a teenage girl that never opens her eyes.'

'Oh, well,' she was told, 'there's a million people in Blackpool, they'll turn up.'

Alex was astonished. They weren't her kids, she didn't have any idea where they were or what they were doing, and one had never opened her eyes. What would happen if they decided to go to the seafront for a midnight swim? What would happen if they went on the road?

'How can I tell two sets of parents that I've lost their children in Blackpool?' she was thinking. 'That was the worst thing that had ever happened to me. But the police just said, "OK, love, we'll watch out for them."'

So Alex walked backwards and forwards along the Golden Mile for three hours – the longest three hours of her life – asking passers-by, checking the pubs, hotels and shops, and eventually a penny arcade, where Alex finally hit the jackpot.

'The first slot machine place I walked into, the very first one – and there was the security guard holding on to the girl's hand. She still had her eyes closed – three hours later she still had her eyes closed! And I said, "Oh thank God you've found her."

'"Is she yours?" he asked. "She's been wandering around this place with her eyes closed for hours."'

Now there was only one of them still lost – a little boy of 8 or 9, who was very hyperactive. He could have been anywhere in Blackpool, but Alex thought, 'They were holding hands, there's a chance that he's in here, too.' So she combed the arcade and found him sitting under a fruit machine, watching the numbers going round. He'd been there for hours, too, while people were putting money in, and hadn't missed Alex at all.

'I shouted, *"John!"*

'He just went, "Hiya."

'So I got hold of these two kids and I said, "Oh thank you God, thank you God." I did tell the parents, I'm terribly honest. I went back and said to the parents, "I've had a terrible weekend with your kids – I lost them."

'And their attitude was, "What's the problem – you found them again." That's all the parents said to me. "You found them again." That was a terrible experience – I learnt an awful lot from that.'

Above all she learnt that the whirling dervish had to slow down. The Blackpool experience brought home to Alex that she could attempt too much, that she had gone beyond a reasonable limit with four children on the Golden Mile. Two would have been sufficiently difficult, but four sets of parents had said their kid would like to go to Blackpool, and four would fit in the car, so she took four. A lesson had been learnt – when to say 'No'.

The next two years were a period of growing experience, confidence and professionalism. The initial eager-to-please mayhem of taking everyone's special needs kids home became the organised chaos of the committed care worker. She didn't ask for money, the kids would bring soup, or steak pies, or whatever the parents could afford to send with them.

'I don't think there was ever a weekend when I was on my own. I had about ten children, and they sort of rotated, so I always had somebody. There was one particular boy that I had every other weekend. At the time there was no such thing as respite for his parents, and this was a difficult child. It wasn't that they didn't want to be with him, they just needed a break so they could spend some time with each other.'

A new kind of logic began to grow. Rather than the unpredictable comings-and-goings of reacting to random requests, why not put the arrangements onto a firmer footing? In any case, although she loved having the kids with her, sometimes for up to three weeks, she could become distressed when they left. Alex wanted more certainty, more maternal control, and decided that being a foster parent to a special needs child would provide security but not be too ambitious – she thought adoption would be rejected out of hand. Then, being Alex, she didn't approach a social worker; she went straight to the top and made an appointment with Val Scerri, Director of Salford Social Services.

Val ran social services in Salford for over thirty years and he's still a legendary figure, a Maltese immigrant who came to England in his youth, and went on to change many lives. One was Alex.

'He was wonderful – a director of social services meeting somebody who was 23 – and he took two hours to talk to me.

'"Why do you want to do this?" he said. "What's your motivation?"

'At the end he said, "You don't want to foster, you want to adopt."

'I said, "They won't let me adopt because I'm single and I work full-time."

'He said, "I'll recommend you to an adoption agency and we'll see what happens."'

Alex was both thrilled and daunted to be invited to a training group at an adoption agency although probably only because the big boss had recommended her. Indeed, the initial letter set the tone. Written at the top was 'Dear Mr and Mrs …' which they had crudely erased and replaced with 'Dear Alex Bell …'

In fact it was not so much a training group as an induction and support group for all the couples intending to adopt – all couples, that is, apart from Alex.

'I can see the scene like it was today. I can even remember the dress I had on. We were in this big, boomy room, with people sitting in a circle, in couples. It was man–woman–empty chair; man–woman–empty chair: man–woman–empty chair ... all the way around the room: and then it was empty chair–woman–empty chair – *me*.

'This lady leaned across and said, "Could your husband not come then?"

'"I'm single," I said.

'And she said, "Oh, you've got no chance then."

'Next, the social worker came in, took every couple's name and when she got to me she just said, "Alex Bell?" and I said, "Yeah," and she said, "Single people don't adopt, you know." Like "What the hell are you doing, this is for married couples." And I thought, "What does she think I'm here for, then?" Typical social worker.'

That was the beginning of a lifelong love–hate relationship between Alex and social workers.

In fact, today Alex gets on well with the senior, experienced social workers, but sometimes the relationship is strained with the middle ranks, invariably because the nanny-knows-best, hierarchical culture of social work has reservations about spirited and opinionated individuals. Alex is not so much rebellious as unable to accept dogma or rules that must be obeyed for their own sake only. As a lively woman in her early 20s, she must have seemed just like novice nun Julie Andrews, alternatively charming and scandalising the more conventional older nuns.

'How do you solve a problem like Maria?' they sing in *The Sound of Music*, and they could be obedient social workers referring to Alex.

Man–woman–empty chair; empty chair–Alex–empty chair.

Back then, in the late 1970s, Alex smiled at the couples around her single seat in that draughty, unfriendly hall, and knew that she wasn't like them, and was comfortable about it.

'People said to me, sadly, like, "Can't you have kids?"'

'I replied, "Never tried." Never wanted to try, but as far as I know, yeah, I could.'

When Alex got up from the inward-looking circle of chairs and headed home through the Manchester fog to her empty house, she was more determined than ever, single or not. Alex was already constructing her own world: a world of practical solutions that break rules; a world of putting the child first; a world of staying up all night; a world of risk; a world of love, whatever the consequences – the world Alex Bell yearned for.

However maddening these sessions were for Alex, they were the best route – the only route – for Alex to go down. So she continued to attend the meetings every month.

'I knew what I wanted to do, and I was very excited about it, but I also realised there would never be a man who wanted to share that, so I never bothered even looking. I was Von Trapped, but happy.'

Chapter Four

A bloody long pregnancy

By 1980, Alex was 25, but with permed dark hair, no make-up and a preference for plain dresses and slacks she looked younger, certainly very young to be a special needs teacher with several years experience. Many of her colleagues were surprised to discover that 'young Alex' had her own car and – crucially – now owned a three-bedroom semi-detached town house in Swinton, 'a bit rundown, with dreadful purple walls', she says. The girl who helped out in the long-stay wards had come a long way.

The word most commonly used to describe her was 'independent'. Apart from a mortgage she was financially independent; though she lived alone (albeit often looking after children on evenings and at weekends) she was socially independent; and though she seemed like an average teacher, she was most definitely independent-minded.

As always her mother was hugely supportive in this, but she still found herself in conflict with her father. He regarded Alex as being so contrary as to be unreasonable and he never tired of letting her know, at the top of his voice, that his view was in the majority.

Although institutional care was being transformed, broader social attitudes were slower to change. In 1980 there was still only one accepted reason for adoption: because a husband or wife was infertile and therefore a couple couldn't have children. For a single, fertile woman to want to adopt was highly unusual, but to want to adopt a 'mentally handicapped' child was almost unwholesome. The accepted wisdom was 'Surely, nobody in the their right mind would deliberately seek out and demand to adopt a stranger's Down's syndrome child, would they?'

In fact nobody did, but even if they had tried it would not have been allowed.

Until young Alex. She was one of the first. And all the more surprising because she was attractive, intelligent, and had no visible hang-ups – indeed, she was happier, saner and more normal than many of the people who came to assess her.

During that period, from 1978 to 1980, Alex continued, constantly, to put herself in the frame for adoption – even if she couldn't put herself forward formally. It was a kind of purgatory, an awful, monotonous limbo of waiting, of dull, deadly meetings, of form-filling and more waiting, and more meetings.

And their answer was by now becoming only too predictable. It was always 'No.'

The Adoption Agency didn't even seem to consider it – they just said 'No.'

But Alex had never heard 'No' very clearly. To her, 'No' came before 'Why not?' And 'Why not?' are Alex's favourite two words.

'The Adoption Agency said disabled kids aren't up for adoption because nobody wants to adopt them. I told them, "Well, I do." And they said, "Well, you shouldn't. So they aren't available. Just forget it."'

Alex would have shocked them even more if she had told them that she did not want normal children. If she wanted normal kids, she would have had them herself. But Alex specifically wanted special needs children, children who didn't have many options, children who fascinated and enthralled her, the kind of children she taught, that she took home at the weekends, and that is the only reason she wanted to adopt.

'At that time, before IVF, almost all adopters were infertile people going after beautiful healthy little pink babies. But I find normal kids very run of the mill, they've never appealed to me. You can imagine; the agencies were wary about somebody who would prefer to adopt when there is no physical reason not to have their own kids, and adopt disabled kids at that.'

But immediately after the word 'No' left the adoption officers' lips, before Alex could even muster her logical arguments, a Government social policy review committee re-reviewed the review and pronounced not just a shift of direction, but a complete U-turn.

The argument was mainly economic: The expensive long-stay hospitals were closing fast, so social services would be required to find somewhere else for babies with Down's syndrome. Somebody very senior must have said, 'Well now, because of the contraceptive pill, we haven't got any healthy white babies to adopt any more. Let's try Down's syndrome babies and see what the reaction is.'

The upheaval for adoption agencies was absolute.

A whole wave of otherwise healthy babies with Down's became available all of a sudden. Social policy was saying, 'We'll dabble our feet in the water and see if anybody picks up on these kids.'

By happy coincidence, Alex was still attending the monthly adoption evenings, a rough diamond 'sitting between a dozen Mr and Mrs Perfects', but now Alex herself became 'Miss Perfect', at the head of this new queue, ready and waiting – the most obvious person to try out first.

Finally in 1980, the Manchester Adoption Society were commissioned to vet Alex, in the person of Betty Morgan, their most indefatigable, 'bomb-proof' adoption officer – probably of all time. Two women with very different temperaments were about to collide.

* * *

There is a touch of Miss Marple to Betty, who has described herself as the oldest adoption officer in the North West. Now in her 80s and only recently retired to the Lake District, Betty is like everyone's favourite grandmother: grey-haired and respectable, but progressive and unconventional, kind and mumsy, yet tough as an ox, she is a good listener, but capable of scandalous asides. Betty and Alex were either going to be best mother–daughter friends or hate each other on sight, not least because of the huge generation gap between them.

Betty didn't begin working in adoption until she was 52, and even then more by accident than by design, a story Betty still delights to tell, in her soft, exacting voice.

'You see, I wanted to stay at home while my children were growing up, be an old-fashioned mum, and hadn't ever seriously considered working, let alone a career, but when my son was at university he had a friend who was a volunteer with the NSPCC [National Society for the Prevention of Cruelty to Children], who kept on at me and said, "Now both your children are away at college, there's a little girl in Pendlebury Children's Hospital who needs you."

'Mary had been taken from her parents because she'd been so badly treated and couldn't sit up though she was about 14 months.

She was scared stiff when I first went but it
she used to scream when I left her, so the h
and I applied to foster her; that's how I becan
the area officer for the Manchester Adoption So
me one day when Mary was at home. He was lo   ail my
books in the bookcase, and he asked, "Have you eve considered
training to work for us?"'

After beginning training in the early 1970s at the age of 50,
Betty worked first as an assistant, then as a placement officer, for
the Manchester Adoption Society, which had moved away from
its Christian founders to become the most go-ahead adoption
agency in Britain, dominated by a committee with dynamic min-
isters and formidable vicars' wives, who fluctuated between the
play-safe traditional and the outright radical.

At that time, many decisions about more humane approaches
to the disabled were being driven by religious groups in the North
West who flouted the conventional wisdom that the disabled
should be hidden away in hospitals and care homes. For instance,
they were beginning to push for new, educational opportunities
for children with special needs, where conventionally all 'solutions' had tended to be health-based.

But even adoption agencies like the Manchester Adoption
Society were still subject to the ancient, paternalistic attitudes of
the judges who let all concerned know that the courts were in
charge of adoption and still firmly grounded in the past. Some of
their pronouncements scandalised Betty.

'Everyone, especially the judges, talked about HWI, which
didn't mean a thing to me. Then I discovered it meant "healthy
white infants", which the judges definitely preferred, and that
shocked me, because the courts would not allow you to place a
child that was mixed race, or had health problems.

...e judge might say, "You can't place this child, he's got a lung complaint." It might be a simple complaint but he considered the child was "not adoption material". This was back in the early 1970s, it was ridiculous really, but if it had been a Down's syndrome child it would have been very, very difficult. It would have been easier to place the child in a fostering situation rather than adoptive.'*

That was the combustible background to the first meeting of Alex and Betty: a 26-year-old hot-headed, single young woman with exceptional qualifications, determined to adopt a Down's baby, and a much older but equally strong-minded woman having to make the critical recommendation. Both of them were subject to inflexible, ancient attitudes, going through rapid change.

So one morning in the spring of 1980 Betty Morgan got in her little car and went off to meet Alex Bell. Their first encounter was at Alex's parents' house. Alex opened the door and said, 'Don't tell me I'm too young because you're older than most social workers.'

Betty wasn't entirely surprised. For a start, she *was* old, over 60 by then, but more importantly, a young single woman trying to adopt was bound to be defensive.

'I wouldn't dream of telling you you're too young,' Betty replied.

---

*The reasons why Down's children – like 'unhealthy children' and 'mixed race children' – were not considered suitable for adoption were, of course, embedded in prejudices about the kind of children who would benefit from being brought up within normal family life and, equally, prejudices about who might be regarded as suitable carers for them. And whereas adoption by definition represented a permanent solution to the caring of 'unwanted children', these same judges were only prepared to countenance fostering, which was strictly under the control of the social services – who were still the legal carers – for the kind of children that Alex was aching to adopt.

However, after several further meetings, that is exactly what Betty decided – that Alex was too 'immature, too inexperienced in the ways of the world' to become an adoptive mother, ironically because of Betty's own maternal concern. It didn't seem to matter that Alex was confident, and had gone out of her way to become experienced with special needs children, or that she had a car and house. Indeed, as Alex drove and showed her around, those were the very things that counted against her with Betty. Alex may have appeared to be financially independent, but Betty saw her possession of a house and car rather differently – as financial millstones around her neck; along with Alex's relative youth they made her a bad risk.

'I had a daughter more or less the same age as Alex,' said Betty, 'and I thought, "How would I feel if she was single, coming to me and saying she's going to adopt a child with very serious problems?" I was trying to sort out my own feelings. Alex also had a house with quite a hefty mortgage, she'd bought a car and I thought, "Oh my God, financially she was in shtuck really – how's she going to manage?"'

So Betty went back to the adoption committee and expressed her serious doubts. But the committee, in its radical frame of mind and after an intense bout of what Betty called 'bickering among the vicars' wives', told her to persevere, in particular to take a committee member to meet Alex's mother, her headmistress and other supporting friends. Betty was none too pleased, but did as she was told.

And then something unexpected happened. Betty began to warm to Alex. She started to see qualities in her she had missed the first time round – her determination, her single-mindedness, her battling spirit. And Betty was also impressed by Doris Bell.

'Alex's mother was a strong, no-nonsense woman,' she says. 'I remember she put her hands on her hips and said, "Mrs Morgan! It's a pity there aren't a few more people around like our Alex. She'll get all the support she needs." Her mother was tremendous.'

Even so, Betty still had reservations about approving Alex for adoption, and Alex, on her part, had never really expected to be approved anyway – after all, she had been told too many times over the last three years that she didn't stand a chance of adopting, though she was still prepared for a fight.

So the battle carried on, Betty with her 'misgivings' and Alex continuing her pushing – with the radical committee in the background calling for progress. The two women didn't argue, but they didn't discuss either – partly because Alex had an answer for every objection Betty put to her. For instance, one evening Betty challenged Alex that it was all very well adopting a Down's baby, but she was only 26. 'What if you meet someone – a man …?'

'Do you think I would consider anyone who wouldn't take my child?' Alex replied.

And, no, Betty didn't think she would.

Eventually, after further months of checks and interviews, assessments and references, Betty made her final recommendation.

It was … 'No' … ish.

Or was it?

'I had to go back to the committee,' says Betty, 'and give them an unbiased opinion, but my misgivings were that she was so young and it was going to be such a financial blow to give up her jolly good salary and be living on more or less a pittance. But Down's syndrome children were being referred, and we thought, "Well, you know, is it wrong to refuse this girl?" Quite a quandary. And the committee member who visited with me felt as undecided as I did. Well, I think so.'

These days, Betty and Alex are firm friends, with the kind of trusting friendship that goes beyond the normal ebb-and-flow of having to work together. It's a theme that repeats many times in Alex's life. Betty was like a mother from the very beginning, in the way Alex is a mother figure to many of the birth parents of her adopted children. They both acknowledge the 'mother–daughter' dimension of their relationship, but it has not been without difficulties – as Betty's initial concern for Alex suggests.

'Yes, the committee member who visited felt as undecided as I did. I said, "I like Alex tremendously, we get on very well." I said all the positive things about her and I said, "I have no doubts whatsoever, I am not in the slightest bit worried about the *child*. My misgivings are for Alex," and I said it over and over again.

'But we were overruled. Well, not overruled. It was decided that we should see what children were referred and see how things went.'

And with that the process of making Alex eligible for adoption was slowly, almost grudgingly, under way.

For a potential adopter, the first sign of progress is in being embraced – it feels more like a mauling, actually – by the prying officers of the bureaucratic state. Strangers probe ancient relationships, police records are sent for and carefully read. Bank accounts are pored over and questions asked if irregularities appear, and three personal references are chased up.

In Alex's case in 1982 much of the checking had to be done by Betty intruding on Alex's life – 'snooping', Alex once called it with a cheeky smile. As far as Alex's relationships were concerned, there had been a few brief boyfriends, but none was of any importance.

Most adopters welcome the checks, however invasive, because they see them as the last hurdle before the longed-for meeting with a child. It's just the beginning of the waiting-list stage, in which adopters have to do training, with childcare classes that drove Alex barmy. 'I could have taught the teacher,' she says.

Alex was, of course, and still is a qualified special needs teacher. Her knowledge and understanding of this subject virtually make her the equivalent of a university professor, and yet she was being patronised by people with little training, who saw her as a young woman (and later, even worse, as a 'mother'), and therefore assumed she didn't have a brain.

Further, even more detailed assessments were conducted. Alex's house was appraised, to see precisely where the baby would sleep, spend the day, how transport to and from schools would work, followed by a home study, which looked at the kitchen and feeding arrangements, none of which fazed Alex.

'I've even had social workers look in my fridge to see what food I've got, but I understand why it's hard, because it should be hard, because you're talking about vulnerable children, aren't you? But it's harder doing it on your own because you haven't got anybody there to support you.'

At that stage, a comprehensive medical is arranged, which is especially rigorous, on the basis that the child may already have lost one set of parents and it would be terribly unfortunate for them to lose another.

However, when Alex's GP edged towards being, perhaps, a tad too thorough, Alex told him, 'You can put your torch away, Martin. You're not looking anywhere that's dark.'

The assessment takes somewhere between a year and eighteen months until, finally, if all the answers are satisfactory, a potential adopter is 'approved in principle' – and after many months of rigorous screening, intrusion and bureaucracy, Alex finally received a letter saying, 'Congratulations, you've been approved to adopt.'

* * *

The next stage of the process may take many years while the adoption society waits for a suitable child to come along, but Alex, of course, wasn't the kind of person to wait. Now she was officially approved, she had access to adoption magazines like *Be My Parent*, a bi-monthly magazine published by BAAF, the British Association for Adoption and Fostering. *Be My Parent* advertised children from all over Britain, using heartrending photos and sentimental descriptions of 'available' babies – they were invariably cute babies – some with learning difficulties and other 'challenges'.

One night, at her house in Swinton, now refurbished and without purple walls, Alex was reading the magazine from cover to cover, when she came across the picture of a pair of Down's twins – Christopher and Richard – and she fell in love at first sight.

While many people would simply turn the page, Alex sprang immediately into action. Besides, Alex thought they would have few other options, and therefore were destined for her.

'I'll never forget them as long as I live. They were just gorgeous, and I thought nobody else would be interested, being Down's syndrome, even though they were lovely. So I phoned Betty, went round to see her, bombarded her.'

But Betty's reply was unwavering: Alex wouldn't be allowed to adopt twins as a first placement. Her dismissal disappointed Alex, who had set her heart on Christopher and Richard – Down's twin boys were Alex's ideal, her perfect family; indeed, Alex still has the magazine. But she's long ago forgiven Betty, telling the story with a knowing smirk rather than with rancour, as if to say, 'Betty turned me down for two – and now I've got nine.'

During this time, Alex was driving into Salford at least once a month for group coffee evenings with other approved parents, observing the highs and lows of the process and to see how different couples coped with the waiting period. The Adoption Society tried to create a supportive, almost club-style atmosphere in which the group as a whole shares the joy when one couple gets a baby. But as supportive as they could be, the reality was that some couples would occasionally become irritated, jealous, even aggressive, turning away when previous members brought in their new child.

And all the time, Alex was the only 'individual', the only 'non-couple' on the waiting list.

She continued to teach at her special school, she continued to have special kids home for the weekend, or the school holidays, only now 'home' was the three-bedroom house in Swinton. But still she waited, as the weeks became months, became a year.

Then in December 1983, Betty Morgan called round to see Alex.

'I was at home in the evening after school when Betty came with a photograph. A black and white photograph of this baby, and she said, "This is the baby that you're going to have."'

In the picture (page 52) David, as he was then known (now Matthew), is sitting on a carpeted floor, in a corduroy jumpsuit, face turned to camera, with shiny, longish hair, a half smile, his tongue out – indeed, a gorgeous little boy – soon to be her own little soul to 'have and to hold'.

'I hadn't seen him in the adoption magazine – this had all been discussed without me knowing it had gone through. Not even "Do you want a boy or girl?" They'd had a meeting with the child's social worker before anybody involved me. They decided this was the child I was going to have and everything was done, all the decisions were taken. And then I was shown a picture and I was told that this is yours, this is the child that you're going to have. And he was beautiful, he was absolutely beautiful.'

At last, after three years' hard labour, Alex now knew she would soon be a mother. Even though this was her dream come true and her life was to somersault and never be the same again – and she of all people was well aware of the fact – her reply was typically matter of fact.

'I said, "Oh, right, OK."'

But she had no idea of the perilous journey David had taken, or that he was, in fact, a twin.

At around 16 weeks, just about the time when the baby begins to wriggle, David's mother had an amniocentesis, a simple procedure to syringe off a sample of amniotic fluid to check for chromosomal abnormalities. As the baby grows, the foetus naturally sheds small numbers of cells that remain suspended in the fluid, and these can be cultured in the laboratory until there are enough to be harvested for testing. Then they are dyed and put under the microscope so that the chromosomes can be identified and counted. Down's syndrome is indicated in most cases by an extra chromosome 21 in every cell. To the relief of David's parents the amnio-test was negative – the baby would be normal.

The baby was normal. But the baby wasn't David. It was Robert – David's twin brother.

In hindsight it's probable that the needle had entered Robert's amniotic sac, drawing an ounce of fluid with the normal two copies of chromosome 21. If the needle had strayed a fraction and picked out the sac containing David, the cultured foetal cells would have revealed the three copies of chromosome 21 and raised the question of a termination. A tiny deviation of fate: life or perhaps, in some cases, death, decided by a millimetre.

David was born on 24 April 1982, in the maternity wing of Watford General Hospital, arriving over an hour later than his brother, Robert (not his real name). Their birth was essentially normal, but even as David was still adapting, like every new-born baby, to the miraculous state of being alive and out of the womb, doubts were beginning to set in among the maternity staff.

After the birth, David's mother was told the ultimate good-news-bad-news. She had a normal baby boy. And a not-quite-so-normal one. It was apparent that David had been born with Down's syndrome and his life would never be the same as that of her normal child.

Three days after giving birth, David's mother left hospital, taking her normal baby home; but David was left behind.

For the next nine weeks, David was kept in limbo – in an acute paediatric ward, surrounded by premature and desperately ill babies in incubators, although he was healthy. Inside his birth family, a battle was raging. His mother wanted to keep him, but his father, who had started a new business, felt it would be difficult to cope. Gradually, as the hospital began to begrudge the ill-baby space, he was put in a crib and wheeled down the corridor to the laundry and linen area, while social services started to look for a temporary foster home.

*   *   *

Janet and John Cornwall lived six miles from Watford, in the leafy suburb of Rickmansworth, about 30 miles north west of London, in a 1960s large semi, with a long garden, which is still their home to this day. Back then, in the summer of 1982, their four children were still at home when the hospital's social worker phoned Janet to ask whether she and John would consider adopting David.

Janet, a polite, neat woman, at the time in her late 30s and now in her 60s, is chatty and open, very much at ease with her husband John, a quiet man with a beard. Before giving up work to have a family, Janet was a nurse at Great Ormond Street Hospital, the most famous children's hospital in Britain, so in theory she had the necessary skills for caring for a child with special needs. As far back as she can remember, Janet had been baby-oriented – she ran the church crèche for the Sunday morning service at the age of 16 – and still describes herself as 'permanently broody'.

However, none of her family knew anything about Down's syndrome so she and her husband arranged a family conference, to go through the pros and cons. Their two daughters were fine with the idea, but the two boys weren't quite sure. They didn't know whether they'd want to hold 'a baby like that'. So they piled into their estate car and drove to the hospital.

They looked in the main ward but couldn't find David. They asked a few nurses, without any luck. Then an administrator realised who they meant and escorted the Cornwalls to a huge, out-of-the-way room at the end of a corridor – a working laundry. All the hospital linen was stacked up in old canvas bins. And there, in a transparent plastic tub, in a bleached-out space, Janet saw baby David for the first time.

'It was terrible,' she says. 'He was lying on a white sheet, with a white baby-grow, in a white room, right up to the top, absolutely nothing, no toys, no nothing, just this little baby lying there, bright red hair stuck right up, looking terribly Down's syndrome.'

'In a white-sided bin and a high white ceiling over his head, nothing for him to focus on,' John added.

Though 9 weeks old, David weighed just 7 pounds; he was listless and floppy until Louise, the Cornwalls' 18-year-old daughter, picked him up and snuggled him to her T-shirt. He nuzzled his tiny head into Louise's shoulder – it was the first time he'd responded, his first experience of the warm comfort of human flesh. According to the nurses, until that moment baby David had never been cuddled.

Louise remembers it well. 'When I cuddled him, he was floppy, no control over his arms or legs, and I could see the smiles on the faces of the nurses, with their full-sleeved gowns, that someone was able to touch him, flesh to flesh – and I just didn't want to let go.'

Before they went, the social worker told Janet, 'When you see him, that he's got disabilities, you may not want to take him home.' The Cornwall boys had been nervous, uncertain. But now Louise couldn't put him down, they agreed to take him home, and within hours both boys loved David almost more than Louise did, and wanted to keep him forever.

Dealing with a Down's syndrome baby is like dealing with any baby, except they're slower to learn, and they grow in a different way. With David, this was made worse by his solitary nine weeks in hospital. Twenty years later, Louise Cornwall, now a GP in Banbury and a mother of four, well remembers just how small and delicate David was when they got him home.

'If any baby was stuck in hospital for nine weeks you wouldn't expect them to be doing a great deal, but he was only 7 pounds. That's new-born baby size – the average birth weight is about 7 pounds 4 ounces, so he was smaller than newborn. Normally by six weeks they can smile, they can make some sort of noises, and they'd be responding much more. But he wasn't doing any of that. He had been fed, changed, all the things that you have to do, but I don't think there was any kind of stimulation.'

The Cornwalls – especially Louise and her mother – are a baby kind of family. They have dozens of photo albums, always on hand, packed full of smiling children and happy memories, so that what appears to be a simple picture of a baby sitting on a carpet dribbling was, according to Janet, a significant moment of outstanding achievement. 'That's when he first sat up. Just for a second,' she remembers.

On the next page, another picture of David, still sitting up but leaning forward, then another, with him lolling over, about to fall down, a favourite of Janet's.

'He had such little arms he couldn't stay up but had to hold on to his tummy. We propped him up and used to do exercises with a plastic roll thing; we'd throw him over it and then when he came back he'd be sitting up, only for a second, and then he'd tumble again.'

The Cornwalls used to fight over who was going to cuddle him, feed him and stimulate him.

'Louise would come home from school,' Janet remembers, 'and it would be, "Well, it's my turn. You cuddled him yesterday."

'"No, I want to have him."

'It was like that, the boys as much as the girls. I offered the children 50p for the first one to get him to turn over. We all used to lie on our side trying to get him to roll, and Louise put him on a cushion and he fell over and once he got the idea he did it again.

But it took us about a month to do that because he was usually on his tummy. Louise reckons I never gave her the 50p.'

Although the Cornwalls adored David, Down's children remain dependent on their parents much longer than ordinary children – if not forever – and John in particular felt they were too old to adopt him. By the time he would be in his 20s, they'd be 'pushing 70', and they didn't want to pass a dependency onto their children. So throughout the period in which they were fostering, Watford social services were looking to place David for adoption. Early in 1983 they told Janet Cornwall that a family had been found, a couple who already had a 4-year-old daughter with Down's syndrome.

'He wasn't walking, of course. But when he first left us, if you held him up, he would put one foot up after the other. We had taught him to kick, well sort of, to put his feet against the wall and make him push himself back. Not a lot, but when he left we were very proud of ourselves.'

After eight months of constant stimulation by six highly motivated cuddlers and prodders, they drove him off to his new home in Essex. When they arrived, the woman said to her little girl, 'Oh, here's our new boy, David,' and put him in a playpen in the corner. Janet was not impressed; she felt that if a person desperately wanted to adopt a baby they wouldn't just leave him in the playpen. The journey home with Louise was sombre.

They were invited back in the April for his first birthday but the visit was even more harrowing. Still in that playpen in the corner, David had retreated into himself. Louise and her mother hardly recognised the almost catatonic baby who was propped up against the wall being fed jelly. The greatest shock was that his new parents had strapped heavy iron callipers to David's legs that held him rigid from hip to toe, and dragged him down when he tried to crawl. Janet wanted to cry – after all their work, all the fun of trying to get him to use his muscles, he had gone backwards. While telling this story, Janet points once more to her photo album and shakes her head slowly, sadly.

'Look at his legs hanging down like that, and his tummy was hanging out, and he was dribbling. And his little arms wouldn't move, it was so distressing.'

Louise was even more upset: 'I was really choked the whole day because I knew he wasn't happy. I just refused to speak. OK, it was an immature attitude, but I was gutted, I just didn't want him to be there, so we came back in the car feeling even more dreadful all the way home.'

Despite their feelings of shock and their anguish for David's plight, the Cornwall family were trying very hard not to be judgemental. They knew that the adoptive mother was 'caring in her own way', and was perfectly open with them – they simply had different styles of parenting. Janet and Louise felt that perhaps they were being prejudiced, that no other family would have been good enough for their David. But what happened next was to change everything.

Seven months after being desperate to adopt David, after agreeing to take him forever, his new parents decided to get divorced. The social worker couldn't choose which of the two parents should have David, so she took him back into care. Suddenly, unexpectedly, David was homeless.

'When I found out, there was only once place he belonged,' said Janet.

John, a quiet but strong-minded man, was well aware how distressed Janet and Louise had been when they had to give up David the first time. Then, with the collapse of the adoptive placement, all his protective instincts for the women he loved came to the fore. John thought of the pain when David would have to leave again, and put his foot down. Gently, but firmly, he insisted they should not take David back.

But John Cornwall didn't stand a chance. There wasn't a question in the two women's minds – they wanted David back, especially Louise.

'I've seen my mum cry three times in her entire life and this was one of them. Mum came down the garden and burst into tears and said, "Dad won't let us have him back." Then I burst into tears with her, which was very unusual for me, too. So Mum went back and said to Dad, "Now look, you've upset Louise." And he sort of said, as Dad would, because he believed the best of people, "Oh all right then. We'll have him again." And so we did.'

David was now 16 months old and back at the Cornwalls' home, but it took some time for Louise to be entirely happy.

'I remember bringing him in from the social worker's car, sitting down with him on my lap and at first thinking he didn't look like the little baby that had first left us. He looked so switched off and sad. Then I like to think he remembered that he was back with us, in a nice place. He slept in my bedroom and would wake up early, so I would take him down the garden at five in the morning. It was such a privilege.'

During the rest of the summer, and through the autumn of 1983, the Cornwalls worked as a unit to develop David. His weight had stabilised rather than increased; the callipers had weakened his legs, and his muscles were unused and wasted. Like all toddlers being fostered, David went for regular medical assessments to check his progress – and every single one was an ordeal for Janet, who spent hours trying to get David in optimum shape. Partly, this was the instinct of a proud woman faced with an outsider's judgement; but it was also a realisation that Janet wanted him to 'be something'.

Janet would coax David to stand up by taking the cushions off her sofa and putting a chocolate button on the end, just out of reach, so he had to stretch up, then once he got halfway she put another chocolate button further away, so he had to stretch for that; and gradually he could actually stand up and stretch for the chocolate button at the back. Then he would wobble, still standing. But when he fell, the family would put cushions round him to soften his fall.

'I almost cringe when I think about it. His legs were completely floppy, he couldn't use them at all, so he used to lie on his tummy and go up on his knee if we put the chocolate button in front of him, just a little way out of his reach. I'd just got him to do this without the chocolate buttons, and then went for an assessment.

'The lady said, "Does he crawl?"

'"Well, in his own sort of way," I said, and put him on the floor and he wouldn't move.

'So I said, "Well, actually if I put a line of chocolate buttons he'll go after them" – and of course you don't give babies chocolate buttons because of their teeth.'

Nevertheless, Janet continued to use the chocolate button training method.

'But once he got the momentum he was fine. We had to do this for every assessment. Each time I crossed my fingers and thought, "You've got to do it. I know you can do it."'

During this time, Watford Social Services were again attempting to find a family to adopt David. They advertised him in *Be My Parent*, the adoption magazine sent to carers and adopters throughout Britain.

Be My Parent 94

David

Date of birth: 24th April 1982

DAVID is a baby boy of 18 months. He was born with Down's Syndrome which is frequently known as mongolism. He was placed for adoption some months ago and, although his family loved him dearly, the arrangement had to end because of a change in their circumstances. David, therefore, has a very special need to find another home as quickly as possible.

Fortunately, his general health is good. However, he will always be dependent and will need the continuing patience and love of a family able to cope with his handicap and help him develop to the best of his ability. Like other mentally handicapped children, he will require special schooling.

David is small for his age. He has a mop of fine fair hair and is a lively, mischievous and very affectionate little boy who has become an expert at detecting chocolate! He knows what he wants and will certainly let you know if you keep him waiting!

He is having physiotherapy to increase the muscle tone in his legs and he's responding to this. He loves water and goes swimming regularly with his present foster mother. He may never swim The Channel but it will not be for lack of enthusiasm.

(Profile originally published in *Be My Parent*. Reproduced with kind permission of BAAF.)

DAVID is a baby boy of 18 months. He was born with Down's Syndrome which is frequently known as mongolism. He was placed for adoption some months ago and, although his family loved him dearly, the arrangement had to end because of a change in their circumstances. David, therefore, has a very special need to find another home as quickly as possible.

Fortunately, his general health is good. However, he will always be dependent and will need the continuing patience and love of a family able to cope with his handicap and help him develop to the best of his ability. Like other mentally handicapped children, he will require special schooling.

David is small for his age. He has a mop of fine fair hair and is a lively, mischievous and very affectionate little boy who has become an expert at detecting chocolate! He knows what he wants and will certainly let you know if you keep him waiting!

He is having physiotherapy to increase the muscle tone in his legs and he's responding to this. He loves water and goes swimming regularly with his present foster mother. He may never swim The Channel but it will not be for lack of enthusiasm.

The Cornwall family were in a bind, Janet most of all. They were committed to preparing David for 'that world out there'. A photographer friend from the church took the special photos of David when he was 18 months for the advert, but they desperately didn't want him to go, the cruel paradox for foster parents everywhere, summed up by John, in his characteristically concise way. 'Your heart wants him to stay with us, but your head knows he ought to go to somebody …'

As the months passed by, while they played and worked with him every day to make him stronger, their attachment to David also grew stronger and he became a focal member of the family. He ate with them, slept in their arms, played in the garden and went on holiday with them. There were no longer six Cornwalls, David made them a family of seven. Above all, Louise could not bear even to think of letting him go, and as autumn turned to winter they realised a watershed was approaching – Christmas. In early December 1983, the Cornwall clan sat down for a definitive family discussion, with Louise taking the lead.

'We'd all got so fond of him that Mum and Dad agreed that "if nobody comes by Christmas day we'll adopt him". This wasn't frivolous; they definitely meant it.'

The whole family said a quiet cheer because David would be there for keeps. Louise Cornwall was on vacation from university; this was one of the happiest days in her life and she settled back, looking forward to an extra special Christmas present.

Then one morning, a few days before Christmas, the phone rang.

When Louise recalls the next part of the story, tears still come into her eyes. 'It must have been within days of Christmas – I used to think it was actually Christmas Eve, but it can't have been – we got a call from social services to say that they'd got this young single woman from Manchester who was interested. My mother told us. She tried to be positive, but she was obviously upset and we were all up in arms. I can remember sitting at teatime, all of us there, completely bereft. It was like, "Bloody hell, bloody hell, nearly Christmas, we so nearly got there." We were distraught; and we were furious.'

Given the possessiveness of the Cornwall family and the combativeness of then 27-year-old Alex Bell, an emotional punch-up could have ensued. By the time Alex arrived, a week before Christmas 1983, when Janet Cornwall opened her front door, though seething inside, she managed a smile. But Louise felt differently. Very differently.

'As far as I was concerned, Alex was just a coarse Northerner who was coming to take our baby away. She had on these thick, dark, jamjar glasses and her hair all sort of frizzy permed; and she was a single woman – a man-hater, I had decided, who obviously had huge hang-ups – and was going to adopt *our* child from my busy, loving, warm, lively family – oh, yes, Alex didn't have a hope.'

Standing with Betty, on the other side of the lounge, Alex didn't notice the mood of the Cornwall family. At that moment they hardly even existed. After four frustrating years of hoping, Alex was at last face to face with her first, her very own, child.

'Louise had hold of him,' she remembers. 'She was playing with him, he was sat on the floor, in front of the french windows and a lovely garden, and he was watching squirrels, and he looked at me when I came in the room, and he sort of babbled away, not words, baby talk, blerr-blerr-blerr-da-blerr, like that, and I said, "Are you giving me lip?" – the first thing I said to him – then I picked him up off the floor, took him to the window, looked out, and then Janet said, "Oh, that's the first person who's picked him up and he's not cried."

Before Alex had rung their doorbell the Cornwall family had almost wanted to lynch this young upstart of a woman who had had the nerve to come into their house to remove their beloved toddler, to take him off, up North, and out of their lives. And yet, in spite of this, Janet – charitable, Christian Janet – was quickly able to see only the good in Alex. Meanwhile Alex recalls that the Cornwalls were not just polite but friendly. Janet hid her broken heart with kindness, only remembering how David and Alex bonded.

'I remember the day and the trauma of it,' says Janet, 'sort of half thinking, "Well, perhaps she won't want him after all," but she obviously wanted him and I almost resented Alex. But he was meant for her – you could tell straight away.

'It was David who decided. He was one of these children that if you gave him to the wrong person, he'd squeal and wriggle. But the people he wanted or liked he'd settle with immediately. Of course we gave him to Alex and he settled down fine. *He* decided. And part of me thought, thank goodness.'

Still oblivious to the Cornwall family, Alex just continued to hold him.

'Right away I thought he was gorgeous,' she says, 'a lovely little lad. I didn't go with the thought, "Will I like this child? Is he the right child?" I'd been told *this* is the child, this is your child, this is the child you are having, this is your son, so before I even saw him, he was mine. It wasn't ever, "Do I think I will bond with him?" I knew I'd bond with him, because I've got him.'

There are no hard-and-fast rules governing the handover of babies from foster parents to their adopters. It's usually worked out on an ad hoc basis. The day David met Alex, he was already feverish with a routine toddler infection, but by the evening he had to be rushed to casualty with a raging tummy bug. Later, mainly because of an illness he picked up in hospital, according to the Cornwalls, he needed surgery, so Alex and the social workers agreed to leave David with the Cornwalls until he was fully recovered. For Louise Cornwall this meant they could keep him for Christmas, so at least that part of their wish had come true.

'It was bitter-sweet, smiles through tears. I remember Christmas Day at church, a small church, which was very much part of our family, where everybody knew him. He crawled all the way down the aisle with one leg behind, really fast, everybody watching, and because he'd been really unwell – he'd lost loads of weight – the minister stopped the service. It was a true Christmas Day moment when the vicar said, "Oh isn't it nice to see that David is better." And then he carried on with the service.'

With David recovering, Alex commuted every other weekend the 200 miles from Manchester to Watford, to spend as much time as possible with him, creating a bond, while Janet closed her eyes and enjoyed David while he was still with them. During this time, Janet and Alex became friends, taking turns at being mother, learning from each other about dealing with challenging children and David in particular. At one point, Alex stayed for a week; for the first three days Janet was in charge, then Alex took over, with methods that mildly scandalised the Cornwalls.

Janet had originally tried to encourage David to stand up using her 'chocolate button' method with cushions around him in case he fell. But when Alex took charge, to Janet's amazement, she dispensed with the cushions and just let him fall back and crash his head against the floor. Janet thought, 'Oh, how awful,' but Alex told her, 'That's the only way he'll learn.' Though Janet was doubtful, she knew Alex was experienced with special needs children, and didn't intervene. Then within days David wasn't falling down, which really impressed Janet.

'In fact, we had thought, all the children said, "She's cruel, don't let her have him." But you could see Alex knew what she was doing.'

Although the Cornwall family may have been in denial, closing their minds to the impending departure of David – 'just enjoying him,' according to Louise, finally the day arrived for them to hand David over to Alex. She arrived accompanied by Betty and David's social worker, a 'lovely lady' called Janice McNaughton whom Alex adored.

'I met Janice when I first met David,' Alex recalls. 'Janice was looking for a single person, specifically. Because, remember, David was placed with a couple in Southend on Sea who decided to divorce, and they both wanted to keep him, and Janice said she wouldn't decide between them and took him back, so then she was specifically looking for a single person to have him so that she didn't get herself in that position again.'

On Wednesday, 22 February 1984, after an early breakfast, David's bags were packed, as Janet Cornwall fussed over him for the very last time. To this day, Janet still finds it hard to talk about David finally leaving without misty eyes.

'In a way it was a relief, that our work was over, we'd got him ready for the rest of his life. But, yes, that day we all felt terrible.'

So terrible, that Alex could hardly bear it.

'I said to Janice, "I can't take him away from this lot, they love him too much."

'And she just said, "Go and get him in the car." That's all she said.'

The centre of attraction – David – can't remember a single moment, not surprising as he wasn't yet 2 years old. But Alex recalls every little detail, the colours, the smells of that day, after what had been 'four years in labour'.

'I remember we drove to Hilton Park services, on the M1, where we stopped for a meal, the first meal he had. It was sausage, peas and chips and gravy and he sat in a high chair and ate it all.

'I remember getting him into the house, and sitting him on the floor and just being totally exhausted.

'I remember both the social workers went and left me with a screaming bundle. I didn't know what he was missing, probably everything. I tried to imagine what it was like to be him. You get in a car, go with a person you barely know, to a house you've never been to, and he was horrible at night, woke up every hour on the hour like an alarm clock, really hard work.

'I was, "Oh my God, why didn't they tell me he woke up all night long? When am I going to get any sleep? I've got to go to work in the morning."

'It was a bloody long pregnancy. From 23, when I started, to 28 when I actually got this child – a bloody long pregnancy.

'But he was everything I'd always wanted; he was perfect, there was no other word for it. Now he was mine.

'And I decided to call him Matthew.'

Chapter Five

Mr Happy: Matthew

On that cold February day when Alex brought him to her house for the very first time, Matthew sat on Alex's lounge carpet and cried and cried and cried.

Twenty-eight-year-old Alex was in shock. After all the interviews, the assessments and the waiting, the moment had finally come when she had been given a child. That first morning was sudden, overwhelming, and oddly lonely for a single woman. Between continuous cups of tea that she hardly bothered to drink and wondering what to do next, Alex could only think one thought: 'I'm a family now. Er, fine …'

Matthew was in shock, too: He had lost the people he loved and whom he was used to – his foster family; he had been whisked off to a new home with unfamiliar routines; and though not quite 2, he had to begin school for the first time. And it happened so fast because Alex couldn't have time off from her teaching job at Elmstead for his adoption.

It may sound stark and draconian, but she had to fit meeting Matthew and taking him back to her home into the February half-term school holiday, a single week. So after three days in

Matthew as a baby.

Watford picking him up, four days at home getting to know him, on Monday morning Alex was off to school.

Matthew's response to this trauma? He bawled, long and loud, much to Alex's horror.

'The first few weeks with Matthew were harrowing with him crying all the time, because I thought he didn't like me. He was never in my class, which was even worse because he was in the class next door, and I could hear him crying all day long through the wall.'

The next two years with Matthew were to be a steep learning curve for Alex – difficult, new, but wonderful.

'Matthew was very hard work. He'd lost a lot – all the cuddles of the Cornwalls – and not gained a lot, as far as he was concerned. But he was dead cute, a little sweetheart. I remember him first walking, he first walked at Elmstead.'

A few months after adopting Matthew, the social worker Janice McNaughton got in touch. 'She took me and Matthew to her house in Bushey, Watford, very classy. She was married and had two kids and a beautiful black Labrador called Benson. She was the only social worker who ever took me to her house, because she had gone on and on to her family about this little boy Matthew – well, David originally – and one day she said, "My husband wants to meet you," so she took us to her house.

'Sadly Janice died a few years ago. Betty knows all about her, because Janice went and stayed at Betty's house, and she was a terrible heavy smoker, and Betty was most indignant that when Janice left after this one night she found all these cigarette ends in her pot plants.'

A year later in 1984, when Matthew was three, Alex took him to see 'Jane' (Matthew's birth mother – not her real name) and her husband. Jane couldn't put Matthew down. She hugged and cuddled and kissed him, while, according to Alex, his father sat coldly in the corner.

'Do you know much about Down's syndrome?' Alex asked him.

'Why should I be interested in anything about that subject?' he replied coolly.

Alex doesn't condemn him. She simply remembers feeling sad for him, sad that he hadn't been able to find a way of dealing with a Down's syndrome son, of dealing with the pain, his own included.

Special needs education was still trying to grapple with the political and social changes that were occurring in the early 1980s, not least the thorny question of where such children should be schooled – alongside mainstream pupils, or in special classes or schools? To begin with the decision was fairly straightforward for a toddler like Matthew: he would spend the morning at Elmstead, Alex's special school, then during the lunch hour she would take him to her mum's, where he would sleep all afternoon, before she picked him up and drove him home. Beyond that, his arrival at the school was unremarkable. A couple of teachers gave her greetings cards, but most hardly acknowledged that Alex now had a child, which upset her at the time, 'like he wasn't really my baby, like it didn't matter'.

Alex had already decided that Matthew should go to a mainstream school – he was too bright for her special needs school, which, though excellent, was too basic: Matthew was in the top quarter of Down's children and she thought he should be stretched, so she began to look around.

In 1985 the word 'inclusion' didn't exist. Down's kids were separated – excluded – full stop. Alex had now had Matthew for two years and she wanted him to go to a 'normal' school, so that he could be brought up with ordinary kids, which was unheard of back then. Indeed, it was so surprising that the educational bureaucracy didn't even consider being obstructive when Alex sneaked Matthew in under their defences, one of the first Down's children in Salford to go to a mainstream school. The technique she used was typical of Alex's approach.

When a delegation from an ordinary infant school came to visit the special school where Alex taught, she waited until most of them had passed, grabbed their headmistress and whispered, 'I'm looking for a nursery school for my Matthew.'

'We'll have him,' the headmistress replied, and because her school wasn't in the local catchment area nobody realised what Alex had done until it was too late. Dorning Street Infant School, Eccles, had no idea they were breaking the rules, and certainly Alex wasn't likely to tell them.

'He loved Dorning Street,' she says. 'They were lovely there, they had a naughty tile on the bathroom floor that he had to stand on when he was naughty. Maybe it had a crack on it, I don't know.'

Whether or not Matthew spent much time standing on the naughty tile may never be known, but from the age of 4 a mini-cab would arrive every morning to take him off to Dorning Street to make his little bit of history.

If this doesn't sound exactly earth-shattering, it's illuminating to realise how Down's children were treated only a decade or so before. Janet Pardoe, who had a sister with Down's and was head-mistress at Swinton Hospital School in the 1960s and 70s, remembers the way it used to be:

'They were called "subnormal", and we actually had to learn the difference between a cretin and a moron and an imbecile – which scored the lowest IQ. The kid would spend a few minutes with a psychologist, the parents had to wait outside, and then a week later a letter arrived saying the child was "unsuitable for education – ineducable". What a sentence. What a word – "*ineducable*".'

In contrast, 6-year-old Matthew had done so well at Dorning Street Infants that he went on naturally to an ordinary primary school.

By now Alex had worked her wonders behind the scenes so he was part of an official trial. The school, Wardley Primary, had go-ahead attitudes. With another boy called Michael they had two 'specials', taken on as an experiment, which according to Alex was 'brilliant' for Matthew.

'This was in the days before they had nursery classes in schools. He was at Wardley until he was 12. He had an extra twelve months there because he was twelve months behind the rest of the kids.

'They had full-time support, and the school was very receptive, not like now, when special needs kids are forced on to schools to save money, with only a few hours of special tuition. Matthew had his own full-time teaching helper, and as he moved up the classes she moved up with him. She also helped the other children. It was fantastic, and he did so well.'

A boy with Down's syndrome who, twenty years earlier, might have been condemned as 'ineducable', had a reading age of 9 by the time he was 12 – a tribute to the school, to Alex, to enlightened times and, most of all, to Matthew, who worked hard to learn, and played even harder, to fit in. So much about Matthew was founded in those six formative, challenging but happy years: his cheery confidence to go out into the world on equal terms, his self-worth and, most important of all, Matthew's belief that the other lads would want to be his friends.

'Wardley was my first school,' remembers Matthew. 'I liked it there. I got some mates of my own. I went home with them, sometimes. We had a nice time. They are the best.'

His time there was a triumph, for Matthew and for the generation of 'specials' like him.

Then came the bombshell.

Twelve-year-old Matthew expected to go on to Swinton High School with his mates, and Alex enrolled him. But the headmaster refused, saying their school 'wasn't ready for kids like this yet'. Alex made the reasonable point that he'd been at the feeder school since he was 6 and done very well, but the headmaster simply shrugged. The Education Department backed Alex and said they'd provide special tuition so that Matthew would have someone all the time, but the head dug his heels in even more and wouldn't even consider it.

Alex took a deep breath – and gave up.

'I thought, "If that's the attitude, they don't deserve Matthew." I didn't fight, because I knew that head wouldn't budge, and anyway, if I'd fought and won, he'd have been looking for faults and would have picked at him the whole time until they could have got him out. The head wasn't nasty or anything, just – "We're not ready for kids like him yet." Matter of fact.'

Thus it was that Matthew's efforts to be 'normal' were betrayed by an inflexible man who probably thought he was serving an interest greater than the unwritten contract that says an ungifted pupil who tries extra hard should be treated with respect and encouragement. This was a life-changing decision for Matthew; the brutal truth is that he was never the same again, his momentum was shattered – the delicate impetus to try that bit harder to make up for that extra chromosome had been casually crushed.

Matthew watched his mates, the boys he hung around with and played with, go off to the ordinary school, the one round the corner while, metaphorically speaking, he had to limp off to 'the Special'. It was bad for his friends, because they saw Matthew as one of them, and it was terrible for Matthew. It took away his hopes and expectations. His work ethos went, his philosophy of life changed overnight.

'I don't care where I go any more,' he said. 'I've done my homework all these years and I'm not with me mates. Why not?'

And Alex had to tell him the truth, that the school wouldn't have him.

Worse was to follow. Having left Wardley Primary School, and having been rejected by Swinton High School, Matthew was sent, instead, to a school for 'moderate learning difficulties', called Oakwood, in Salford, which was for people who weren't necessarily disabled, kids from bad homes, or who had never attended school properly. Apart from the fact that he didn't know a soul, that he got no one-to-one help, that he was still pining for his friends, Matthew says he was bullied.

'When I was transferred to Oakwood, I didn't like that. The thing is, I had to go. I was forced to. But there was a boy called Johnny, he bullied me, and told me I had to pull the girls' pants down. Johnny didn't have a life, a happy life like me. That is why.'

Johnny Stevens (name changed) came from a disrupted family; he had a brother who had drowned and the family had gone to pieces, and though he was more a streetwise truant than a bully, he made Matthew's life a misery. He'd wait for him in the toilet, tell him, 'Go and get the girls, do things to the girls,' and Matthew would say, 'I'm not doing that, I'm not.' So Matthew would never go to the toilet. It got that bad.

Altogether, Matthew stayed at Oakwood for eighteen long, miserable months. Given the headmaster of Swinton High School's refusal, Alex had little choice; Salford had no other options – it was either Oakwood or a fully fledged school for 'special needs', which was far too basic. But eventually, when Matthew was 13 in 1995, Alex had to act.

'Every day Matthew came home and said he didn't like being there; he told me that every day since he started. And every day, same as everybody else, I said, "You'll settle, get new friends, you'll be all right. Give it time." But after eighteen months when he said for the 500th time, "I hate this school. Why do you send me?" something in me snapped.

'So I said, "You've not got to go any more, it's not fair, you don't want to go, don't go." And he never went from that day on. I phoned up the Education Department and said, "He's not coming any more." I just told them.'

Lots of parents have had that stomach-churning feeling of being almost persecuted by the school 'system', when they're only trying to get the best for their child. Most are bought off by a loaded compromise, a few go to court, still fewer race round to the school office threatening violence.

Alex had her own modus operandi – she went icy calm and made a cup of tea, controlling her feelings by doodling in the margin of newspapers the names of people she once met who might now help. Gradually, over the space of a day or two, as her sense of injustice built, Alex was consumed by a quiet storm, not for her own sake, but for Matthew.

Without informing Salford, her local authority, she toured a wide area to find the most suitable school. In particular, she visited Tanfield, Wigan, which was a school for children with moderate or medium special needs. The Deputy Headmistress was so infectious with her enthusiasm for drama and art that Alex thought, 'If this is one of the people at the top, anyone would be happy here.' But apart from having a word with the Deputy Head, Alex didn't tell anyone: instead she waited.

Eventually, with Matthew now steadfastly at home, she was summoned to explain herself before Salford's education panel. But Alex was unrepentant, turning the tables on them by demonstrating that Salford had no suitable facility.

Her argument hinged on the fact that, on the one hand, Matthew had a proven school record at Wardley Primary and that since he had been transferred to Oakwood he had been given no incentive to develop educationally, as although Oakwood was essentially a special needs school, it was also the place children with behavioural problems were sent to, which Matthew certainly didn't have; and on the other hand, a fully fledged special school would be quite unsuitable for someone with Matthew's ability.

Finally, as the meeting was ending in acrimony, she casually suggested Tanfield, whose Deputy Head had indicated to Alex that they would in principle be willing for Matthew to go there. It was a solution that would cost Salford thousands of pounds because it was out of their area.

Salford had no option but to agree. The logic of Alex's argument was inescapable; there really was nowhere else for Matthew to go.

So in 1996, now aged 14, Matthew started at Tanfield. It turned out to be a breath of fresh air. After nearly two years of trauma at Oakfield, he was happy from the very beginning.

But two years later in 1998, at the age of 16 and while still at Tanfield, Matthew's heart began to cause concern. Nearly half of children born with Down's syndrome have congenital heart defects, typically, like Matthew, a hole in the heart. Sometimes, they heal themselves, and because Matthew's hole wasn't causing any direct problems, Alex and a succession of doctors had decided to wait and see. But when it hadn't healed by the time he was 16, they knew it would cause heart and lung problems in later life, so it was clear they had to operate.

These days, the procedure is straightforward; a balloon is fed up to the heart through a small incision in the groin, and the heart is sealed using a tiny pad, a bit like a small Brillo pad, so that when the blood congeals around it a sold mass is formed, blocking the hole. By the time Matthew was operated on, the Manchester health authority had performed nearly 200 similar operations, all of them completely successful.

Matthew's was the first to go wrong.

He went to St Mary's, the operation took half an hour, everything seemed fine, so after an night's rest, the next day he went home, and then back to school. But gradually Matthew went downhill, until a week later he couldn't get off the sofa. The hospital suggested a virus and prescribed antibiotics, then back to school – where he collapsed and had to be put in a taxi to St Mary's. By now, Matthew was breathless, he could hardly walk. When Alex met him outside he was taking three steps, then having to lie down.

'The walk from the car park which would have taken us ten minutes maximum took us over an hour, and I thought, I'm not going to get this kid to the ward. I'm not even going to get him as far as the hospital; he can't do it and I can't lift him up – he's 16. It suddenly struck me, God, Matthew is really ill.

'Of course this was something that had never happened to anybody else before so they just said, "Don't worry," until one of the nurses said, "Has he always got a heart rate this slow?" It was 40, and she said it should be about 78.

'A few hours later he went downhill rapidly and his heart rate dropped to about 25, which is virtually not working at all. So he wasn't getting any oxygen and as soon as he fell asleep he just started to go unconscious and his heart was just stopping.'

For Alex this was terrifying. But for Matthew, star of the show as always, he was simply beginning an adventure that he looks back on with delight.

'My heart stopped once, you know. I was dead, just for a little bit. That's not happened to you, has it? I've been dead.' Matthew laughs. Such fun.

Meanwhile Alex was suffering her own kind of heart attack.

'This was the worst night of my life. Here he was going in and out of consciousness, and by that time I had six others who needed looking after. If I stayed with Matthew there'd have been mayhem at home. Anyway, the doctor said, "We'll just see how he goes overnight," and I left him on the night care ward.

'Three o'clock in the morning I get a phone call from the nurse. "Matthew has seriously deteriorated so we'll have to put him in the High Dependency unit. We just thought you should know."

'"Thanks a bunch," I say. "I've got a house full of children asleep. What d'you want me to do?"

'So she says, very breezy, "Oh, he'll be fine, don't worry, we just wanted to tell you where he was so you don't panic when you come in the morning."

'So of course I couldn't go back to bed then at three in the morning. So I ironed. I ironed for four hours. I got rid of all the ironing in the house.

'As soon as I got the kids off to school, it was straight back to the hospital expecting to find this child in a coma. He was in the

High Dependency unit, with all the bleeps and drips and flashing red numbers, sat up on a computer game, apparently fine, saying, "I died, you know."'

Matthew's reaction a week after a routine operation was a mystery. The surgeon phoned every cardiology unit in the country but nobody has ever had this reaction. It continued for several days – one moment he would stabilise, the next he would go downhill with nurses racing around High Dependency in panic. They considered a pacemaker, further surgery, even a transplant, but the rollercoaster continued.

All the while, Alex was going home, trying to be normal, for the sake of her other six. After another week, his heart began to pick up a rhythm, instead of beep … beep … beep, Alex heard beep beep. Then back to beep … beep … beep.

The normal High Dependency stay, even for major operations, was just a couple of days, but Matthew remained wired to drips and machines for over a month. And though the surgeon, the nurses and Alex went almost grey with worry, Matthew adored every single minute.

'Kids in the High Dependency unit are usually unconscious, they don't eat, so no hospital food is brought in. But he was living the high life, because he could order any food any time he wanted and it would be specially arranged. And it was the most wonderful place I've ever been, because it was so safe and so secure and the nurses were one to one obviously with the kids, and had time to talk to you and make you cups of tea. So it was quite a shock, moving into a general ward where your kid is one of twenty. But still, Matthew was happy. "The kids in High Dependency were always asleep," he said – unconscious, more like – whereas the kids on the general ward loved having him to play with.'

To this day, nobody knows what caused Matthew's drastic reaction to his routine hole-in-the-heart operation and because they didn't know why it had happened in the first place they didn't know why it had recovered, so they didn't know whether it was going to happen again. Finally, they took the monitors off and then put him on a kind of treadmill, putting him under stress to see what might happen. It absolutely exhausted him because he was so unfit, but eventually they let him go home. Ever since then he's been fine.

'Occasionally, I still worry. The hole has healed up but he'll still have his little Brillo pad in there, a plug, it will be in there for life. The only thing they can think of that went wrong is that the electrodes, which went through his groin, may have accidentally touched part of his heart wall, enough to send it into heart block, it's called. To this day he has got no idea how seriously ill he was; he was having fun, he was eating, he was sleeping, he felt OK, and he was star of the hospital, with machines and monitors and drips, without which …'

Alex pauses, almost shudders, inhabited rather than just remembering. The cheerful toughness lifts for a moment with the realisation of how much she loves Matthew. Her first, her companion, her Mr Happy.

'… without which he wouldn't be around, he would have been in heart failure.'

She shakes her head. 'It was horrible, it was awful, seeing the other parents. Every day you watch them by the side of beds, their children desperately ill, many die. And you're just thinking, "Oh, God, please don't let it be mine."'

*　　*　　*

Matthew stayed at Tanfield until he was 19, his confidence growing by the day, mainly because the work was too easy for him. At
Swinton High he would have had to run to keep up; at Tanfield
he was top of the class without too much effort. Eventually,
Matthew became Head Boy. Alex had mixed feelings. Academ-
ically, he wasn't stretched, but socially 'they brought him back to
being my Matthew again'.

Nevertheless, the legacy of a single pronouncement, the dead-
ening 'No' from the Headmaster of Swinton High, continues to
this day because Matthew was excluded from the challenges of
being ordinary, excluded from the right to a normal life that Alex
was trying so hard to give him.

'The difference of that one decision by that headmaster is incal-
culable. From that moment, Matthew's confidence crumbled. He
was left out, left behind. And he couldn't understand why. He'd
always tried hard, done his homework, been polite, kind, helpful, always did what he was told, and here he was being totally
rejected. And if he didn't know why, he didn't know what he had
to do to be accepted. Terrible isn't a strong enough word.

'OK, so things have moved on, at least he wasn't chained to a
bed, but that one arbitrary decision by someone that didn't know
him, had never met him, chained him in another way, chained
him outside from his friends. And he's never got over it, never
will get over it. Being told you won't fit in because of what you
are, rather than who you are.'

Matthew may have been Mr Happy but there have been bumps
and scrapes along the way, even though he has a remarkable ability – typical of Down's people – to bounce back and hold on to his
dreams ...

*   *   *

Matthew at 25

Hello. My name is Matthew Bell. I am a student at Eccles College. I have a bus pass and a student card. Today we are going to Camelot. We go on the rides and watch a show called King Arthur and the Knights of the Round-table. *Then we come home to have a Chinese.*

People say I'm mad about chocolate, but I'm not really. I don't eat cakes. My life is happy, because I make new friends.

Sometimes my mum Alex gets a bit hard. I do love her, but she's always strict with children. Apart from that, she's fabulous. She was a teacher and she decided to give up her job and have me instead.

I do music. We are doing Oliver! *I am playing a baddy called Bill Sykes. Last time I was in* Snow White. *I played Happy the dwarf. Because I told them, 'I'm happy.'*

I live in a big house. I have a drum kit. It was my 21st birthday present. I have the best bedroom and the best view. I've got a girlfriend called Leanne. And I've got brothers and sisters. But I'm the second in command.

Matthew left Eccles, the local further and higher education college close to Salford, in 2007, though he still likes to go back now and again. He loved it there. He can read, he can write, and like many youngsters with the world out there in front of them, he has dreams that might be a touch unrealistic. Like being an actor, or working for Manchester United … but more on that later.

'For my job, I want to be an actor, to have a part in *Coronation Street*, I want to be their first Down's syndrome character. They can write a special part. This would be to express the love in me, and to make friends. The main character I like is Lucy Barlow. She'll be my best mate, with Pete Barlow too.'

'They once had a Down's baby on *Brookside*,' says Alex, 'who gurgled a bit, so keep hoping, chuck.' But she's careful not to dash his hopes or the sheer bravado of his ambition. What Matthew needs, though, is practical help, because the denial of a normal high-school life interfered with the evolution of so many everyday systems, which he might have picked up naturally from ordinary mates.

Although Matthew can tell the time, he doesn't fully understand what it means, not in the sense of being somewhere at, say, half-past three. Lunchtime is to do with being hungry rather than being time to break for lunch. However, this doesn't mean he can't learn punctuality, more that he will need constant, repetitive experiences of 'right place, right time' before a regularity will be irrevocably fixed in his mind. As Alex says, the best way for Matthew to get this is through a one-to-one relationship to guide him into the market of work.

'At the moment, you can go to Safeway and say, "My son's a disabled person, he has a right to work here," and maybe they'll take him on. But, of course, the person will fail because they haven't got the same initiative, the same simple skills, as other people. They need one person to say, "Right, you've done that job, now what's the next job? Go on, do that."'

Such a mentoring scheme would transform the working lives of the more gifted Down's people. Simple things, like taking the bus to work, showing them 'this is where you get on, where you sit, get off, turn here, through this door', repeated for weeks until it sticks, will create a sense of independence, which in turn would allow them to be fully productive members of society; and that matters to proud people like Matthew.

Alex, of course, has a plan. 'I'm going to approach Manchester United, because it's Matthew's great love and he would make a brilliant tour guide. He can talk the socks off anybody about the team, the history, and most of the guides are older men, real fans, and they love Matthew whenever he goes, and could say, "This is my assistant Matthew, he's going to help me with the tour."

'He would be within a secure environment that he knows well, with people who will appreciate that he might need a little bit of extra help, while they can stand back and let him do his own thing, say three mornings a week – "Right, Matthew will tell you about the players' room" – and that would be so lovely for him, and very good for the club, because a lot of people do those tours; thousands of people every year from all over the world. It's a Mecca, is Old Trafford, and my God, he'd be over the moon, he could be doing that for the rest of his life.

'At the beginning he may need somebody to take him and be there in case there's a problem, and bring him home, but eventually, with a routine, he might just be dropped off at the club, picked up at the club, and the club would take him under their wing because people are great with Matthew, they will love him to bits. He's absolutely besotted with the whole place and I think that it's a real possibility for Matthew, and so good for everyone …'

Phew. Wayne Rooney has nothing on Alex in full flow.

The key to Matthew having a happy, productive life is for him to have routines and stability in which everything has to stay the same – his base mustn't change too much. He is bright for a lad with Down's syndrome, but he's been held back by a naturally conservative nature, and by being at a school and within a family which didn't really challenge him. (Matthew is by far the most capable of Alex's children. He's the only one who can read and write – though Emily is beginning to – and is physically pretty coordinated. Hence he can seem way ahead of the rest without even trying.) Alex knows this has been a block on his development, and would love to push him out into the world more, though there will always be limitations – not least because Matthew, like many Down's people, is so trusting and obedient.

For example, Matthew could learn to drive a car and would obey the Highway Code meticulously but he'd be lethal on the roads because he'd expect other road users to be absolutely reliable too. The moment they swerved suddenly or – unthinkable to Matthew – broke the law, he couldn't cope and might inadvertently cause an accident. He cannot anticipate the unexpected. It's the way he is – he will always be reliable, do the right thing, so he can't expect that other people will do odd or bad things.

Maybe because of that extra chromosome 21 Matthew believes that people will help him out, that the world is wonderful, and because he's rarely met nasty people he doesn't understand that there are predators who would prey on him, with bad intentions, that he's only safe up to a certain point, beyond which he'd be putting himself in harm's way. Down's people don't know there's a line. And he won't become streetwise because, like many people with Down's, he wasn't born with suspicion, and hasn't been on the street enough to learn it.

So he doesn't have a realistic concept of evil. He understands villains in films, or that murderers are bad – for instance, he might see Peter Sutcliffe (the Yorkshire Ripper) or Osama Bin Laden as a baddie, but he couldn't imagine someone that he might meet on a bus as evil. And he is very black and white – 'Good and bad to him is like pantomime,' says Alex – anything subtle or theoretical is difficult for people with Down's to grasp, so Alex helps him out.

'Some parts of Matthew are less developed than other parts,' she says. 'Abstract things, like money. He understands the concept of why we use money, what it's for, but not what money really represents. If he had a £20 note, he could use it to pay for, say, a magazine, but he couldn't understand the change. If someone short-changed him, he wouldn't know, which makes him vulnerable. I only let him have a pound at a time – unless it's something specific that I know the price of, so then I can send him with exactly the right money.'

Alex thinks that Matthew functions around the mental age of 11 to 12, but there are bits that are 7 or 8, those abstract bits, the difficult concepts of life. And though it would be very easy for him to stagnate, stay exactly as he is, she believes that one day he'll grow to live apart from them, still within the family, but apart – with his own flat, but broadly looked after. And supported forever.

Matthew agrees. 'I definitely don't want to live on my own, but I will move out when I get married. To Leanne, we're engaged. I'm going down to Bristol to church, and then get a flat together and have kids.'

Matthew and girls – this is familiar territory for Alex.

'That bit certainly isn't 7 or 8. That functions at 25 – the sexual bits – because he wants a girlfriend, wants to get married, and all that. There are girls at college – he's marrying a different one every week. He's very caring, very compassionate, very friendly, very protective – if that's what women want. Very reliable, but also very moody – doesn't take criticism well, never lashes out, never screams or shouts, just moody.

'And very loving – a childlike lovingness, very trusting. But most of it's words, he just wants girls as friends, he likes talking to them, but he's not into "action", he never wants anything other than a drink of Coke.'

That may be so, but apart from Alex there is still one other woman who features very significantly in Matthew's thoughts.

'People say it's a dream ...'

The story of Matthew Bell would not be complete without knowing that one word – a name – is ever present on the tip of his tongue. The word is Jane (not her real name), his birth mother. If you ask him a general question, like 'Are you happy, Matthew?' he will answer, out of the blue, 'Yes, because of me mum Jane, she's a nice lady, and though I don't see her, she thinks about me, every day.' That is what he says, misty-eyed, unprompted.

Or if you ask, 'Who is your favourite person, Matthew?' back comes the same answer – 'Me birth mother, Jane.'

Or, 'What's your first memory?' he answers, 'Me mum, me first mum, Jane. I remember meeting her. People say it's a dream, but it's not.' Yet Matthew has not met her since he was 3 years old, and can't have a memory of her.

At first sight, this is a tragedy, a heartbreaking story of unrequited love. But on deeper examination, it's an opportunity – to settle a host of painful demons from the past and to reach forward, to see if there can be a pot of gold at the end of Matthew's particular rainbow. The agony goes well beyond him, or even his mother, to a birth family who have carried an unbearable burden for far too long.

Alex still feels sad for both his birth parents when she recalls their meeting when Matthew was 3. Matthew also has an older brother, and most crucial of all, a twin brother, a young man exactly the same age, who has not met Matthew.

This is a fairly typical Down's syndrome state of affairs: one twin baby taken home and the Down's twin left behind at the hospital. A mother pining with love for a child she isn't able to see, a father who has rejected him, and brothers who may know little of his existence.

With such a background, the obvious temptation is to avoid raking over potentially distressing emotions and move on, but that would disregard Matthew's feelings. He desperately wants to meet his birth family, especially his mother and twin brother. So, before his 18th birthday, Alex took Matthew to After Adoption, a charity who specialise in helping adoptees find their birth parents and counsel all parties through what is often a delicate process. Over the last century a million children in the UK have been adopted, and After Adoption have acted as intermediary in thousands of cases. They have a huge archive of birth, marriage and death certificates, which they provide to people who are researching their personal history.

Matthew's birth family had disappeared. Alex did not have their new address, dates of birth, or even his father's full name. All she knew was a surname, that his mother was called 'Jane' (to repeat, this is not her real name), and that Matthew had a brother two years older, presumably born in 1980. The best starting point was to find their full names from the marriage certificate.

With Matthew as her assistant, Alex combed through tens of thousands of certificates looking for their surname – conveniently slightly unusual. 'If they'd been called Smith, we'd have been there for years,' Alex remembers. No luck for 1979, so then backwards to 1978. Still no luck. They returned the next day, and halfway through the marriages for 1977 the name leapt out. Now they had the father's full name; for confirmation they went back to cross-check that he had fathered a son in 1980. He had. They had the marriage and birth certificates for the right family. But that didn't provide an address.

To locate addresses, After Adoption have their own town and street database, but they do not open it up to tracers. Their deal was: 'Now we know who we have to locate, leave it to us; we will find them, contact them on your behalf, and try to get you all together.' But first, Alex had to provide them with a biographical package.

'We wrote a letter to them, a positive letter, with Matthew's school results, his hobbies and interests, things he'd written, this is what he's like, that he's a fantastic personality, that he's funny, very happy. And we put a picture in, along with stories and news of his 18th birthday, that he had his mates over, had a little party, all those little things that they'd want to know.'

The package was put together by After Adoption, who sent it to Matthew's birth family, suggesting they get in touch. To Alex's delight, the response was immediate.

'After Adoption got a wonderful phone call from Matthew's mum, saying she thought about him every day of her life, especially on his 18th birthday, because, of course, her other twin shared the same birthday. And – fantastic news for Matthew – she'd love to meet him. So After Adoption contacted us and told Matthew to get ready to see his mum, maybe a big get-together late birthday party …'

Then … nothing.

Alex phoned After Adoption. They were very sorry, but they had received no further contact from Matthew's parents.

Alex kept badgering until eventually After Adoption said that they presumed Matthew's parents had simply changed their mind. And it was their policy not to pursue families who did not respond.

Matthew was devastated.

One moment the highest of highs; the next moment, the coldest of cold shoulders. According to Alex, 'you could physically see him drop'.

'I think somewhere out there is a damaged lady who is desperate to meet Matthew, but can't – probably she had no choice, and I don't want to cause her any problems. Or the boys. We don't know they weren't told that "one twin died at birth", that's how they explained only bringing home one twin. This probably isn't a case that she's wonderful and he's horrible, I bet it's more complex than that. But hopefully she did get that letter, and his photo, and hopefully she's hidden it somewhere, and she looks at it, and that she feels proud of him.'

Alex fluctuates between being philosophical and wanting to take direct action, but Matthew isn't so restrained. He's all for finding their address, knocking on the door and saying, 'I'm Matthew, I'm your son,' but, so far, Alex has dissuaded him.

'What would it do to his mum and dad if they were actually confronted with him in circumstances like that? And what would it do to Matthew if they shut the door in his face?'

Matthew is left with a legacy of anguished disappointment, which may one day turn bitter. He has been rebuffed. All adopted children would find it hard to understand, but for a person with Down's, programmed by that extra chromosome to love and be loved, it is beyond comprehension. So Matthew furrows his brow, lets his bottom lip hang down and thrashes around in his pain with a series of disjointed spits and spats – it's the only way Matthew knows how to deal with the hurt of rejection.

'My first mum was a nice lady, but my dad was a nasty piece of work, who has stopped me seeing my true twin brother. My life is rotten because someone has wrecked it for me. My dad wrecked my life and my dad hates me. Because he didn't want my mum – my real mum – to have a Down's syndrome kid.'

Alex treats this philosophically. 'I've always known that his mum has had constant problems getting access to Matthew, so one of the reasons I do media work, go on the telly, take Matthew with me, is so that his mum sees him. I don't think anyone could ever feel bad about Matthew, so I hope she sees her kid from time to time on television, or in a magazine. That's all I can do.'

Does this story have an unhappy ending? We'll have to wait and see. Though it may be beyond Alex and Matthew, it's not difficult to find people with slightly unusual names these days, especially using the Internet and Google.

Certainly, it wasn't hard to find Matthew's twin brother – two years ago he signed a chatty letter about deodorant to a men's health magazine, which included the town he then lived in. Next, it was off to a local council office in the Home Counties for two hours combing through the electoral register, which gave the address of a detached house in which he lived with his father and mother and a brother.

This leaves one crucial decision. To approach, or not to approach?

The answer must be to balance the pain versus the possibilities of joy. Let's say there *is* an approach and it causes discomfort or anger or perhaps even outrage to his birth family – how long will that last? A few days? Weeks? A couple of months? That is not to marginalise pain, especially if caused by intrusion, but it is with a purpose.

Because if there is *no* approach, the gnawing, aching pain will go on forever, and not just for Matthew or his birth mother. What about his birth father? His purpose all along may have been to protect a family he loves. He may have felt desperately sad and lonely in forcing through the decision he made, and it's unlikely he's had any kind of closure. In short, he has lived with a decision for twenty-five years now, a decision he would have thought was for the best for all concerned. That must have hurt, must still hurt.

So, to leave matters as they are will continue to cause pain. But if an approach is made and it works, not only is the release of that pain a major positive, the possibility of long-term, lasting joy is enthralling. For Matthew's mother, Matthew's family and most important of all, for Matthew himself. Given the balance of possible short-term pain versus possible long-term joy, it's difficult to do nothing.

In his broader life, the busy life of a go-ahead young adult, Matthew is having fun, and getting 'out there'. If Matthew's appearing in a play or musical, which he usually is, he'll want to do the dance, sing the song, rap the lines in Alex's kitchen, and he doesn't wait to be asked. From Bill Sykes in *Oliver!*, to a villager in *Puss in Boots*, he'll press the button on the CD and jiggle in front of the microwave, head down in concentration. This won't only be a verse and chorus, he'll do the whole number, sometimes waiting in silence during a section that belongs to a co-star.

When it's done, he doesn't expect applause or praise, that's not his purpose; he's doing it for the doing, 'because it's good', as he often says. And it *is* good, of course, because it's Matthew. He brings out the best in himself and in other people. Everybody likes him; though he can ramble and rabbit, and though he makes things up, no one could feel badly because of Matthew.

Take Leanne he mentioned earlier as his 'girlfriend', for example. She's Nathan's older sister, training to be a nurse in Bristol, quasi-engaged, and though she adores Matthew, it's not as a boyfriend, not even as a friend, but as a boy in a man's frame, who feels somehow, as a young man, that he 'ought' to have a girl-friend. That's a major part of Matthew's charm, and he is charming, being so youthfully easy-going – though, these days, he can become tetchy when his eight brothers and sisters turn the decibels of their constant playtime up too high, or when Chloe, especially Chloe, interferes with his 'things'. A momentary cloud might frown over Matthew's sunny, fleshy face as he grumbles off to his own space downstairs. But fifteen seconds later it will be gone, forgotten, because he's incapable of a grudge, unable to harbour ill feelings.

After a shaky start, and a major hole-in-the-heart scare, Matthew's life has been a hard-earned success. Fifty years ago he would have been locked away; now he's heading towards a fulfilled life. None of it has been easy; often it's been downright hard and sometimes unfair, but he's reached the age of 25 in good health and with a hopeful future.

As he says himself, 'I was a dwarf in *Snow White*, I was Happy. That's me, Mr Happy.'

And, yes, he is. Happy.

But there's still one hole in his heart that hasn't been repaired.

Chapter Six

'You won't be keeping this one': Simon

Discovery Bay is a shimmering enclave of upmarket houses and apartments tucked away on the ocean side of Lantau Island, Hong Kong.

Although the city, bustling and booming, is only a 25-minute ferry ride away, the resort is a haven of peace because no cars are allowed among the decent parks, the ex-pat golf course, the marina club or the long sandy beach. Family life here is easy. There is an ample supply of inexpensive Filipina amahs (women who were hired to suckle babies) and nannies, a spotless day nursery, and an international primary school based on the English curriculum. Trouble, when it occurs, usually comes from the urban turbulence of Hong Kong city, or when a signal 8 typhoon sweeps across the choppy South China Sea.

That was the case on 27 June 1984 when Adam's mother took the ferry and checked into the maternity ward of Matilda Hospital, on Victoria Peak, high above Hong Kong, for what was expected to be a routine delivery. She was 30, living with her husband, a British solicitor from Devon. This was to be her second child; they already had a 5-year-old daughter who was being looked after at home by the amah.

Adam weighed 2.895 kilograms at birth, with a colour that was distinctly blue. He was immediately diagnosed as having a congenital heart condition and Down's syndrome. The next day he was transferred to Queen Mary Hospital. After fifteen days he was sent home, stable, with slight cyanosis but otherwise healthy.

For the Chinese, the birth of a baby is a magical but superstitious event, tied up with favourable signs or dark omens. Seconds matter, as can the weather or tides, and the actual demeanour of the baby can be significant, too. A Down's syndrome child is considered lucky. It's said they give more love, stay with their parents forever and are happy children.

In British hospitals, in theory at least, there are procedures for telling a mother that her baby has Down's syndrome. Essentially, after an initial cuddle, the baby is spirited away 'to the nursery' until the birth processes are finished and, ideally, until after the mother has had some sleep, before a dedicated team of senior nurse and consultant can gently, and very supportively, break the news. However, according to reports, Adam's mother was told enthusiastically of his condition within moments of his birth by a Hong Kong maternity nurse, as if it were a matter to celebrate.

Her response was to reject him. She never recovered from that initial shock or formed a bond with her child. Where there is no love, no amount of counselling will help. If a mother cannot stand to cuddle her baby, there is nothing she, or anyone else, can do about it. Any attempt to keep mother with baby is only the cruel prolonging of an inevitable rejection followed by institutionalisation, or adoption.

However, for Adam all was not lost. After two weeks he went home to Discovery Bay and was met by Cara, a Filipina amah, who was thrilled to have a tiny baby all to herself. Cara could have held him forever. Like many Down's syndrome babies he was highly responsive; though floppy, he would laugh and giggle and smile – always smile. Cara talked and sang to him and gave him the physical hugging and maternal love that the often broken-hearted mothers of Down's babies simply can't manage, and he thrived on it.

As the weeks passed, although Adam progressed well, the strain at home became intolerable. His parents considered having Adam put in an institution or adopted in Hong Kong, but the island was soon to be taken back by China, so they decided, instead, that he should be flown to Britain, initially to Adam's grandmother's home near Plymouth, and while back there, that his father should approach the Local Authority for help.

On Saturday, 15 September 1984, Adam said goodbye forever to Hong Kong. Cara carried him onto an airliner and then cuddled him all the way to a new homeland, his mother travelling separately with her daughter. Three days later, still only 3 months old and tiny, he was taken into the care of Devon County Social Services. In their report, put before the courts, they describe him as slightly cyanotic – the old-fashioned term used to be 'blue baby' – 'but remarkably alert and mobile for a Down's syndrome baby. He is responsive and laughs and giggles a lot. His responsiveness is probably due to the very high degree of loving care provided in the first few weeks of his life by the Filipino amah.'

But what the report does not say, what nobody knew, was that Adam had been born with a death sentence. He had Tetralogy of Fallot, basically a hole in the wall of his heart separating the left and right ventricles – serious, but ultimately treatable. However, in Adam's case it wasn't only one hole – it was four.

*   *   *

Temporarily back in Britain, Adam's father told social services that he wanted to sign a 'Freeing Order', a rare and unconditional procedure by which birth parents relinquish all control or responsibility over their baby son; they would have no say over his life from the moment it was signed.

The Adoption Worker for that part of Devon was Hester St John Ives. Though now in her 70s, she still works part time for Devon Social Services, and well remembers when she first heard about Adam.

'I took the initial phone call from an absolutely distraught elderly woman, who said, "My son in Hong Kong had a Down's child, and wants to have him adopted." He came over, stayed with his mother, went through the rigmarole – which was quite unprecedented. Most of us hadn't heard of Freeing Orders. What they didn't want was to be saddled with the child. So he signed, then the mum came over – I don't think she ever touched the baby, couldn't face it. And she signed. So the Local Authority became the parents.'

Hester is warm and engaging, old school upper-class, but free thinking and mildly scandalous, with a round handsome face and bustling, muscular manner. As exotic, down-to-earth and well bred as her name, she lives in a country house just up from the main square in a perfect Devon market town.

'The Filipino amah adored him. She had flown over, helped me take him to Pam Smith, his new foster mother. Filipinos and Chinese regard Down's syndrome as lucky in the family, I don't think she could understand why anyone would want to give up a lucky baby. And the grandma, she was very keen on the child, too. But had to keep quiet. The mother was vulnerable and tragic, and only just in control of herself. I didn't warm to the father, very protective of his image.'

Adam's life is full of ironies: the most rejected baby, the most cuddled, with much more to follow. But when in October 1984 foster mother Pam Smith, then 33, studied her angelic, delicate charge, she got more and more panicky.

'I'd said yes to fostering, because I was really up for a baby. But when Hester brought him round, I was thinking, "I've never done disabled, I don't know, can I cope?" Then my daughter Karen, I can still see her, he was in a pram at the bottom of the garden, and she went, "Mum, I thought you said he was Down's syndrome."

'"He is, sweetheart."

'"Well, he doesn't look it."

'And I thought, "Right, I can do this."

'So I picked him up, and never put him down.'

A determined though nervy woman, Pam was an assistant dinner lady at the local school and, at that time, had little experience of fostering. Now in her 50s, she still lives in the spotless post-war terraced house on the edge of Plymouth where Adam came to her twenty-two years ago. He's still part of her, still her 'cheeky babe'.

It was in this house, lying on a blanket in front of the gas fire, that Pam first noticed that Adam's breathing was irregular. His stomach had caved in, he was gasping, struggling for breath. She raced him to the doctors, they diagnosed heart failure, the hospital carried out a routine procedure, and he was back in front of Pam's fireplace within a week.

'The nurse came with this A4 sheet and a drawing of the heart and was explaining to me this was that, that was this, and here is where the hole is. And because I'm quite into medical stuff, I asked, "So how big is the hole?"

'"Oh, we don't need to go down that road, that will be a job for the consultant ..."

'I thought, "Ah, they're not answering me, there's something wrong here," but I didn't push it, I couldn't push it, because I was on a positive at the time, and I had to be strong enough to bring him home, get him spruced, have Adam ready for a family, for adoption.'

In March 1985, Adam was first advertised on page 26 of *Be My Parent*, the adoption magazine (see page 92). He was eight months.

After a few weeks, Devon Social Services had several enquiries from approved adopters and Hester was beginning to arrange interviews when Adam turned very blue and virtually stopped breathing. What the adoption advert had described as 'a heart murmur' became progressively 'serious', then 'life-threatening', then 'probably terminal'.

There was only one hospital in the south of England equipped to deal with his condition, only one consultant prepared to give it a go – Barry Keaton of Southampton General. With the adoption put on hold, Adam was rushed off by ambulance in Pam Smith's lap to begin the most harrowing few months of both their lives.

If this is a book with no villains it certainly does have heroes – souls prepared to bear pain so they can give love. Like foster mother Pam, who wore her heart on the sleeve that cuddled and caressed a lonely baby as he went in and out of life, in and out of death. It's far easier to be a doctor or a nurse at such times, easier to be busy, diverted, professional, easier to be at the sharp end.

Pam was at the blunt end, down the corridor by the tea machine, always waiting so that when Adam surfaced – *if* he surfaced – she was there with a snatched kiss, a coo and comfort, while flicking away the tear that's part of the deal. Pam had to cry, because she had to care – they complement each other like the two sides of Adam's oh-too-softly beating heart – a tick then tock, care then cry.

Adam

Date of birth: 27th June 1994

(Profile originally published in *Be My Parent*. Reproduced with kind permission of BAAF.)

ADAM is a cuddly 8-month-old baby who was born with the mental handicap known as Down's Syndrome. He is quite small for his age, but is making good progress in his foster home. He focusses well, his muscle tone is improving and he is beginning to sit up and to make efforts to roll over.

Adam loves being cuddled and delights his foster family with lots of happy cooing and burbling. He is used to having older children around and really enjoys company.

Adam has a heart murmur, and has twice been admitted to hospital when a virus infection put his heart under strain. The condition is still being investigated, but the current view is that it may prove inoperable. If so, unless the condition can be controlled by medication, Adam's life expectancy might be limited to his mid-teens.

Because Adam tires easily, feeding can be a slow process, and his mental handicap means he will probably have to attend a special school.

Everyone who knows Adam is won over by his engaging personality and ready smile. When he was in hospital he was a great favourite on the children's ward, with the young nurses competing to look after him.

Adam is an alert and responsive baby with a contented nature. He needs a family who can accept his handicaps while encouraging him to live life to the full. In return he will bring them great happiness.

Pam kept a diary, her blow-by-blow account of Adam's odyssey in the hands of a committed surgeon who probably should have given up but just didn't. And while his team, also heroic in a seven-days-a-week, routine kind of way, bustled and pumped and connected machines, Pam sobbed in ballpoint onto an economy jotter. Yellowing now, brown round the edges, it's a testament to faith and persistence, spirit and prayer, to science and love.

The Diary of Adam by Pam Smith

Thursday, 16 May 1985
Called at 6 a.m. Walked to operating theatre with him – flat on his tum, head up, almost to say 'Where are we going?'

See you later kid – steal a kiss. Tears.

Later, shock of the face blanked out. More tears.

Friday, 17 May
Tried to have a cuddle, got too upset as he was so cold. Went for cig, waiting. He's back on a ventilator, fighting. Dear Lord, will I ever forget the feel of those cold lifeless hands. Night, night Adam. Stick in there kid.

Saturday, 18 May
Heart failure on right ventricle, infection on right lung. Sitting with him in the afternoon, noticed his right hand twitching. Poor little lamb, if only I can do something – it's enough to see your little face with tubes, without it contorting with fits. Now midnight. Must get to bed. Night, night. Stick in there kid. Steal a kiss.

From the very beginning, Adam was fighting for his life. Still a baby, his bright eyes now dulled, his smile hidden by a bright red dummy, his tiny heart became a hotchpotch of patches as he went on the ventilator in Intensive Care.

The initial operation, these days quite standard but in the 1980s still life-threatening, was to place a pad alongside the walls of his heart, essentially to stop used and oxygenated blood from mixing before beginning its journey around his veins. Initially it worked. Though still very weak, and suffering from fits because of lack of enriched blood, Adam stabilised and even started making progress.

For Pam, keeping a bedside watch, or out by the entrance having a smoke, the tension and tears seemed to be worth it.

Saturday, 25 May

He's off the ventilator! Cup of tea and Kit Kat to celebrate. Tears of happiness – brave strong little fellow. Joy of joys I had a cuddle. Can give you kisses now instead of stealing them through the bloody tubes. Well done little one. Stick in there kid. GIVE you a kiss night night.

That was the high point of Pam's vigil at the hospital. Some time on the Monday, the pad shifted and Adam's heart stopped. He was rushed back to theatre for an emergency operation. The surgery team attempted more complex procedures, with Barry Keaton rewriting the book as he went. After every operation they seem to discover yet another hole, which in turn put pressure on the hole they had just repaired. Still Adam fitted, so more pads were needed, but his little heart could not cope, and shut down. He was resuscitated, then it shut down again; and again; and again. Eventually, when the surgeon had tried everything possible, Adam was wheeled back to Intensive Care.

Tuesday, 28 May

Devastated.

Doors shut with screen out. Elaine stopped me. 'I'm sorry, Pam, he's not too good, we have to reventilate him.'

Can't – or won't – take it in.

As Elaine explains, the tears flow. The right ventricle is in failure, pneumonia has spread down and he's needing a lot of oxygen.

Damn tears – will you never stop? A cup of tea appears from somewhere, they do their bit to comfort me. Special times of the past few days come back – helping to wash him, feeding him through the tube, brushing his tuft of hair on the top – and that special cuddle. Hold on to those – pull on the strength they can give me.

Hester calls – 'A nun and the Sisters are praying – all in the office are thinking of us. Can I see about getting him christened?'

I feel quite composed – although numb – Hester rings off in tears. It must be worse for her being so far off. Go back for a while. He's quiet – all checks are stable. Night, night, Adam. Stick in there kid. Steal a kiss.

Wednesday, 29 May

Went down 6.30. Not much change.

Ask Barbara about christening him. 'We can get that done for you.'

It's Hugh's (the Priest) day off but he arrives. Laying his hands on my shoulders he talks quietly, compassionately. 'So sorry for Adam – for you – don't give up, he's not left us yet.' 'If he dies – well there is a reason Pam – you won't see it now but in time you will – maybe he was just too good for this world.'

He takes my hand and we go back in.

[Intensive Care Nurse] Julia has gone up to [ward] El borrowed a vase and some flowers, someone's Polaroid and a nightie cut up the back. One of the treatment trolleys is covered with a white cloth, Hugh's candlesticks, and water bowl and flowers at the side.

Hugh starts and I'm conscious of Julia at my side with her arm round me. My tears flow gently at the start then sudden uncontrollable sobs – I just feel we're putting home the last screw – as if we were giving up. Towards the end an inner calm came over me and I felt quite warm. You're not on your own now little one. Just as He's guided and watched over me He's there now with you. This time the ventilator is in your nose so I've two little cheeks I can kiss. Put you back on the bed with girls holding all the tubes. He's quiet in the evening, not twitching so hope the fits have finished.

Hester phones and I relate the day to her.

Night, night. Stick in there kid. Steal a kiss.

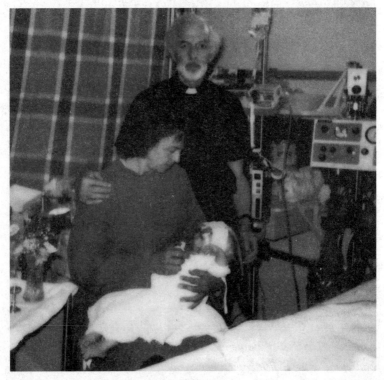

Adam's baptism.

Adam was only just clinging to life, with more serious neuro-logical damage than first realised. After he had been connected to machines for nearly a month, the consultant decided that there was little purpose in keeping him alive artificially, so baby Adam left Intensive Care and the ventilator, and went back to the general ward, probably to die within the next few days. Pam was 'completely drained – emotionally, mentally, physically' – overwhelmed by the endless bleep-bleep-bleep, highs-and-lows of such a brittle life. The hospital expected nature to take its mortal course, but still Adam continued to cling on to life.

And then, against all medical logic, he stabilised.

This took Pam by surprise and shook her spiritual expectations. A superstitious woman by nature, and religious by conviction, Pam felt as if she had said her last prayers for him, had accepted living without him, had come to terms with his death. So, as Adam revived, her slight confusion was reflected in her diary.

Friday, 14 June

The joy of seeing his little face without ventilator was indescribable. 'Do you want a cuddle?' DO I!!!!

Long talk with Paul. 'What's the neurological damage?' – 'Too early to say yet.' Mixed emotions – so sad to see state of Adam, but relieved to have talked it out.

Baby Adam now weighed 5.5 kilograms. With no more surgery possible, the acute hospital needed the bed and wanted him to leave – but to go where? His birth parents were back in Hong Kong with no responsibility, he was an administrative orphan, under the overall charge of Devon Social Services. So it was down to Hester St John Ives, and she decided that he would be sent back to Plymouth, to a long-stay hospital called Freedom Fields, which functioned as a convalescent home and sometimes as a hospice.

To Pam this was good news – after nearly six weeks camping out in Southampton she could now look after him from home, but underneath her breezy optimism, anger was building at the cruelty of fate, that he was now 'a brain damaged mite, just sitting there'.

Sunday, 23 June

Had a lie in!

Adam sitting in bouncy chair head to one side just lolling. Tell me Hugh, what's the point of him living? What have you been left with now and for how long little one?

Monday, 24 June

In his bouncy chair fast asleep with eyes open. As far as I'm concerned Adam died weeks ago. Squeeze of hand – walk away choking. Ordered first birthday cake – can't bring myself to make one. Sorry little fellow but it was done with as much love as if I could have made it.

Pam was caught in a trap. Unable to bear Adam's brain damage, she had reached the end of her endurance – but still thought of herself as his mother, felt that she had a duty to look after him, and couldn't desert her baby until she was able to pass him on to an adoptive family.

The social services support team understood this, and decided that Pam should go home. At first they only dropped hints … she had done all she could … she should put her own family first – but still she went in, wandering the corridors at Freedom Fields like a dazed corpse, causing the staff concern that Pam herself needed help.

This culminated in a choreographed meeting in the office of Dr Pelham, the head of Freedom Fields, which was specifically called to help deal with Pam, and to help Pam deal with herself, although she had no idea that was the purpose.

Thursday, 27 June
Adam's first birthday.

The big meeting. Dr Pelham kindness itself. Won't resuscitate or use injection if Adam goes into heart failure. 'Can't tell the extent of brain damage, not for a while.'

Dawning realisation – they're talking of him making it and then him leaving hospital. Oh God, what are we doing? I cried out – 'But I can't take him home!'

All four at the meeting virtually together say to me 'No you can't.'

Dr Pelham: 'We've called on you to do more than enough, and you've done it. We wouldn't expect you to do any more.'

Feel worse than I did – the full force that this time I won't be handing the baby over to an adoptive family. My first boy – and I can't see him on to a happy couple.

Go back in the afternoon with birthday cake and cards. Told Adam how many cards he had and described them. Had a short cuddle but moaning all the time – with this morning's conversation going round and round in my head I can take it no more and have to leave.

While Adam continued to survive, but lie almost lifelessly in his cot, Hester St John Ives had been working behind the scenes to find a long-term home for him, finally coming up with Parkview residential children's home, the first time he would be out of hospital for three months. The journey to Parkview was Pam's opportunity to say a final goodbye, to hand over what she called 'my lifeless bundle', so Pam got up early to gather his toys and clothes – most of which she and her family had given him.

Tuesday, 23 July

Felt a bit down first thing.

Adam sitting in his chair with blue two-piece romper suit on. Packed all his bits, then took him out for a cuddle. Back in his cot to change him. Lying there in nappy – turned to get vest – AND HE COOED. He did it for quite a while. When I rudely interrupted and lifted his head to put the vest over – HE CRIED. Real noise – real tears – with me joining him! Oh little one you'll never know what that meant to me – and today of all days! How I've ached to hear your voice – to see and hear you cry – ever since May 15th little one and today – the very day I needed it you gave it to me. Carried on dressing you – all-in-one romper Pen got, socks 'Auntie' Gail gave you – all in blue and white. Have lots of cuddles and especially shoulder cuddles – and kisses.

That's about as far as I can take it. I don't think I can see him again.

Hester said she'll let me know how you're getting on – and I'll be thinking of you and praying for you often. Maybe I'll soon see the 'reason' Hugh spoke of when he christened you. Maybe you might yet get a Mummy and Daddy. Maybe …

The next morning Pam woke up both depressed and relieved, purposeless but free, so the renewal process could start, so she could begin contemplating fostering another baby, perhaps not so traumatic next time.

Hester St John Ives examined the prospects of Adam being adopted, and was doubtful. The optimism of the previous spring had melted away with every heart operation and resuscitation, and potential adopters had melted away as well.

'He wouldn't have been that difficult to place before the hole-in-the-heart surgery, but after – I thought it was a lost cause. But there wasn't any option except to try. Parkview made progress with him, so a bit before Christmas we had another photo, and we agonised over the words, then he was put back in *Be My Parent*, though who'd be brave enough to reply, I couldn't imagine.' (See page 102.)

There was one phone call. Just one. And Hester was very, very sceptical. A single mother living near Manchester who already had an adopted, three-and-a-half-year-old son.

Alex Bell still remembers when she first read the advert.

'I saw him in the magazine. And everyone said, "After Matthew who's so vibrant, so bright, so full of life, what do you want this one for, that's obviously got a death sentence on him? How can you put Matthew through losing a brother?"'

'It was a huge battle to get him. I didn't battle for Matthew, I was presented with a baby, but with Adam, I chose Adam, I said, "This is the child I want," and I was positive about it, and I wasn't persuaded out of it. And his social worker said, "We're looking for a nurse or a doctor," and I just said, "Well, when you don't find a nurse or a doctor, give me a call."'

Hester accepts she was against Alex having Adam. She agrees that her reasons, in hindsight, were based not so much on the personalities involved, but on good, old-fashioned prejudice, with, perhaps, a dollop of West Country alienation at Alex's heavy Manchester accent, very different from the plummy accent of Hester. Alex was only 30 years old, and with her soft voice and slightly hesitant way of talking, seemed even younger and came across to Hester as 'a slip of a girl'.

Adam

Date of birth: 27th June 1984

17-month-old Adam is a lovable, affectionate baby, very small for his age, who is adored by everyone who knows him.

He was born with both the mental handicap Down's Syndrome and a serious heart condition. He underwent surgery for this and during the operation suffered a lack of oxygen which left him with additional brain damage. At first it was thought Adam might need total nursing care for the rest of his life but he's now beginning to regain some of the ground he lost. Almost every day shows a little improvement.

However, Adam's operation was only partially successful and his heart condition may still limit his life span. Adam's vision, too, may be impaired. This is currently being investigated. Certainly Adam will need special schooling and also regular physiotherapy for some years, and he may remain dependent on adults all his life.

Adam – who's fair-haired and blue-eyed – is very responsive and loves attention. He's just cut his second tooth and now laughs and chuckles all the time. But he tires easily and feeding is a slow business. Despite his problems Adam is a real fighter and seems determined to live his life to the full. His parents feel unable to cope with his handicaps, but adoptive parents who are prepared for the challenge that Adam represents will surely find great rewards and joy in watching him respond to the love and security they give him.

But no one else called.

When the phone did ring, it was always Alex. She was using a technique from the past, the one she first used on the matron at Swinton Hospital.

'I pestered that woman. I used to phone Hester up and say, "Have you got a nurse or a doctor yet?" And eventually, after so many months, it was, "No, we don't think we're going to find a nurse or a doctor," so I said, "Well, what about me? I'm still here."

'And then I was told, "Well, this child needs a full-time mother."

'"Well, what do think I am?" I said.

'"You're working," she said.

'"I'll take the kids to work with me," I said.

As usual, for every objection, Alex had an answer, until finally she had a breakthrough. A secretary gave her Hester's home phone number. Fom that moment it was just a matter of time before Hester capitulated.

'Yes, Alex pestered me. I mean she was perfectly polite, but I'd say, extremely persistent. I must have told her a dozen times – oh, probably more than that – the child was too damaged, and eventually I said, "For God's sake, come down and see for yourself." I think she came almost the next day, and I must say they did hit it off. I found it quite moving, actually.'

Alex put Matthew in the car, went down to Plymouth and knew the moment she arrived.

'He was the one I loved from the second I set eyes on him, he was such a beautiful little thing and he smiled as he came in the room, he was just gorgeous.'

After that, Adam was a relatively easy adoption. The Freeing Order meant that Devon Social Services were solely in charge – if they were satisfied with Alex it would be a simple process.

*   *   *

During this time, Pam Smith had put her tear-stained diary in the bottom drawer of her bedside chest, too emotionally beaten to write any more, but gradually she came to terms with the trauma of those nine exhausting weeks. She had kept in touch through Hester, popping in to see Adam about once a fortnight, watching him gain weight, seeing him grow those all-important first few teeth and taking him Christmas presents from herself and most of her friends. By early March, the recovery cycle was almost complete; the very day she heard about Alex she began to write in her diary once again.

Thursday, 6 March 1986

Bumped into Hester. A single-parent mum, who has already adopted a 4-year-old Down's child, has clicked with Adam! They get on really well. Hester goes to panel on the 19th. If it's passed the mum will come down on the Sunday and stay with Adam, and 'go home' the following Thursday.

All along our prayers were answered – at times beyond our understanding – but this time – if God's willing – Adam will at last have a home of his own. It's no more than you deserve, little one.

At Adam's baptism ceremony in Intensive Care, Hugh the priest said, 'There is a reason, Pam – you won't see it now but in time you will.' That day had come, the day Pam had longed for, the day she did not think would ever occur. She handed over her first-ever baby boy, Adam, to his adoptive mother, Alex Bell, on Tuesday, 25 March 1986.

Tuesday, 25 March

Just before 3.30, Hester's car drives up. In they come with Matthew holding Alex's hand and Hester carrying Adam. What a sight. Even more improvement – eight teeth, 20 pounds and a lovely pair of real boots on! He can clap his hands now and makes the 'oo-oo' noise he used to when he gets excited. I'm sure great happiness will come from the pain and heartache of ten months ago.

Go down to shops and Post Office, with Alex carrying Matthew, and Adam in my arms. Everyone marvelling at how well Adam's come on, leaves me feeling very elated – so happy I could burst!

Help Hester load the car. Words can't express how I feel, darling Adam, as I stand in the road watching you sitting on your mummy's lap with her arms around you and your big brother at the side. I know you're going to be happy little one – you deserve it.

God Bless.

One of the first things Alex did when she adopted Adam was to give him a new name. She decided to call him Simon.

Twenty years later, Pam still mists up when remembering the rollercoaster of 1985 and the fact that Simon is alive and thriving. She hadn't read her diary for many years, and the memory had exhausted her, as if the scribbles in that jotter had wormed their way back into her system and reawakened memories that still pulled her down.

'You can't foster without pain,' she says of the trauma of mothering an ailing baby like Simon, or the grief of handing over a temporary part of your family to strangers who come to adopt. 'You accept the pain, or you wouldn't do it.'

As she talks she turns page after page of baby snapshots that are at the core of her life.

'All the time, I felt so useless. Useless. That was my baby on that bed in intensive care, wired up, being ventilated, and I couldn't do anything. Everybody else was doing it. You feel distraught.

It was as if I was outside my own body, sitting there, watching, and "Hang on, they're talking about my baby."

'Then after the baptism, I sort of accepted it, let it be with God – that's how I think I coped. That was the warm feeling. Acceptance. Like it wasn't up to me. After that, I could sleep, I wasn't tense, I was just really sad. For him.'

She sighs. 'Still it did all work out fine. Yeah. Well chuffed.'

Memory awakened, memory put back to rest; time to move on and let another mum deal with the everyday life-and-death struggle that is Simon Bell.

With Simon at home in Swinton, Alex's life became a good deal more complicated. She now had two children under the age of 5. Both were difficult, although in Matthew's case the problems came from outsiders, rather than his own behaviour. For instance, the headmistress of Matthew's school had very little sympathy for parent-teachers, especially when they had chosen to be single mums. Alex describes her as 'very bolshy', occasionally illogically so. For instance, she forced Alex to abide strictly to a rule that teachers had to be at work *before* nine o'clock, but children could not arrive at school *until* nine. This led to one of the most ridiculous, and wasteful, school-runs of all time.

Alex would have to wait at home with Matthew until a taxi came, and then put him inside. Next she would jump in her car and race the few miles to the school, go inside for a couple of minutes. Then she would come outside to find Matthew waiting in the taxi with the driver, and take Matthew inside the school. The taxi was paid for – by the Education Department, of course, and a complete waste of money.

'Is that sad, or what?' asks Alex.

Although she still adored teaching, the petty rules were beginning to irritate her, things like the dress codes. The school couldn't dictate her appearance – she had hugely permed, black curly hair like an overgrown show-poodle, and big glasses 'like Deirdre in *Coronation Street*' – but staff were required to wear dresses every day, 'boring, uncomfortable dresses'. And tights (pantyhose) that were 'hell, horrible – oh, yes, I looked like a tee-churrr'. She says this with an ironic, exaggerated, Manchester monotone.

But essentially she was happy, living in her own semi-detached town house in Warwick Avenue, an independent, bustling 30-year-old, always contemplating a new idea or venture: like the first of five extensions to her house – a bedroom and disabled bathroom for Simon – or the extension of her family. At that time she wanted four children – 'I didn't know why then, I still don't, but four seemed perfect, a challenge, but manageable.'

So in the evening, when Matthew and Simon were in bed, she began combing 'the book' again, turning the pages of *Adoption Today*, wondering if each smiling face would be her next.

The house was big enough and she had the support of the neighbours and her family, especially her charitable but practical mother, who was now the pillar of Alex's life, delighted to take the children whenever Alex could spare them. But her father, who had become even more old-fashioned and paternalistic as he grew old, still expected his daughter to find a man, get married and have her own children, so he found it almost impossible to approve open-heartedly of Alex's life.

'When I adopted Matthew, I thought, "I'm a family now." My dad got on well with him, said, "Very nice little lad, but when's he going back?" He didn't understand this was his grandson, that I'd have Matthew forever.

'Dad said, "But no man will want you if you take those kids home, no man will want to take you out."

'So I said, "Well, that's all right then."'

Alex wasn't interested in going out, or a relationship with any man, she was far too self-contained, and in a sense too liberated – not from the responsibilities of family or being 'tied down', but from the conventions of breeding, reproduction, and therefore needing a man.

'From the day I met Matthew and Simon,' she said, 'they were my children, just somebody else gave birth to them. That's the way I look at it.'

She was looking for an older child, perhaps a 10-year-old, one who had missed out on adoption when being a baby, and cute. There were still kids like that around, more physically independent, 'a boy who could stand up', to complement the two under-5s she already had, each of whom was difficult in his own particular way. Matthew, because he couldn't or wouldn't sleep, and could only be pacified by sharing a bedroom with Alex, and Simon because he never stopped sleeping, sometimes so deeply that it brought Alex almost to her knees.

'When Simon came to me he was on six medications for his heart, and that was really hard because it emphasised to you six times every single day that this kid was dying. The doctors and paediatricians were all saying, "Don't expect to keep this one." People actually said it. "*Don't expect to keep this one.*" They'd never have said that to a birth parent, would they?'

Alex learned a lot from caring for Simon in those early days. She learned to stop panicking. She used to stand outside his bedroom door and if she could hear him gurgling, making a noise, that was fine, she could go in. But if everything was quiet, she used to think he'd died. Then she realised, whatever the truth, whether he was dead or alive, she still had to open the door and go in.

'So you go in, and he was lying there quietly, smiling at you. This sweet, lovely kid. And that way, day after day, we gave each other strength, because he's such a determined character, it makes me want to go on longer. If he can do this against all the odds, and he can fight, and he can survive, then I can do the same. Fight and survive.'

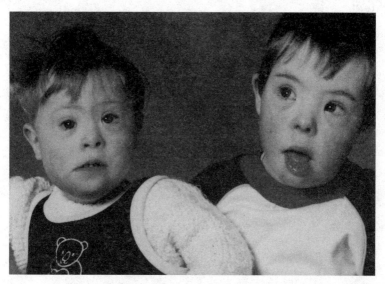

Simon (left) aged 2 and Matthew (right) aged 4.

A couple of decades later, Simon had a very special celebration. His 21st birthday probably didn't mean a lot to Simon – a day of even more noise than usual, a special cake, a day of extra love and fuss – but the fact that he's here at all is a tribute to an enormous cast who worked to the limit of their resources, to the brink of their hearts. People like Cara, the Filipina amah, Hester St John Ives, Surgeon Barry Keaton, a dozen nurses, Dr Pelham, Norma at Parkview, and a handful of anonymous carers, all acting together to help one little baby survive, and eventually to go on to live a happy life. But it wasn't only his physical being, it was his sunny spirit and his smile that was saved too. And he wasn't saved by the machines and the professionals; he was saved by cuddles and kisses and love – and Pam Smith.

'What's the point?' Pam asked in her diary at the depths of despair. 'What's the point of him living?', at that time a fair question.

The answer: what's the point of a smile?

Chapter Seven

The lodger: Adrian

After breakfast on 16 April 1988, a short, stocky 9-year-old boy helped his foster mother, Jenny Walker, pack his battered cardboard and plastic suitcase. Adrian Smith was leaving forever the house in Town Moor, Doncaster, that had been his home for the last two years. But with the packing finished, he just wandered nonchalantly into the lounge, to sit cross-legged in front of the television without a care in the world.

Mid-morning the doorbell rang; Mrs Walker greeted a slightly shy, round-faced younger woman who had come for Adrian. Mrs Walker handed over a few documents and a letter from Adrian's social worker, and then it was time for him to leave. He shook Mrs Walker by the hand, picked up his little suitcase, and then politely went out to the car with Alex Bell, his new mummy.

As Alex fastened Adrian's seatbelt, Mrs Walker called out, 'Bye, bye, Aid-ee,' but Adrian didn't look back, or wave, he just stared at the car dashboard, fascinated by the dials and clock-faces.

A couple of hours and a hundred miles later, Alex drove up to her house in Swinton, took Adrian by the hand and led him to his new bedroom, a permanent home for the first time in his life.

Together they unpacked his clothes and put them tidily away in his own chest and cupboard. Alex saw how few personal possessions he had, no sentimental keepsakes, hardly a photo – he could have been one of those nameless secret agents who weren't allowed to carry clues about their past.

Then she introduced him to his new brothers, a podgy, friendly boy who was nearly 6, and a 3 year old with a blank, rather babyish face, who even smiled though he was sleeping. They all sat together as Adrian grunted through an early tea, then he politely excused himself and went off to Alex's lounge to watch television. That was the day Alex Bell adopted her third son, Adrian. But to Adrian, it was just another day.

Since the 1970s it has been a social services requirement that all children who are leaving care for adoption must have a letter to refer to in the future about their past. The letter is usually written by their social worker, and should include the colour of their mother's eyes, her build, the colour of the father's hair, his temperament, even whether he speaks with a regional accent. But Adrian's social worker had never met either parent, since she came on the scene when he was six, and they had left Adrian behind in the hospital the day after his birth.

The letter is included here in full because it's an excellent example, well-written and sympathetic, of the difficulties faced by an honest social worker in telling the story of a rejected childhood.

Adrian's social worker doesn't write, 'Your parents knew you were Down's syndrome and had already decided to dump you before you were even born'; instead, she writes, 'they felt that adoption would be better for you'. On the face of it that might not

17 February 1988

Dear Adrian,
I have been asked to write to you with the story of your life up to February 1988. This I am very pleased and happy to do.

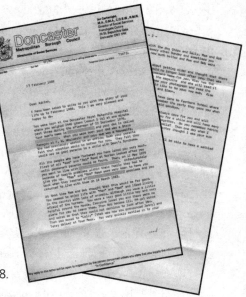

You were born at the Doncaster Royal Maternity Hospital where you weighed 2440 grams (about 5lb) at one minute past three during the afternoon of 23 September 1978. Your mum's name is— and your dad is called—. When you were born your dad was a Store Manager at F. W. Woolworth and your mum was a Housewife. She had previously worked in an office. Both your parents felt that adoption would be better for you. They felt they would not be good parents to a child with Down's Syndrome.

All the people who have fostered you have loved you very much. First of all "Mam" and "Bob" Reed at Norton looked after you until permanent parents could be found. Then, on 11 May 1979 you went to live with C and D—. Unfortunately because of health problems within their family they had to give you up. "Mam" and "Bob" Reed were very keen to have you back when they learned of C and D's problems and you returned to live with them on 18 March 1983.

At that time Mam and Bob thought that this would be for good. You seemed to enjoy life with "Man" and "Bob" and liked living in the country with lots of animals, although you were a little afraid of the

---

Adrian's letter from Doncaster Social Services.

horses. You were a very good little boy and very helpful around the house. Everyone loved you and there were no plans for you to leave them. Then Bob became ill. He got worse and worse so that they could not continue to look after you. Then you moved to "Lolly" (that was how you pronounced Jenny) and Terry Walker at Town Moor. You very quickly settled in to your new home, enjoying walks with the dog Chips and Sally. Mam and Bob continued to take you out every other Sunday and sometimes you would sleep there. Bob was now much better and Mam and Bob were sorry they had let you go.

Lolly and Terry were worried about getting older and thought that there could come a time when they could no longer look after you. That was why they asked me to find a permanent home for you. Alex has the advertisement that was placed in the magazine and she will read it to you if you want. When Alex saw your photograph and read the advertisement she decided she would like to be your new mum. Also you would be a brother to Matthew and Simon.

Since you were three years old you have gone to Fernbank School where you have been well liked. Do you remember the party they gave you when you left? Everyone kissed you and said goodbye.

Lolly and Terry and Mam and Bob will always care for you and will keep in touch with you. I will visit you for a while and will have many happy memories of times we have spent together. Do you remember having your photograph taken and you wouldn't smile? Then one day when I took you to see Alex in Manchester the Porter thought I was your mum and I felt very proud.

Good luck, Adrian, I hope this time you will be able to have a settled home.

From your friend and
Social Worker

seem to matter, but it amounts to an avoidance of uncomfortable truths while papering over cracks that might become fault-lines later in Adrian's life.

In the next paragraph she writes about Adrian's first potential adopters: 'Unfortunately because of health problems within their family they had to give you up.' However, that is contradicted by the Social Services Form E, which states: 'Adrian was proving too rough for a newly born child to the family. [So] he was returned to the Reeds who decided to keep him long term.'

Then, later, according to that letter, the Reeds also had to reject Adrian because Bob got ill. 'Bob got worse and worse, so that they could not continue to look after you.' But the Reeds do not remember it like that.

So what was going on during those nine years in which Adrian moved four times and was eventually turned down by three adoptive families? The answer is not contained in that letter, not even by reading between the lines. Alex had to find out for herself that Adrian, while being sociable and perfectly affectionate in a childlike Down's way, was inflicted with an emotion bypass, an impenetrability that won't allow anyone in, including Alex. In short, he seems to be incapable of showing or receiving love – because he was also autistic.

When you know that, there's something very admirable, and a bit sad, about Alex's relationship with him. At the core, unrequited love – and Alex can be almost physically hurt when her love isn't returned. Although the story has tragic overtones, along with a completely happy ending for Adrian, Alex has had to gather up all her resources to give him the life he needs – 'a life', she says, 'of detached, remote, uncomplicated support'. Note the word 'support'. Not love. For Alex, love would be far easier, but love, in the normal sense of the word, wouldn't work with Adrian.

Instead, out of a sense of duty in some ways stronger than love, Alex has found a way to allow him distance, without it breaking her heart. With a long-suffering sigh, a tight smile and eyebrows arched as high as the sky, she calls him 'The Lodger'.

'He treats everybody exactly the same, whether you are family, a total stranger, whether he has met you once or a million times. No moods, no depth, no attachment. But that's not a mother and child relationship, you see. That's landlady and tenant. I put that down in a report once, Adrian is a lodger. I'm committed to caring for him but that's what he is, he is a lodger.'

Alex's honesty, even if blunt, is better than resigned cynicism, and it's a measure of her that after twenty years of being rebuffed by Adrian, day after day, she is just as committed to providing the best life he can have as on that day, in October 1987, when she first saw his unsmiling photograph in her bi-monthly copy of Be My Parent.

Like the letter that would accompany Adrian six months later, the magazine accentuated the positive – fair enough for an advertisement. 'He is a Down's syndrome child with very good general health'; and 'he is a loving and lovable boy'. As always, Alex swallowed the hook, which had been baited by the adoption magazine advertisement.

'I rang up. Adrian had three enquiries, which is quite a lot for an older child. One a couple – yes, really, a couple; another single person; and me. And I know I'm right at the bottom because I've got two disabled children already and they're tiny, and, "she works full time – how bad can it get?" So I was at the bottom of the list, and rightly so.'

But very soon the couple dismissed themselves out of the situation, saying that Adrian wasn't the child they wanted after all, so Adrian was offered to the other single person, but she'd just seen 'a cute pink baby', so then there was only Alex.

ADRIAN is a stocky, though short, 9-year-old with light brown hair. He is a Down's Syndrome child with very good general health. He came into care shortly after birth, and has now lived with three foster families who unfortunately have been unable to care for him permanently.

He is an active boy who wakens early, but sleeps well. Normally he is well behaved. His speech, though poor, continues to improve. Adrian loves to watch sport on TV, especially swimming and wrestling. He likes singing, and has good concentration if interested! His imaginative play is highly developed, with a lovely sense of humour. His comprehension is fairly good, he tries hard to he helpful, and enjoys performing simple tasks.

Adrian attends a special school for children with severe learning difficulties. His teacher is generally

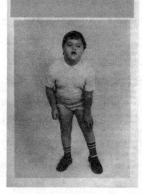

ADRIAN [23.9.78] is a stocky, though short, 9 year old with light brown hair. He is a Down's Syndrome child with very good general health. He came into care shortly after birth, and has now lived with three foster families who unfortunately have been unable to care for him permanently. He is an active boy who wakens early, but sleeps well. Normally he is well behaved. His speech, though poor, continues to improve. ADRIAN loves to watch sport on T.V., especially swimming and wrestling. He likes singing, and has good concentration if interested! His imaginative play is highly developed, with a lovely sense of humour. His comprehension is fairly good, he tries hard to he helpful, and enjoys performing simple tasks. ADRIAN attends a special school for children with severe learning difficulties. His teacher is generally pleased with his progress; with constant encouragement he tries hard to co-operate, though has to be reminded occasionally not to be too forceful with other children. Although ADRIAN can be over boisterous at times and is extremely active, he is a loving and loveable boy with an outgoing, friendly nature. We would like to hear from a lively family who could offer ADRIAN a permanent, loving home.

(Original advertisement for Adrian in *Adoption Today*.)

pleased with his progress; with constant encouragement he tries hard to co-operate, though has to be reminded occasionally not to be too forceful with other children. Although Adrian can be over boisterous at times and is extremely active, he is a loving and loveable boy with an outgoing, friendly nature. We would like to hear from a lively family who could offer Adrian a permanent, loving home.

'The social workers are completely blunt about all this, they tell you, "Oh God, we're left with you now." And as soon as I knew the kind of life Adrian had had, which was three placement breakdowns, I thought, "Yeah, I've got to go for this one, because no one else will."'

So began the regular process of stilted introductions, 'informal get-togethers' over gallons of tea, assessments and reports, and the endless to and fro of people and paper that is adoption today. Alex was right, no one else did want Adrian, but not only because of the broken placements. Alex noticed a detachment in Adrian from the very start, rare in a Down's child because they are usually especially affectionate; so she raised it with his social worker.

'I liked the social worker, she wasn't bad; however, she wouldn't look at Adrian as being a damaged boy. To her, Adrian was an ordinary 9-year-old Down's kid full stop, and she couldn't see beyond that. I'm saying, "Wait, he's got huge attachment problems."

'"No, he's totally uncomplicated," that's all she said, "totally uncomplicated", meaning he didn't have a heart condition or any of the associated problems with Down's syndrome, which was true – he'd been given huge emotional difficulties instead.'

But, as usual, Alex's wouldn't be put off. Adrian needed a permanent home and no one else would provide one. Even if Adrian didn't understand, his need was all that mattered. So the piles of paperwork were completed, the formal meetings with all-powerful social workers became chatty, a familial teamwork took root, all of which inexorably led to that long-anticipated day – a massive day in the life of any child – in which he left a home of two years for a lifetime with his new family. With Alex.

'Adrian got in the car and never even waved to his foster parents – he just moved on.'

He settled in well with Matthew and Simon, didn't make demands, didn't argue, ate what he was given to eat, behaved politely, went to bed when bidden, woke with the dawn, brushed his teeth, was ready on time – an altogether perfect boy. Except … every perfect second, every distant perfect minute, every distant remote perfect hour, every distant remote infuriating perfect day – broke Alex's heart. She tried so hard, but she couldn't make him love her; and therefore she couldn't love him.

'He doesn't understand other people's needs, so therefore he's not got any compassion in him. If an old person fell down in the street, Matthew would rush over and say, "Are you OK? Do you want me to get you a doctor?" Adrian would just walk over that person as though they didn't exist. This shows me that Adrian isn't connecting with anybody else in the world. It's very distressing when you put a heart and soul into a child and you get Mr Blank.'

There is another view: the view of two sets of foster parents, who had at one time been expected to adopt Adrian – the Walkers of Doncaster, and the Reeds of Norton, a village deeply rooted in the harsh but big-hearted Yorkshire coal-mining community.

Sheila Reed, known to all as 'Mam', is especially indignant at any suggestion by Alex that Adrian wasn't loving. 'Nonsense! Rubbish!' are among the milder words she uses, while her husband rolls his eyes in supportive admonishment. 'I admired the woman for taking him on, but saying he couldn't bond – oh, my.'

Mam is a 'big' woman, as grittily Yorkshire as the now-closed pits, tough and motherly in a single stare. She has not forgiven Alex for seating them on a side table at Adrian's christening, and makes it plain that she no longer merits her approval.

'Alex is a typical schoolteacher, kids must do what she says, regimented – and it's not normal to have nine children in a family – with an unmarried mother. It's an institution, not a family.

A schoolroom.' Indignation flies around the tasteful, aged wall-paper, with Bob nodding along in the corner, Mam puckering her lips every time she uses the words 'unmarried' or 'normal'.

'Alex had no intention of ever getting married, you know, of being what I call a "normal" mother. No intention. I know Adrian's disabled mentally, but I wanted him to have a "normal" family. But, of course, it's got nothing to do with us now. Nowt.'

Mam isn't comfortable with the idea that Adrian now belongs to another woman with similar strong ideas – albeit more softly stated by Alex. But the difference between the two women, apart from Mam being of an earlier generation, is to do with the concept of failure, in particular failure as a mother. Mam couldn't conceive of that. To her motherhood is instinctive: all you need is to care – and Mam certainly cares – then the rest, including love, will slot into place. Of course Adrian was loving – he must have given her lots of love – because Mam was not self-conscious enough as a mother to have noticed otherwise. Their relationship was just mother–son natural.

The Reeds are into their 70s now, healthy and busy, living in a bustling farmhouse with a dozen doors, where the phones never stop ringing and people are forever rushing through, asking for a screwdriver or a copy of the *Sporting Life*. Mam recalls how she came to foster Adrian twice.

'I had a friend in the village and we both fostered. Sometimes, when there were two, she'd take the brother, I'd take the sister, and one day she met me in the street, and said, "We've been asked to have a Down's baby but me husband won't have him in the house, won't have owt to do with Down's."

'"Oh, we'll take him," I said, and that's how we got Adie. I don't think he'd been born then, but they knew he was going to be Down's.'

'His mother and father told rest of family that he'd died at birth,' Bob agrees. 'With him being Down's. What I heard.'

'I got some clothes to pick him up from the hospital,' says Mam. 'Looked like any other baby.'

According to Bob, from day one – literally, as he was one day old – Adrian was well behaved.

'He never cried. I always say – no disrespect to me own grand-children – but I could manage six of Adrian rather than one of me own.'

'Yeah, he was very obedient,' Mam agrees, 'but he did take longer. In nappies – longer; in a pushchair – longer; can't do things – for longer. Needed extra, and longer. He never had speech, took us time to understand his ways. But I know he showed love – in his own way. Even if he had a problem showing affection, and he did – he weren't different to any other child. But slower, yes.'

Adrian's first stay with the Reeds was a temporary fostering placement. At 7 months he was driven down the road to Bentley to begin life with a new, permanent family who had agreed to adopt him. Mam talks about them with a scornful shake of the head.

'It didn't work out, because the woman became pregnant. After a year or two. And she already had one of her own. Said she wouldn't be able to cope, what she told social services.'

Mam's thunderous expression melts as she remembers how he was returned to them, still an infant.

'By chance I was talking to social worker and she said Adrian was coming back in care and she couldn't get anybody to have him because of his condition, and I said, "I'll take him back."'

'"Well, go and pick him up from school," she told me. It was done like that. I picked him up after school, which isn't bad from here, brought him home, sat him down, gave him tea, and every-one came in and said, "Oop, see our Adrian's back."'

Social services seemed to believe that Mam and Bob would now adopt him themselves, as written in his social worker's let-ter: '*At that time Mam and Bob thought it would be for good. Every-one loved you and there were no plans for you to leave,*' but the Reeds have no memory of that.

'We were far too old,' Bob says.

Nor do they have a recollection of '*Bob became ill. He got worse and worse so they could not continue to look after you.*' This produced another bout of incredulous eye-widening from Mam.

'Was that your epilepsy?' she asks Bob, but he shakes his head.

'Not the right time.'

So why did they let him go?

Mam points at Bob. 'He said it. We'd have been over 50, Adie was 5. We'd have fostered him forever, but they wanted him to be adopted. Didn't make sense. Not at the time …'

The way she says 'at the time', it is clear that now – with hind-sight – it *does* make sense. She's worked out what 'they' were up to.

'Comes down to one single word,' she says as if it were obvi-ous. 'Money. Social services have to pay for long-term fostering. Adoption's free. If they can get them adopted, great – they're off their books forever.' Mam nods at Bob, who nods obediently back. Point settled, then.

Could that be true? Could it be that Adrian got moved around so the local authority could save cash? Well, that's what Mam thinks, and it's difficult to find another reason, because left to their own devices Adrian would have stayed with the Reeds as a paid-for foster child – and none the worse for that. Theirs was a hectic, brusque kind of love, with three generations of the family living in a warren of farm buildings, detached but close, hard but warm-hearted. Given the busyness of their lives, they may not even have noticed if Adrian had been remote or loving, normal or compulsive, which might have been just as well, because his behaviour was becoming increasingly obsessive, as witnessed by his next foster parents, Jenny and Terry Walker.

Adrian was 7 when he arrived at the Walkers' home – a solid terraced house not far from Doncaster Racecourse. At first Jenny Walker was impressed.

'Adrian was the kind of child you only dream about, he was perfectly behaved. When he came in, he'd hang his coat up, take his shoes off, put his slippers on. This is just what he did, we didn't have to tell him, not even once, he just did it. Mr Perfect, he was.'

So far, so good. But Jenny began to notice that Adrian could take his need for perfect order too far.

'He would get upset if the pantry door wasn't closed – he had to get up and shut it. And when he went to bed, if his duvet cover wasn't absolutely spot-on in the corner, we had to spend blooming ages doing it and redoing it until he could see it was perfect. Or "our" slippers had to be exactly side by side. Or his music player, the right way round, exactly in line.'

Adrian used to go into the kitchen, come back with a folded tea-towel, and sit down crossed-legged in the dog basket and then just throw the tea-towel from one hand to the other, for ages, just back and forth, back and forth, for ten minutes, fifteen minutes, in front of the television, back and forth, absolutely in a world of his own. And sometimes he'd flick his fingers, on and on. When he first started, the Walkers wondered if he was signing, trying to communicate, then they realised he was making waving move-ments, staring at his fingers.

'… the most beautiful movements, fingers and hands, for ages, on and on – where he got that from, I've no idea. I'd let him get on with it for a little bit, then distract him.'

Whether the Walkers told Adrian's social worker we don't know, but she would have recognised that Adrian's behaviour was a sign of mild-to-mid autistic tendencies. The 'signing', the waving movement of fingers in front of the face, concentrating on them for minutes or longer, is a way of locking the world out by focusing inward. Mild autism would explain Adrian's other, non-Down's eccentricities, and go some way to explaining his ret-icence at showing love, bonding or forming attachments. But the word 'autism', however mild, does not feature in any of the many social work reports, or the advertisement in *Be My Parent*; if it had, Alex's attitude to taking Adrian would have been different.

Instead, the internal social work report says of Adrian going to live with the Walkers: 'this placement was considered to be a long-term arrangement', meaning adoption, but, like the Reeds before them, the Walkers deny this. And the ultimate reason given in the report for the Walkers not going through with adop-tion?

'Two hospitalisations and Mr Walker's health.' Terry shook his head, as if that were a complete mystery. 'Nothing that I remember. Just we were too old for adopting. Always had been.'

During the two years that Adrian was with them, the Walkers regarded him as a complex, sensitive boy, who didn't communi-cate his feelings.

'He'd sit there all day, not doing much, in a world of his own, but he'd be happy.'

And though he didn't react to insults, never ever had a tantrum, Jenny Walker could tell when he was hurt.

'In the school holidays, up at the main school, there was a sand-pit, so I took him up there, but when he went in all the other children left the sandpit, and they didn't go back in until Adrian got out. And their mothers were with them, and did nothing.

'Adrian knew. He just knew. And he looked at me and he said, "Go home, mum, go home."

'After that, he didn't show anything, but he would never go back there.'

In February 1988, when he went to live with Alex, the Walkers missed Adrian a great deal. Like Alex, they remember that on the day he left there were no hugs or tears, but they interpret that as typical Adrian, quiet and dignified, although Terry Walker did have doubts for months afterwards.

'He was fine, but you're never sure if they're feeling some kind of rejection – "Here we go, they're chucking me out again."'

Alex agrees. 'He was passed around terribly and nobody ever told him anything, because he was disabled and they didn't think he understood, or he didn't verbalise well. It was, "Pack your bag you're moving on again," without an explanations as to why he was moving. So why should he build a relationship, because it wasn't going to last as far as he was concerned. This was life. You moved on regularly.'

Back in Manchester, Alex continued to teach at her special school and juggle the education of three challenging children: Mathew (6), Simon (3) and Adrian (almost 10). The boys couldn't have been more different.

Matthew, at the higher attainment level of Down's, emotional and curious, learning to read and talk and play football, trying hard to be 'one of the lads'.

Simon, cherubic and cute, smiling and giggling from his wheelchair, touching and cuddling and hugging everyone within reach.

And now Adrian, fitting in, getting up, going to school each day, polite and undemanding – but, to Alex, something very important was missing.

'Six weeks in I can remember saying, "There's something wrong. I don't love this child and he doesn't love me." But the social workers didn't listen. They said, "It will work, it will grow."

'"There's no bonding with him," I said, and all I got told was, "It takes time." Then I realised, he can't give and he can't receive either, he's totally independent. Like he actually came out of the womb preparing his own bottle. He's a total complete entity in himself and nobody else matters in his world.'

Brutal, if sad, words.

Adrian at 29

Nineteen years later, Adrian comes across as a bit distant, a self-contained adult – 'a whippet and flat cap kind of old man', Alex says, not entirely affectionately, like an ex-Yorkshire-miner enveloped in his own world – companionable, without actually being there. Short and stocky, in another era he might have said, 'Where's me tea, woman?' while flicking through the 'local' morosely in the corner. It's this remoteness, of being treated like a taken-for-granted wife, rather than a loved mother, that some-times overwhelms Alex – and makes her wonder out loud about rose-tinted social workers.

'It's what they don't tell you that matters,' she says, with a knowing glint, 'maybe because they don't notice themselves.

Maybe …' she adds, letting it hang, not quite managing to hide her doubts. 'Maybe', and as Adrian approaches his 29th birthday, Alex has not changed her view.

During that time Adrian has not made a single friend; it simply isn't in his make-up. Nor has he revealed any dependence, except the obvious – food, clothes, warmth, a place to sleep and a television to watch. But in his way he's a character, a companion rather than soul mate, a vacant though affable presence. Among the few things that stand out, that define him, are a remarkable ability to know the time, days and dates, and a fanatical love of James Bond.

If you sat him down and read those words to him he would agreeably mumble, 'Yeah …? That's so …? Yeah …? That's so …?' then he'd get up and wander off, without understanding a single word.

Adrian is the family timekeeper, as if born with a clock inside his brain. If the younger kids are going swimming, Adrian will tell them when to get ready; ditto, any event where punctuality is important. This is all the more odd because Matthew, who's much more advanced that Adrian, has no concept of time at all and constantly needs prompting by his slower brother.

But it's on dates that Adrian really comes into his own, as a classic autistic savant, like the Dustin Hoffman character in *Rain Man*. Give him any date in any year – say, 18 February 1923 – and he will know the day of the week. Instantly, without thought, he'll mumble 'Sunday'. It's uncanny. Perhaps one in twenty autistic people have truly exceptional calendar memories like this, and Adrian thrives on the audience that gathers to watch him perform.

As for James Bond, that has an unreal quality, too. Adrian knows most of the films off by heart and, though he can't read, he seems instinctively to know when they're coming on TV. In his nasal, Yorkshire accent he'll say, 'Dames Bond on tonn-ite,' as he tidies away someone else's clutter.

It may be fanciful, but it's easy to see why James Bond would be an Adrian type of hero. Bond came from nowhere. He does not have a home, a base, a mother or father, a background. Bond does not form attachments, he has only acquaintances, rather than friends, people in Bond films do not display real emotion, Bond is a loner, and happy to be so.

All this drives Alex mad, including the irony that Adrian is himself unable to … *bond*.

'Matthew would fall apart if someone took his roots away, he's a real home person. But to Adrian, home means nothing. It took two years of him saying "Are we going to Alex's house?" before he used the word "home"; and then it was "Are we going to Alex's home?"'

To love and be loved

The most controversial aspect of Alex's relationship with Adrian is to do with her – not his – need to love and be loved. It's what lifts her assorted children into being a family, lifts being a carer into being a mother, it's what makes her house a home. Love, and therefore security. And it's probably that security, the security of the true loving family that can criticise and purge itself in public, which allows Alex to be so forthright about the hurt Adrian inadvertently causes to her feelings.

'I'm totally committed to caring for Adrian but I don't love him at all, you know I don't. I've said it many times. There are things about Adrian I don't even like. I don't like his total unconcern for the rest of the world; I don't like his lack of compassion, this "I couldn't give a shit about anybody else." He never says that because he hasn't got the words to say it, but it's the way he acts.'

Alex doesn't blame Adrian for this. From the time he was moved around, staying a year here, a year there, Adrian was destined to be a person without the emotional certainty that having a firm foundation brings, and Alex could see that after just a few weeks. She freely admits that she might sensibly have said, 'It's not working with this child,' and sent him back, but her pride would not allow it: she'd have been no better than the person before her, or the person before them.

'Once I commit myself to a child it's forever, and the only thing I can say I've done for Adrian is to have stopped the cycle of rejection. So this is a successful adoption for Adrian, very successful for him; it's just totally unsuccessful for me.'

Should we believe Alex when she says she doesn't love Adrian?

Well, it would be wonderful to ask the man himself, but he wouldn't understand the question, let alone know the answer. 'Love me mum? Yeah, that'll be good, ten past six ...' So no help there.

Louise, Alex's forthright helper, turns her nose up at Alex's bluster. 'She's been his mum for twenty years, what's she going on about?' Louise does have a point.

But the final word on whether she loves him or not must be with Alex herself. 'I mean nothing to Adrian, and when you're a mum it matters so much. If he left tomorrow, he would walk to the car and say, "Where are we going?" and he wouldn't look back, he would never say to anyone, "Where has Alex gone?" or ask about me. To me, that is failure, Adrian is my failure, of all of them.'

Yet compared with what might have been, Adrian has had a remarkably happy life. He's older than the rest, part of the 'in-between' generation, coming on the scene after the beds had been unchained, but before the adopting of babies with Down's syndrome had become accepted, when social workers still thought it was a miracle to get anyone to take a disabled baby.

Had he been born ten years earlier, Adrian would have been dispatched off to a long-stay hospital in the Yorkshire Moors and institutionalised. And when the last of those institutions closed in the early 1990s, he'd have been turfed out to drift through a series of antiseptic hostels, unable to adjust to family life. On the other hand, had he been born a few years later, the process of adoption for Down's syndrome babies would have bedded in, and a life-family would have been selected and 'signed up' while he was still a pink little baby, to maximise the chance of bonding. Timing is everything, and Adrian got his half right.

But Adrian's life is not a failure. Not for him, not for the still-learning social workers, not for the hesitant foster parents, not for the rapidly changing system, and really not for Alex, because every day that he wakes up like a 29-year-old geriatric, exactly on time, in his perfectly tidy room, in a house with brothers and sisters, Adrian is testimony to a wonderful, loving revolution, not by individuals but by society, our society. For all our short-comings, we've done him proud, especially Alex.

'Sometimes I can see that he's a success, for us as well as himself. There are things he's very good at. Tidying up. He puts all the videos in perfect order, I never have to tidy his room, there's nothing, ever, out of place. He's like that little thing on *Teletubbies*. Noo-noo. It's a little blue vacuum cleaner, and it goes round and Hoovers up all the mess after the Teletubbies have been there, and just puts everything back in place. That's Adrian, he's a Noo-

Three in stripes. From left: Matthew (5), Simon (3) and Adrian (9½).

noo. So, yes, I do miss him when he's not around, because the whole place becomes like a tip.'

Alex has given Adrian the best life she can give him and stopped the cycle of an innocent Down's boy, born a bit autistic, never settling down, forever moving from place to place – she has stopped the cycle of damage. And although Adrian might never understand what it means, and Alex may shake her head in frustration, he's been under her roof for twenty years now: and that just has to mean The Lodger has found a home at last – even if only as live-in cleaner.

Chapter Eight

'To say goodbye':
Nathan

The story of Nathan – Alex's fourth – began with the collapse of his mother's self-confidence amidst feelings of overwhelming guilt and pain; she was rescued by the burgeoning confidence of Alex, so that a saga which might have had a tragic conclusion came to a heart-warming ending. But that isn't the story of Nathan; it's the story of his mother, Sue Gane (now Lester), who lives in Kingswood, near Bristol.

Sue was 25, and already had a 5-year-old daughter, Leanne, when, on 9 March 1989, she checked into Southmead Maternity Hospital with her husband Trevor. Although the pregnancy had been restless, the birth was routine, but as she lay back exhausted Sue began to have the nightmare feeling that something wasn't right. The usual maternity bustle had become a hush, the nurses were avoiding her gaze, and the baby had been spirited away, 'for tidying'.

Lying there quietly in the recovery suite it was as if the sea had retreated and was poised, dark, silent, waiting – to come crashing back on Sue as a tidal wave.

'People were coming in, and going, and I was half awake, half asleep, and I kept asking, "Is the baby all right?"'

'They said, "Someone will get to you in a minute."

'"Is the baby all right?"

'"Someone's coming."

'"*Is the baby all right?*"

'Then they said, "The baby's on special care," and all the time my mind's racing and I'm thinking, "This is wrong, this is wrong."

'The nurse grabbed my hand and looked at me … I can remember the sadness in her eyes. I was terrified. And she asked, "Do you want to hold him?"

'But I was too scared, so my husband, my ex-husband, Trevor, held him. I couldn't look at this baby, because I knew they were going to tell me something so awful.

'The doctor sat opposite and he said, "I'd just like to say first thing, he's not going to die, what he's got is not life-threatening." Next he said, "But he's got a condition, though you can't see what's wrong with him."

'I'm looking and think, "What do they mean?"

'They said – well, they mumbled, "He's a Mongol, Mongolism. Down's syndrome."

'I was like – "Oh my God."

'You see, by coincidence, when I was pregnant, I'd seen this chap up in Kingswood, and it was the first time I'd ever seen a Down's kid, never noticed it before, and this chap was probably about 30; he was walking along with his mum who was probably 60 and he was holding her hand and I was thinking, "God, that's sad, so sad." Instantly, in that little room in the hospital, my mind went back to that picture, thinking, "That's what he has: that. He's like *that*.'

'I said, "Can you let him die?"

'"No, he won't die."

'"I can't take him home," I said.

'"We'll talk about that."

'They put me in a little room and I just kept saying, "I can't look after him."

'I felt a failure. What had I done wrong, what had I done wrong?

'I did nothing different with Nathan than I did with Leanne, why – why? – did he turn out like that? I was only 25, what made him like that? Why can't I have a normal baby? This isn't supposed to happen to me, this is meant to happen to older women.'

In that little room, Trevor, Sue's husband, sat mutely by her side, without uttering a single word. As the nurse offered Nathan to her, Sue put her arms in front of her face, closed her eyes, and refused to take the baby, so the nurse handed him to Trevor.

'I sort of picked him up and held him and I couldn't see nothing wrong in him. I was fine with it and when Sue said about letting him die, well, it was a life, wasn't it? All right, she couldn't accept it at the time, but I think the hospital just left us to stay on, get our heads round it, talk to people, give us time.'

In the mid-1980s, Frenchay Hospital, like many hospitals in Britain, was still developing procedures for dealing with birth 'complications' such as Down's, especially the immediate post-natal aftermath. While the social workers would be sent for later, Sue discovered that the practice at that time seemed to be: let the parents fend for themselves.

'The hospital gave me three leaflets on Down's syndrome, and put me back in my room. That was that. And they put us next to the nursery – which was great! My husband sat on a chair all night, just sat, didn't say a thing. I don't know how we got through that night.'

Trevor agrees. 'We still had the emotions of him being born. We were upset, we didn't sleep, and right next door the babies were crying all night. Sue was crying all night and I expect I cried as well – because of the upset, I suppose – and the emotion, it runs through you. Like it's the overwhelming emotions of a baby being born what you brought into the world and then being told, you know – there's just so much flying around, you have to try to take it in, but you can't.'

The next morning, Sue's heart was even darker. Now she had to face the world, feeling she had failed. She didn't want anyone to know, she wanted to wake up from this nightmare as if nothing had ever happened, that she had never been pregnant.

'I didn't want to tell my parents. I didn't want anybody to know. I rang my sister and told her. I didn't want my mum to come in because I thought she'd say, "He's your baby, take him home." But when Mum came to the hospital, she said, "You don't have to do anything you don't want to do." She was brilliant.'

And so began the first of the endless tussles that would come to dominate Sue's life for the next ten months. To start with, whether to take Nathan with her when they left the hospital or to leave him behind.

'I left hospital the day after Nathan was born, without him. Every five minutes I had doubts. That I wanted him home. How could I leave him? My God, he's my baby, what have I done? Panic. Then panic became: I'm never going to be free of this – forever – I'm going to be that lady of 60 walking through the precinct, and he's going to be that 30-year-old boy holding my hand. I couldn't see this baby, I could only see this 30 year old. I couldn't let myself see him as a baby, because it would have taken over, I would have had to bring him home, I would have got used to him, then I would have had to love him.'

As Sue and Trevor thrashed around, another dimension of their grief began to surface. Trevor couldn't see the problem – Nathan was their baby, full stop. This began to infuriate Sue, all the more so because Trevor didn't seem capable of seeing her side, or even speaking at all.

'I still don't know the reason today why she couldn't take him home. Frightened, I suppose, stigmas and things. To me it was just "Take him home, that's what you do." But yes, I tend to clam up, bottle things up, so I wouldn't have talked, would have seen it as up to her.'

Sue agrees. 'Trevor went into a shell, and I went into my own little world, and neither of us ever came out.'

Gradually, as the pain of the actual birth receded, Sue provisionally decided against having Nathan at home. So the hospital and social services did their routine conjuring trick, moving him from the maternity ward to a foster home without fuss or ceremony, delivering him to a tried-and-tested partnership – Anne and Roger Pullen, a couple in their 60s, now retired, who still live just up the road from Sue.

During thirty-one years of fostering Anne has cared for 185 babies. In the lounge there's a higgledy-piggledy collage of baby faces, gummed together by Roger, which Anne will chat through, still remembering the name behind every newborn smile.

'Seen all kinds of babies, all kinds of mothers,' she says, 'seen them all. All the babies are good, most of the mothers are good, too, in their way, most confused. But I always know, don't I …?'

'She does,' agrees Roger.

'You see, my job is to give the mum an opportunity to one day take their baby home. That's what we do. Give them space. Time. Which is great for me, because I love babies. Absolutely love them. Younger the better. I once had one only two days old, beautiful, not much bigger than Roger's hand. He likes babies too, don't you?'

Roger nods. 'She's had so many babies, for so long, that when she changed to disposable nappies, and there weren't any terry-towelling on the line outside, our neighbour knocked on the door and asked, "Is Anne all right?"'

'So, I've dealt with enough mums now to know – when they've gone through all the tears, the soul-searching – whether they're going to come here and take them home. If they've got a home. Which most don't. Most aren't like Sue. A lot are drug addicts, or only 16, or babies who were just relinquished, that's the legal term, "relinquished", there's usually no hope for them – but we still have to give every mum every chance, although sometimes I'd like to …'

Anne paused for a moment. The 8-month-old baby girl at her feet had started to grizzle, so she picked her up from the car-pet.

'This one, for instance. Mum should have been here an hour ago, take her for a walk—'

'But she's only 16—' Roger interrupts.

'*I* was only 16—'

'She was,' he says. 'Our first date was taking the neighbour's baby out—'

'I was 13 then—'

'—so I always knew what I was letting myself in for.'

As the Pullens' story unfolds, the truth becomes apparent. Anne had two babies while still a teenager, and then no more. Hence, the fostering – but only babies.

'Yes,' Anne says, 'I always know about the mother. We shed tears of joy when a baby goes to its natural home, which is quite rare.'

Roger nods. 'She plays "Congratulations".'

'I've dealt with enough mums to know from the minute I first see them, I could go to a judge and say, "This baby's going home, or this one's going to be adopted." And with Sue, I knew, too.'

Anne sighs, shrugs, folds her arms and slowly shakes her head. 'The clouds were hanging over,' she says, with a resigned smile, 'from the very beginning.'

While baby Nathan bedded in with the Pullens, the hospital social services strategy began in earnest. Give Sue time. Give her space. Let her come to terms with the initial trauma until the continuity of everyday life could begin to soothe the constant, empty pain. Meanwhile, keep her gently informed about Nathan's progress at the Pullens' house, tantalisingly only ten minutes along the road.

Up until this time Sue had still not seen Nathan, let alone held him, and was literally fluctuating by the minute. She became obsessed, beginning to walk to the Pullens' house, then turning around; dialling their number, then hanging up the phone; making an appointment to see him, then hiding under the bedclothes. And all the while, she was frightened. Frightened what others thought of her, frightened that Leanne would be taken away, frightened that she would never be able to cope again.

Finally, a month after the birth, the social workers suggested Sue might like to meet the Pullens. Anne, veteran of so many mother-and-baby get-togethers, has a well-rehearsed, easygoing procedure.

'Nathan was in the big Silver Cross pram in the corner of the front room, and we were all very chatty, especially Sue, but not mentioning him to begin with, then I think Roger said, "Do you want to see him?" Sue was very nervous, not sure whether she did want to pick him up. Then she changed her mind, picked him up at last, and we all cried, didn't we, Roger?'

Roger smiles enthusiastically. 'And I'd won money on the pools, or something, and took us all, and the young 'un, out for a meal. We got on brilliantly …'

'… and when we got back Sue bathed him, and changed him, and she kept the wet wipe, didn't she, the wipe that she cleaned him with she kept, and slept with it under her pillow, she just wanted to feel close to him.' Anne misted up at the memory, overwhelmed at the pain and power of mother love.

When Sue talks about this, she can't keep still. She's tiny but energetic, still thin after a recent operation, and has the sense of a woman burning from the inside out. She rubs the back of her slender hand, then puts her arms across in a self-hug, then comes forward in her chair, then back, then she rubs her thigh, next her cheek, then brushing back her short brown hair, now touching both shoulders, arms tightly across her chest, not so much agitated as inhabited, as if she were still hugging a baby to her chest, still feeling him – eighteen years later.

'I started wanting all this contact with Nathan. I wanted to hold him with no clothes on, when I had no clothes on, like you do with a baby – skin to skin. I wanted to push him in the pram. I wanted to change his nappy. I wanted to bath him. I wanted to pack as much as I could into the short time I had with him. And Anne was absolutely brilliant, she let me do whatever I wanted with him. If she had hospital appointments or anything, I'd go along.'

The fluctuations deepened and even Trevor became caught up. He'd come home and say, 'I've been thinking about it all morning, and I think we should keep him.'

Sue would immediately back away and say, 'I can't.' Then later, he would say, 'No – I don't think we can,' while Sue would be thinking, 'You know, maybe we could.' They were shadow boxing, using each other to challenge their own feelings, while trying to work out how they really felt. Finally, this culminated on a decisive day when they both did agree, as Trevor arrived back from work.

'I'm sure it was a Wednesday – we spoke and Sue said, "Let's have him home. We'll phone Anne and Roger now. Let's go and get him."

'So we phoned them up – but no reply. Then an hour later – it's "no" again. If they'd answered the phone Nathan would have come home that day, and he'd be with us still. That's what I think. But they'd gone out shopping or something. She wanted him, really wanted him. Just she was afraid.'

But all the time Anne Pullen was sure – her sixth sense had spoken – that Sue wasn't ready and never would be. Whatever the bonding with wet-wipes and cuddles, those 'clouds' would not blow away. Sue couldn't enjoy the baby side of Nathan because of that image of him 'later on', the image of him at 30, holding his mother's hand. Anne explains this with the compassionate nod of a woman who's seen it all, and mostly it's worked out right.

'Because I knew that at some stage someone, somewhere, was going to be there for him long term, which is why I still love to foster.'

The deep post-natal shock and depression had started to lighten, the problems were more practical now and Sue knew she had to make a decision sooner rather than later because Nathan would be beginning to bond and needed a stable long-term home. In this situation, the family get two social workers: one to advise if they are keeping, the other to advise on placements. Sue and Trevor began to see more of Brian McWhinney – the carer who would advise on adoption.

This was the moment, by a thousand-to-one chance, when Sue first encountered Alex.

'I was doing my ironing one morning, and Alex came on the telly, talking about fostering and adoption. I thought, "Down's kids, quick, tape it."'

Alex was on *Good Morning*, the ITV show presented by Judy Finnigan and Richard Madeley, sitting on her lounge floor with Matthew, Simon and Adrian. She'd just been approved to adopt another child, and was reciting her mantra, that a baby was 'somewhere out there in the world', and although somebody else had given birth to them, they were always destined to be hers.

Sue couldn't take her eyes off Alex's lovely house, the pictures and paintings and special equipment, with everything dedicated to the kids.

'I thought, I'd love Nathan to go to a family like that, that's where he needs to be, and all the things Alex was saying I thought, "She's talking about Nathan, she's talking about my son." But, of course, I knew there wasn't any chance …'

When Nathan was four months, Brian McWhinney sent out a flyer, essentially advertising him for adoption. A month later, he told Sue that out of a hundred that had applied, three families had been approved.

'The first family were Mormons, they had a little boy and wanted to adopt another, but I just thought, I'd been brought up in the Catholic religion and maybe a Mormon family wasn't right. Then there was another family and they had a Down's child as well, who seemed fine. But finally Brian said, "There's a single mum with three adopted boys—"

'I grabbed him and shouted, "*Stop!*"

'The tape of Alex was actually still in the video. I played it and said, "That's not her, is it?"

'Brian threw his papers in the air and he went, "Yes."

'Which to me was fantastic, amazing, the best news I could ever have.'

When Brian called Alex in Swinton, she was astonished. Although she had been approved to adopt a fourth Down's syndrome child, Alex assumed her application would be rejected, especially for a healthy Down's baby. So she raced to Bristol the day after Brian's call, for the all-important first face-to-face meeting with Brian, Anne Pullen and, of course, Nathan. Anne was used to couples coming to see their new baby, rather than a single working mother in her 30s, with three young children already – but that wasn't what caused such a great surprise. Alex asked to meet Sue. 'Seeing as I'm here, and she's just up the road. I think she deserves to meet me, and I deserve to meet her.'

The usual practice in adoption until relatively recently was that there should be no bridge between the past and the future, so that once the process was underway the birth parents were expected to fade swiftly out of the picture.* The emphasis shifted to

---

*The Adoption and Children Act 2002 amended the Children Act 1989 to provide for the new special guardianship order which, among other things, would allow the child's legal relationship with his or her birth parents not to be severed. This of course indicates a radical rethinking of the role of the birth parent in the adopted child's life that had been going on for a number of years before that. Even so, back in 1989 birth parents were generally not encouraged to play any further part in the future life of any child they had given up for adoption.

helping the new mother build a relationship. If necessary, subtle hints were dropped to the birth mother that she should stay away from the foster home, but Sue understood this instinctively anyway, and had simply stopped visiting the Pullens, however much she still itched to hold Nathan.

But in response to Alex's request, Brian – experienced and rebellious in his own way – wasn't the kind of social worker to say 'that's unheard of', or to care about setting precedents or breaking rules, so he phoned immediately. Sue burst into tears.

'After Brian rang I had to sit down on the sofa, wondering what this woman was going to think of me. Nobody meets the birth mothers, we disappear, nobody ever sees us, we live with our grief and our guilt of giving up our child forever, we never get to be part of their lives. I thought, she's going to absolutely hate me, because she's going to look at me and think I've got a lovely house, just one child, why can't I bring up Nathan, what is wrong with me that I conceived, but I can't do this?'

'So when Alex arrived with Brian, I was absolutely terrified. But it was a nice sunny day and when she came in the door she just said, "Put the kettle on," and a huge weight lifted off my shoulders. I felt that for the first time since Nathan had been born someone was helping *me*, someone walked in and took this pressure away. The whole time since his birth I'd felt like I just couldn't breathe, it was hurting so much that this child was desperate to be with somebody, but I knew I couldn't be that somebody. And she walked in and I just thought, "It's my mum. My mum's come to take him off me."'

This unique meeting between Nathan's two 'mothers' was the beginning of a relationship that has grown closer and more complex over the years. Alex remembers that Sue was gaunt, terribly stressed, shaking, and sat in the kitchen over that cup of tea, crying. She had expected Alex to disapprove, but Alex was far too grateful to Sue for having 'her' baby, and Alex doesn't do disapproval anyway. She doesn't do 'mumsy' either, that was probably Sue reaching for what she needed at that moment – someone to drink her tea and say, 'It's all turned out fine, hasn't it? Stop feeling guilty.'

Now Sue only had to cope with loss. The loss of her baby.

So, the agony was not over for her, and Alex understood that she was now part of the problem. She was taking Sue's baby away, so Alex had no choice but to keep a distance for the moment, to let Sue deal with the loss on the inside, within her own family.

One of the abiding consequences of Down's syndrome is that there can be pain and heartache, and yet nobody is to blame. While the baby-Nathan caravan prepared to move efficiently out of town, Sue would remain at home with storms raging through her. Trevor tried to help her deal with the loss, but he's a man of few words, and, in truth, he had his own issues. He wanted to keep Nathan, so Sue rolled up into an emotional ball – smiling by day, silent tears at night – all the while wondering what was going on down the road at the Pullens' house with her own flesh and blood.

'The day Nathan left, on 3 February 1990, I could see him in my mind. I knew his car seat, it was blue checked, and I could picture him, with Alex, parked outside Anne and Roger's house. I could see the pushchair, I could see his baby clothes, I knew every single top and bottom. I sat on the stairs and cried my eyes out all day, awful day, just cried. He was going to live in Manchester, he wasn't in Bristol any more.

'It was like a death. That's what I kept saying. "If he'd have died it would have been easier." A hundred times easier, because I could turn round to people and say he died. People wouldn't have been judging me, saying, "She gave up her baby."'

Usually that would be the end of any contact between mother and baby until he turned 18 and might go looking for his parents. It's what Sue expected, because it's the nature of adoption. Nathan now belonged to Alex. Sue and Trevor had no rights – from a legal point of view it *is* a death. Alex understood that, too. But now she could help.

A few weeks later she sent Sue a postcard. Nathan had settled in well. He was happy. He loved the other three boys, and they loved him. At Christmas, Alex rang Sue and said Nathan was the best Christmas present she'd ever had. Sue remembers, 'I thought, how special is that? I just stood there, gobsmacked on the phone, thinking, "Thank you, oh thank you, oh thank you so much."'

Just before his first birthday, Alex suggested they meet. She'd bring Nathan down to Bristol, and social services agreed to provide a room for Sue to spend time with him.

For Sue it was a turning point, a watershed.

'Nathan was lying on the floor, wearing a beautiful little suit, cream with navy blue. We had the most fantastic time. I've got hundreds of photos upstairs. Then Alex left, went back to Manchester, she came all the way down for three hours. Nathan couldn't have known who I was, so Alex did it for me.

'And then, later, the parties began.'

Mother and child reunions

The Bell family parties are almost unprecedented in anyone's experience of adoption, and began with Nathan. Alex had virtually no contact with the birth parents of Matthew, Simon and Adrian, but by staying in contact with Sue she was able to develop special days – often coinciding with birthdays – on which the parents could have a party with their birth child. The upside of these days goes beyond simple 'get-togethers' because it creates a sense of extended family. Sue and Nathan were the guinea pigs as Alex tried to build long-term, loving relationships between an adopted child and his birth parents.

This started as a simple day to celebrate Nathan's second birthday. Alex travelled down from Manchester again, but this time she brought all four boys, along with a cake, so they could have a proper party at a small hotel in Chippenham. Sue took Leanne, her mum, and Anne Pullen went too. The social workers held their breath: few people had heard of the birth relatives and the adoptive mother getting together, and the mixture of emotions could have been explosive.

To everyone's relief, the day was a huge success and, on the surface, Sue had a wonderful time. But underneath the joy of cuddling her son, of being a mother to him for just a day, there was a cost to Sue, too.

'I was on a real high, I was buzzing, I was sobbing, I was absolutely adrenalin flowing – like I'd just run a marathon type of thing. Cramming, cramming and cramming, months and months, years, into those few hours, doing anything with him, just trying to be with him all the time, soaking up every little bit of him. And I'd leave him and still be on an absolute high.

'But, then, a complete slip the next day. Missing him. And though I knew I'd done the right thing leaving him with Alex, it was just that he'd gone again. I couldn't see him again for a while, that was hard; that's still really tough now.'

Alex talks about Sue being physically sick. 'She would be very upset, really ill, depressed and crying. Probably because Nathan was growing up so beautifully, he was a lovely toddler. And that constant doubt, too. "Could I have done it? Did I need to give him away?"'

The answer, though complex, was clear.

Keeping Nathan would have destroyed Sue because she could not adjust to being a Down's mother and might have started blaming Nathan rather than herself – saying, 'Why is this not-normal child blighting every day of my life?' and that would have been unfair on Nathan. It was fairer to blame herself for giving him up than to blame Nathan for being what he was.

Instinctively, Sue knew this about herself, and took the tough decision to let him leave her. Tougher still was to let him go to another woman who seemed like the perfect mother, as if to show her up even more. And if that wasn't enough, she gritted her teeth to stay lovingly in touch, but therefore to be reminded month-by-month what she had done.

For Alex the challenge was different. It's difficult enough to bring up a Down's syndrome child, but an open adoption would mean the birth mother looking over her shoulder the whole time, approving or disapproving of every outlandish outfit, schooling decision, or just every childhood cough, so at first it wasn't only Sue who was nervous; Alex also wondered if she'd have 'the bottle' to pull it off.

'It took me a while to try an open adoption, because I wasn't so confident of what I was doing. It wasn't until Nathan that I actually said it's important for his mum to know where her baby is going. I thought you can never alter the trauma that the family has been through, but you can make it a little easier.'

Neither woman could help herself anyway. Once they had met, once they had handed Nathan between them like a loving charge, they simply had to put him first, and come together as required. The word generosity doesn't do it justice: this was maternal love at its most powerful and refined. And as they passed their precious package across, all of the other adults involved also had to put him first too. At the centre a little boy would grow up stronger as an example that others could follow.

'No dark secrets'

Over the years, Alex has built on the success of her early dealings with Nathan's birth family, so that now she has made open adoption a part of everyday life.

'Some adopters want to play happy families – want to pretend the child is their own to everybody, including the child most of the time, but that's never been our way. We talk about adoption, talk about fostering, so my children will never be confused about who I am, who they are, and why they've all got two mums and a dad. We even play games.

'I'll say, "Right, hands up if you've got a mummy called Sue – well done, Nathan."

'"Whose name is Smith? Adrian …? Adrian, don't be a cloth head."

'These things are positive reinforcements that they've had a past life and that's OK with me. So I'm open, not only with their

From left: Simon (5), Nathan (1), Matthew (7), Adrian (12).

parents, but with my children, and we look through the adverts in *Adoption Today* together and my children know that the kids in these books are looking for new mums and dads – and I never just say mums – and they'll say, "Were we in that book?"

'And I say, "Yes, once you were in the book. And I found you and decided to have you, because you were so beautiful …"

'Some people say, "That will upset them." But it doesn't, it makes them more secure in who they are and how they got here.'

Alex is saying this in the kitchen, as her family sit at the big wooden table, gulping down tea, and there's no doubt they can understand – because Down's syndrome doesn't blunt emotional receptors. So this is a powerful demonstration of what she's saying, that there are no dark secrets in the Bell family.

Why does this seem strange, perhaps even insensitive? Probably because adoption is also about rejection – all of Alex's children have been 'relinquished' by their birth parents. But here they are, nine happy 'victims', almost relishing their very different journeys to get here.

'You chose us, didn't you, Mummy,' says Emily, in her very best cutie tone. Then the penny drops. They don't feel rejected, they feel chosen.

'Who was Adam?' Alex asks, warming to her theme.

Simon howls and shrieks, so she continues.

'Matthew, where did I get you from?'

'Mummy Jane, and my foster parents, the Cornwalls.'

'Where were you born?'

'Watford.'

Alex leans over to give Simon another cup of orange juice. 'They know that I had nothing to do with them originally, but not one of my children has ever said, 'You are not my mummy.' And I would expect them to because everybody who is adopted at some stage says, "Don't shout at me, you're not my mum – you're not my mum!" But I've never ever had that.'

Matthew looks up from flicking through a Manchester United programme. 'I've got two mums, you know. And a twin brother.'

Bell family open days

By the early 1990s, Matthew had three brothers – Simon, Adrian and Nathan. Alex stopped wondering if she could cope, and became more adventurous, especially about dealing with extended birth families. With four difficult youngsters under 15, she gave up full-time work so that she could care for them at home more easily and build more purpose into their development, including contact with an increasingly wide circle of family and friends. Hence, the annual birthday parties soon became weekends, and by the time Nathan was 5, whole weeks in the country, which eventually led to the Bell family open days.

At first, these were held at the holiday house outside Chippenham. Nathan's immediate family went, including Jake his younger brother, Sue's mother and father, her sister and brother and their partners and children, and Anne and Roger Pullen. Next, the Cornwall family started going to see Matthew, along with their four children, and even his social worker. Later, when Alex adopted Andrew, his parents, foster parents and their seven children wanted to come – so the house in Chippenham became too small, and she had to search around for a new, larger venue.

So for the last nine years Alex has rented a series of converted farm buildings near Stow-on-the-Wold, Gloucestershire, for two weeks in the summer and, on the Sunday in between, the entire extended family travels from every point on the compass for fun and games and afternoon tea.

The two-week holiday itself is no minor piece of logistical planning. Packing the individual requirements of nine complex lives into two large vehicles and driving 200 miles is just the beginning. Characters who have vastly different sleeping habits, medical needs and eating regimes have to adapt to unusual routines – and that's before the issue of Chloe's need to run off without warning. The farmhouse is open plan, there's no area with only a single door in which she can be contained, so Alex sums up the holiday in one word: exhausting.

'You have bag after bag after bag with special medications, and things like nappies – because you can't just go to any chemist and buy the right size nappies for large kids, they don't stock them.'

At home they're each used to their own bedroom, so on holiday they wake each other up, which means that Nathan and Adrian, and particularly Thomas, don't sleep well and go around in a mood. But in spite of the problems, it's a place that can accommodate two wheelchairs and, even rarer in Alex's experience, the owners enjoy having a lively, disabled family.

'They're brilliant. They really welcome us and say, "Your kids are well-behaved, easy," and that makes it the best place we've ever been, and we go there every year.'

The holiday is expensive – over £5,000 – partly because the whole family go on day-trips, swimming, to the cinema, riding donkeys, to Bristol zoo, to the seaside, virtually every day. And back at the farm there's a bouncy castle, pool tables, table tennis, a playground, fields, because … they're on holiday. Alex believes they should have the best possible time even though a 'cheap lunch is £80 plus' – because there are 'twelve of us, with the helpers, and that's what a family that size costs when we eat out'.

Then, on that middle Sunday, when the whole team are already 'terminally whacked' – a couple of dozen cars arrive for the Bell family open day. In the grassy fields beside the farmhouse the parents of Chloe talk with the parents of Nathan, talk with the parents of Andrew, who talk with Emily's grandma, while watching their birth children scream and run. It's like any extended family gathering anywhere, with in-laws and relatives asking, 'So how's the last year been? I heard you've got a new car/job/house. Lovely to see how he/she has grown.'

You have to pinch yourself to believe that most of the parents here have willingly given up their child, it's so ordinary, and yet so extraordinary – altogether, over seventy people come, just to be with the kids.

There are five sets of birth-parents and step-parents, eight uncles and aunts, six grandparents, seven brothers and sisters, ten foster parents, and perhaps a dozen foster brothers and sisters, some of whom have their own children.

For instance, Louise Cornwall – Matthew's foster sister, now a GP in Banbury – brings all four of her children, Matthew's foster nephews and nieces, who treat him as an uncle and then fall off swings and scrape their knees like kids everywhere.

'If only more people could see this open day,' Louise says, while administering first aid, 'they'd have such a different attitude to adoption. And Down's.' Louise frowned sadly, disturbed at prejudice and the steady increase of Down's-related abortions.

Inside the farmhouse, Alex would be in her element if she wasn't so 'knackered', surrounded by a sea of home-made sandwiches and stodgy 'fill-them-up' snacks. Ironically, she can be quite shy on such occasions, at home next to the teapots, but from time to time there's a glint of pride in her weary eye. All these people, all these caring, happy people, here because of me.

Outside, a cricket match has been organised and Nathan is attempting to catch. It seems like half of Bristol has turned up to see him. His grandparents, his aunts and uncles and cousin, his mom and stepfather Simon, his dad and stepmother Marie and her kids, his sister and brother Leanne and Jake, foster parents Anne and Roger and Nathan's famous uncle John, who's in a band and seems to be bowling with a sausage roll. Matthew is batting but keeps missing the ball and hitting Emily, who is temporarily behind the stumps, then leaves because the Cornwall baby is on the bouncy castle and that's much more interesting.

Later, after the last of the 'relatives' has left with a thousand goodbye kisses, and the kids are watching *The Sound of Music* on the DVD, Alex collapses in the kitchen with Louise. They survey the tables, still piled high with leftover sandwiches.

'Right, you lot,' shouts Louise, 'pyjamas and toothbrushes.'

No one moves. On the video, the Mother Superior is belting out 'Climb Every Mountain'.

'I know how she feels,' mutters Alex.

The song freezes abruptly – in mid-phrase. The silence is astonishing.

Louise has pressed the remote controller and switched off the video.

'I said pyjamas and toothbrushes. Now!'

Alex smiles. 'There. Told you it didn't pay to get too sentimental. Not with this lot.'

The day is summed up by Nathan's father, Trevor.

'When Nathan was born he was part of our lives for a short while, and then this wonderful woman stepped in and took all that pressure away so I didn't have to think of him every day, I knew he was safe and looked after, and loved, with a great life – I don't know if we could have given him that.

'But with this open adoption it meant we could still see him. I suppose the first time was strange, but then it became "we're all part of one big family". I feel no different towards Matthew or Adrian and all Alex's others, I feel as though we're all together. Yeah, it's nice to see Nathan and find out what he's doing, but often you might only spend five or ten minutes with him and he's off doing what he wants to do because he's having a whale of a time. All the children are part of all the other families and all the carers and all the grandmums and granddads, and it makes you feel like you're fitting in, not kept out.'

For Sue, still raw after eighteen years, the meaning of open adoption is also therapeutic. She's seen every stage of Nathan's life, from baby to adolescent now, and she feels 'less of a baddie, the one who gave him up', that it all came out so right. Indeed, there are days when she believes that open adoption saved her life.

'In my heart I knew I could not keep Nathan, but I did love him, just couldn't cope. I thought if I don't hold him, don't touch him, don't see him, I wouldn't love him – but I did. I loved him 100 per cent. Nature gets you. And that was killing me, would have killed me forever, still does sometimes. But now I can speak to him, it doesn't take me away from the pain that's buried so deep, but I can feel part of him, and he can be part of me – that's what Alex has given me. She's a brilliant best friend magnified a million times.'

Nathan at 18

Big and bustling, Nathan is whizzing through adolescence as if it's been specially sent to persecute him. He can switch from Mr 'Smily-Full-of-Charm' to Mr 'I'm-Really-Aggressively-Angry' in a single breath, but it's probably a passing phase. Alex treats his nasty moods as juvenile tantrums, as do the rest of them. Sometimes, Nathan tries especially hard to be bad, really bad, spitting out wicked words he's just learned like 'bitch', or crashing a kitchen chair against the table, so Alex calls out, 'you big baby,' and sends him to his room; but five minutes later he floats back, smily and cuddly and eager to please Alex again.

'It's like living with a volcano, and he's getting worse as he gets bigger and stronger. Nathan is like two separate people. One minute he bows and he kisses your hand, and equally he can be an evil little … person. He turns if somebody has said "no" to him, or somebody has taken something that he wants, or removed his video. He usually takes it out on something like a door, he'll slam doors, and lashes out if he's walking past one of the younger kids and they're in the way. He doesn't ever go for the two wheelchair kids, never ever, he's really good with them, but he just can't handle his fury.'

Adolescence can be particularly confusing for Down's teenagers. It's difficult for them to understand what's going on or to appreciate that temperamental swings are a natural part of growing up. Adolescence is an abstract concept, whereas anger or, in Nathan's case, rage, is here-and-now real, and he is big enough and fit enough to act in response to the uncontrollable emotions bubbling up inside. Nathan becomes unreasonable because the forces devastating him are unreasonable too.

At times, this seemed more like a serious behavioural problem, rather than routine teenage tantrums, especially when he discovered a new swear word and sat there shouting it out, time after time. So Alex had him tested for the neurological condition known as Tourette's syndrome, but the psychiatrist said it wasn't Tourette's, 'because Nathan chooses when he shouts out'. Conclusion: he's just a big, badly behaved juvenile delinquent.

Thankfully, in the last few months the shouting and aggressive behaviour have begun to wane and the swearing is morphing into catch phrases such as 'you're joking', or 'ah-ha' or 'hi hi hi', nodded out, half a dozen times a minute like a one-sided conversation. Alex nods back with her 'wondrous smile' face, an inscrutable mixture of scepticism and mischief, framed by arched eyebrows, knowing that Nathan can't grasp words, but is highly sensitive to gestures and expressions.

'Nathan would be a perfect only child. He finds it stressful to live within a large family. And he doesn't cope well with problems, he can't talk things through, his communication is quite poor, so he can't get his message across. You can talk to Matthew, you can talk to Emily, you can work through with Adrian or Chloe, but you can't do that with Nathan. He's got limited understanding and is quite limited in his speech, so he gets frustrated and takes it out on himself and anybody that's within hitting distance, which is a bloody shame because he's a really great kid but he's giving himself a bad reputation. I adore him anyway, absolutely adore him, but I would love somebody to come along and say, "If we give him this pill, or whatever, he's going to be fine." Like a magic wand.'

Nathan is stubborn, pushy, selfish, belligerent – but if Alex or Sue or Louise put their arms around his shoulders and say 'I love you', he melts in an instant, adolescence overwhelmed by the baby still inside.

Anything for you

Eighteen years after that terrible night, tossing and turning with Trevor, next to the newborn baby ward, a magic wand has waved for Sue, too.

Time has allowed her to disengage the self-blame, as if shedding a former person a skin at a time while growing a replacement she can be proud of. The confident matter-of-factness of Alex has played a part, along with an unquestioning, supportive family, so that Sue can now reach out to help others.

She's still brittle, but it's a surface fragility; underneath she's fulfilled and strong, perhaps stronger than ever because of the journey she came through while facing her demons. The pain, when it comes, and it does still come, floods through her rather than crushes her, more like sadness than grief, because she knows

Alex

The house is hushed now. Only the sound of Andrew gulping, and gunfire on a distant TV; even cats Max and Milly have gone to sleep outside in the shed. Alex folds Andrew back in his cot with a soft 'goodnight', then picks up part of the six-foot pile of ironing and drops it on the kitchen table. In her practised hand the iron caresses a set of Jungle Book pyjamas, smoothing out the wrinkles from a day of bumps and scrapes. Alex smiles slightly at a fleeting memory, before reaching for a pair of children's jeans. She's managed to iron two inches of the pile. Only five foot ten inches to go before bedtime. So much ironing for so many children. And so many memories. Perhaps she was recalling one particular memory – of a young girl wandering into a hospital …

Matthew

The painting doesn't quite do him justice. The likeness is there, the open but slightly sullen look, the unsure pride of a person who's been knocked around a bit, the hint of Down's in his face, with more in his neck, a polite formality that comes from being eager to please. Artist Norman Long has captured all that, which is probably why it has already been hanging at the National Portrait Gallery in Trafalgar Square. But it's too inward for Matthew: it doesn't show his myriad moods, most of which are outward. Matthew is a doer, a talker, a performer. He calls himself 'a star', a 'one-off', 'special'. He's incapable of bearing a grudge or harbouring ill feelings. That's the extra chromosome 21: it might cause Down's but it means he will always be open, simple, kind and nice, and also innocent and naïve. Today, aged 25, Matthew is as vulnerable as he was that February day in 1984 when, as a just-adopted toddler, he sat on Alex's lounge carpet and cried and cried and cried.

Simon

Simon cannot talk. Yet he can communicate. Indeed, he is very noisy – especially when one of Alex's kids is up to no good. Then he shrieks to the roof, like an angry goose. Simon is the house prefect, the telltale, the snitch. Because he enjoys being in the middle of things, ever watchful, Alex can leave him in charge, on sentry duty. He lolls in a wheelchair in the centre of the room while the world revolves around him. His head is never still: bowed to one side, then the other, listening, seeing and computing. He loves to touch, shake hands, and lean forward to be cuddled. When he's excited, he bangs his thighs with his fingers and sometimes tries to clap. But his hands usually miss. Although he can't frown, a natural radiance comes from deep inside and so he smiles. He lights up a room and everyone in it. And in spite of the pain, he doesn't cry, because the pain is on the outside, from things that just simply won't work. Everyone who meets Simon loves him, he's Alex's soul mate.

Adrian

These days, Adrian comes across as a bit distant, a self-contained adult – 'a whippet and flat cap kind of old man', Alex says, like an ex-Yorkshire-miner enveloped in his own world – companionable, without actually being there. Short and stocky, in another era he might have said, 'Where's me tea, woman?' Adrian is the family timekeeper, as if born with a clock inside his brain. If the younger kids are going swimming, Adrian will tell them when to get ready. Give him any date and he will know the day of the week. As for James Bond, Adrian knows most of the films off by heart and, though he can't read, he seems instinctively to know when they're coming on TV. It's easy to see why James Bond would be an Adrian type of hero. Bond came from nowhere. He does not have a home, a base, a mother or father, a background. Bond does not form attachments, he has only acquaintances, rather than friends. Bond is a loner, and happy to be so. Just like Adrian.

Nathan

Big and bustling, Nathan's whizzing through adolescence as if it's been specially sent to persecute him. He can switch from Mr 'Smily-Full-of-Charm' to Mr 'I'm-Really-Aggressively-Angry' in a single breath, but it's probably a passing phase. Alex treats his nasty moods as juvenile tantrums, as do the rest of them. Sometimes, Nathan tries especially hard to be bad, really bad, spitting out wicked words he's just learned like 'bitch', or crashing a kitchen chair against the table, so Alex calls out, 'you big baby', and sends him to his room; but five minutes later he floats back, smily and cuddly and eager to please again.

Andrew

Andrew can't see, beyond a vague sense of light or dark. He can't feed himself, he has very limited understanding of people or the world around him, and he can't move without assistance. So after school he sprawls in his cot, listening to music and family clatter, until Alex picks him up for a late supper when the rest are watching *Coronation Street*. The size of a 5-year-old at 17, he has a mobile, mischievous face with a smile of impish cheeriness: if he senses that someone is in his room, he will splutter three words into his bed blanket: 'Hi-yah. Mum-ma. Bye'. Yet everyone adores Andrew, especially Nathan. Yes, that boisterous, hormonal hurricane looks at the tiny tangle of misshapen arms and legs and scrap of spiky hair he calls 'An-roo' – and loves him to bits.

Chloe

Chloe is such a beautiful child. Norman Long's portrait shows the sulky, 'I'm going to get my way' naughtiness that Chloe wears like a uniform. She's a scamp – mischievous, unkempt, wilful, noisy and wilful. Yes, wilful twice over – that's Chloe. But she's also a delight, a hyperactive, kittenish girl whose playful curiosity keeps getting her into trouble and sometimes danger, who grabs your hand and won't let go, who demands all your attention and shouts when she doesn't get it, who causes Alex more bother than the other eight put together. 'You have to watch her at all times. Don't leave a door open – or she'll be off. Don't put anything down – because Chloe will have it. Leave a mobile phone – Chloe will be pressing every button. Leave a glass on the table – Chloe will throw it. You don't leave scissors around because she'll start cutting off her hair. Dynamite. She's Little Miss Dynamite.'

Tom

Thomas Johnson? Well, perhaps. Or maybe Thomas Bell? Or Thomas Noname? Or Thomas Nowhere? Yes, Mr Nowhere, that's Tom. Unable to talk or read, to understand speech or sign his own name, at the age of 24 Thomas is in limboland, and always will be – the only certainty is that he lives with Alex. His parents did their best to see him right, to straighten out his future, but they were almost powerless as adoption societies, social services, fostering committees and anonymous bureaucrats used him as a punch-bag. Whack! this way – whack! that way – 'Who cares about Thomas, it's the files that count.' So when he was settling down with the Bell family in Swinton, happy and growing for the first time ever, while Alex and his mum Patricia pleaded and cried – they came for Tom with an order, and carted him away. Leaving Tom as a nomad, too old to be adopted, without a name, Mr Nowhere. But now he's back with Alex.

Emily

Trying to stay solemn, the senior magistrate managed to sniff and smile simultaneously while pronouncing the adoption complete, and inviting Emily to come forward and collect her certificate. But Emily had other ideas. She leapt up from her chair beside Alex, rushed forward and hugged the magistrate, even giving her a gentle kiss on the cheek. She is practically perfect in every way … for now. Alex did have worries about taking a life-limited whirlwind of a girl who's very manipulative and noisy, but she's such a cutie …

Callum

As with many autistic people, no art can mirror the true construction of Callum's mind in his face. Unlike a child with Down's syndrome, Callum has no physical characteristics that mark him out as disabled. He appears normal in every way, with child-model good looks, neatly brushed short hair, a fair complexion, and usually wears a clean white shirt and open collar. At teatime he sits quietly at his place looking straight ahead, elbows on the table and hands holding his head, seemingly in a trance while waiting patiently. He seems like a patient, well-behaved boy in deep thought, innocently beautiful. Then the food arrives …

that the outcome is better than her most hoped-for dream. Most important of all, cantankerous Nathan is happy, even if only grudgingly so, and if she ever doubts that, Sue can just call Alex.

And yet Sue's old feelings hover in the darkness, waiting like ghosts to haunt and taunt.

'I only have to hear one song, and it takes me instantly back to when Nathan was born. We were walking in Tenerife on the seafront last year, on holiday, and a woman in this bar started singing "Anything for You", the song by Gloria Estefan. And instantly I was in floods and floods of tears. It's Nathan's song, it's the song from when Nathan was born.

'I cannot remember for the life of me a song from when Leanne was born or when Jake was born or when I was getting married or anything, but just one little note from one little song from when Nathan was born and the pain is back again. And I just think, "Pick up the phone, ring Alex, speak to him." And that helps. Oh, how it helps.'

And I'd do anything for you
I'll give you up
If that's what I should do
To make you happy ...
I can pretend each time I see you
That I don't care and I don't need you
And though inside I feel like dying
You know you'll never see me crying
Don't ever think that I don't love you
That for one minute I forgot you
But sometimes things don't work out right
And you just have to say goodbye.

Chapter Nine

Touching souls: Andrew

By 1990, although Alex now had four children, she felt able to take on more. Her beloved home on Warwick Avenue had been extended a third time for Nathan, a fourth time to make extra room as the boys got older, and a fifth time after Alex was told by Trafford Adoption Society that she'd been approved in principle to adopt a Down's girl – yes, girl – between the ages of 1 to 5. Alex was particularly looking forward to the addition of a feminine presence to her hitherto all-male brood. With Adrian an increasingly masculine adolescent, and Matthew not far behind, the idea of a girl filled her with anticipation.

So when a friend from Surrey, who had already adopted a couple of Down's children, called to say she was about to adopt a 'seriously disabled' Down's baby boy from Burton-on-Trent, Alex took no notice.

But that baby was Andrew, and the circumstances by which he came to be adopted by Alex are at the same time distressing and heartwarming.

Andrew was born on Friday, 1 June 1990. His parents had previously decided that they couldn't contemplate long-term care for a seriously disabled child, so they left Andrew at the hospital

when his mother went home, and set about adoption immediately. This was not a cold-hearted decision; there was a history of
tragic disablement in Andrew's mother's family, and she knew
that she wouldn't be able to manage.

And then Andrew suffered two cerebral bleeds that left him on
the very edge of death – during which he didn't breathe for
twelve minutes. The hospital advised them that Andrew was
unlikely to live more than a few days, so his parents went back to
the hospital to comfort him as he died.

But he didn't die. Instead, Andrew began making progress.

As he recovered, his parents became so close to him emotionally that the bonding process took over and they changed their
minds, so that in the first week of August, astonished and thrilled
that he had survived, they took him home.

For the next two months Andrew slept twenty-three and a half
hours a day, still fighting to survive. But he was extremely difficult to feed, and his digestive system was defective – hence he
gained no weight. At a routine baby clinic, the paediatric consultant was so alarmed that Andrew had to be re-admitted to Burton-on-Trent district hospital. This proved to be the final straw
for his parents. According to the adoption letter provided for
Andrew:

*This further hospital admission and separation caused your birth
family to think again about your long-term care. They had found it
emotionally very difficult to care for you. It was a painful, distressing
time for them and led their returning to their original plan of seeking
an adoptive family for you.*

That was written by Andrew's social worker, Carol Flock, who
had been keeping a gentle eye on Andrew since the initial request

for adoption immediately after his birth. Now retired in Stafford-shire, she knew the perfect foster family. They were completely bomb-proof, lived nearby and had a reputation for being able to deal with anything – absolutely anything – that could be thrown at them.

Dot and David Coxon are in their 60s. They met at a Salvation Army social in their teens and have remained committed to the Christian organisation ever since. Their ironic mischief and spiritual goodness can bring forth tears of laughter and tears of sadness in the same sentence. Alex, who adores the Coxons, suggested in advance that any preconceptions would be confounded.

'They are wonderful,' she said, 'but do not be fooled by their normal appearance. David makes tea using cold water, then puts the teapot in the microwave. They're a strange bunch.' Alex smirked, landing the first folksy blow.

As a couple, the Coxons appear so ordinary, yet are so unusual, that they seem like a practical joke against expectation. They lived in an anonymous terrace, in an anonymous estate, in an anonymous suburb, on the outskirts of Burton-on-Trent, in Stafford-shire – from the outside the Coxons' uniform house could be a conspiracy to camouflage them in drab, anonymous clothing.

David Coxon, average height, regular Midlands bloke, was himself adopted at six weeks old. His mother was 18 at the time, lived up the road from the prison in Derby, and though he's still got the papers and knows who she is, he hasn't quite got around to meeting her since she gave him away. That was in the 1940s, when nice folk didn't talk about such things. An 'aunt' once said his dad was a doctor, another that he was a Canadian pilot, but David lets you know, with a twinkle, that he prefers the association with Derby gaol.

Meanwhile, Dot's mother had been told there was no chance of having a child, so her parents adopted a girl. But fourteen months later, as if deliberately to confound medical science, along came Dot. Then four years after that, another sister. So Dot has an adopted older sister and a natural younger one, and for the last forty years a husband who was adopted.

'You could say I know a tiny bit about adoption,' she says with such ironic humility that it's funny. 'And that was before our own experiences,' Dot adds, getting ahead of the story.

When they married in 1968, the Coxons tried for a baby, but like Dot's parents, nothing happened. Their doctor couldn't find a reason. 'Keep on trying,' he suggested. After several years 'of nowt' they applied to foster, but even then, nothing happened. Social services had lost their fostering application form. Until, at four o'clock one afternoon, two social workers turned up unannounced, with a child of 13 months, and 'just handed him over, at the door'.

David thought they'd been forgotten. 'We went out and bought a pram,' he shrugged, as if it happened every day.

The Coxons were now on the Register: 'Babies nought to four, any kind, any colour, any background, any condition.' Social services took them at their word, and used the Coxons for the most difficult, the most unappealing cases. Their third was Jason, 'a baby of incest' who was profoundly damaged and blind, whose father-grandfather had been jailed, and the mother was only 13. They considered adoption – 'We're all born innocent, it's not the baby's fault, a child can't choose its parents' – but Jason died before the papers could be processed, just 14 months old. 'Died innocent, too.'

They moved into a bigger house, but still a child of their own didn't 'come along'. They had tests, and were told, 'There's nothing wrong, everything seems fine – it's sometimes like that.

Wait. It'll come.' But they began to think more seriously about adoption, in particular about adopting children they were fostering.

One child, Helen, had been rejected because she was mixed race. Though her father was black, her mother was white and had wanted a white baby. After fostering her for four years, Helen was the Coxons' first adopted child. She's now in her 30s, with her own family.

Next they were asked to foster a baby girl that had been left with the babysitter – her mother just didn't come back. That turned out to be Tania. The same mother's next one, Darren, was also deserted; he came in only a nappy with a plastic bag, exactly 364 days younger than Tania.

'Mum seemed to leave a baby behind about one a year,' David mused.

Finally, Darren and Tania's sister, Marie, whom they also adopted.

Now the Coxons had four adopted children. And then, a huge, wonderful surprise. Out of the blue, after nine years 'of blankety-blank', they suddenly discovered that Dot was pregnant. Anne was born in 1977, much to Dot's delight.

'So we had four young black children, and now a white baby, too.'

David handed over a photograph, with a sardonic smile. 'All the old ladies used to coo in at the pram, then see the other four – dirty looks isn't the word …'

'Must've thought Anne was a doll,' Dot added.

'No,' David said with a mischievous smile, 'I don't think that's what they thought …'

Over the next three years Dot had another two, Rachel and Edward. And all the time they were continuing to foster. Four

The Coxon children. From left: Darren, Tania
(holding baby Anne), Helen and Marie.

adopted children, three birth children, and sometimes a couple of foster babies. But to Dot it wasn't a problem.

'Not even having eight or ten, or twenty – as long as you love them. And when there's enough, they do look after each other, you know.'

By then it was October 1990, the time when 4-month-old Andrew's parents had finally concluded that he should go to a foster home, with the long-term aim of adoption. Dot remembers being called to the hospital.

'They said we've got a baby who's small, can't put weight on. Well, Andrew was very tiny indeed. He was four-and-a-half months, but the size of a three-week-old. We had to feed him every two hours, day and night.'

David would set the alarm, grope downstairs, boil the kettle to warm the bottle, and then take it upstairs. 'Ten o'clock, midnight, two o'clock, four o'clock, six … You get used to it. And then he put on weight, did well.'

The next stage of Andrew's life gave rise to a 'disruptive' episode concerning his first adoptive placement. After the usual exhaustive pre-adoption procedures, in July 1991 Andrew went off to a house in the Home Counties to be adopted by a woman in her 30s who already had two adopted Down's syndrome children. This was Alex's friend. But in the November she returned Andrew to Dot and David with hardly a word.

Recalling this, the Coxons cannot find it in their charitable heart to condemn. David metaphorically puts on his Salvation Army uniform. 'But it did turn out for the best. When she drove away she mumbled, "I couldn't do it." That was good. Better than if she carried on.'

Alex sat in silence for several minutes when I discussed this with her. I presumed that she was deciding whether to comment, or let it pass. 'I'm not the person to ask,' she answered finally. 'I couldn't be objective. That woman sent one of my babies back. No. Leave it to Dot and David, they're more Christian than me.' Her voice was Alex, steady, Mancunian, with a soft lilt that goes up at the end of a sentence. But her face was hard, harder than I've ever seen it. She didn't need to comment.

Andrew was too underdeveloped to be much affected, but there are two people to whom the 'disruption' was not so incidental: Andrew's birth parents. Though Andrew isn't always in their lives, he's certainly in their hearts, and they are shyly present for more of the time than they let on. For instance, they turn up to the open day at Stow-on-the-Wold, during which his birth father plays with him, tickles him, and his birth mother feeds him. Alex reports that they have also recently taken him home for a week.

His birth parents, after years of staying in the sad and lonely shadows, are edging closer, but there's a consensus that the 'disrupted' adoption, interfering with 'closure' at that time, did not help them.

A blob on a beanbag

When Andrew was originally advertised in a social services newsletter, just a few lines, the woman told Alex that she was going to adopt him. Later, when she sent him back, the woman casually told Alex that Andrew was now available again. Alex went to see him in school five days later.

'He was like a little blob on a beanbag. That's all he was, a blob on a beanbag. And I thought, "Nobody's going to have you, mate." That's all I could think about.'

Carol Flock, Andrew's social worker, was with Alex and remembers this very differently. 'Alex turned to me and said, "Why didn't you tell me he was so beautiful?"'

So Alex went back to her adoption officer and said, 'I've found a little boy I've got to take.'

'Even though I'd been approved for a girl. I said, "Andrew needs us more than I need a daughter."'

'So all they could say was, "OK, then."'

The problem was: on paper Alex was like that first woman. Single, several adopted Down's kids, youngish. David Coxon didn't mince words.

'My first thought was, "Why should we trust number two, when we'd all been disrupted by number one?"'

'I said to Alex, "What makes you so sure you're not going to dump him back with us in a couple of months?"'

Andrew's birth parents were worse, partly because they had never really believed that anyone could look after Andrew in the first place. Alex recalls that they gave her a hard time.

'They had put their trust, their faith, in this woman to look after their baby, and after they'd said "yes", she rejected him. That's terrible, and it made life more difficult for me. They said, "Why should we trust you? We trusted the other one …"'

'And I remember saying to his dad, "You will trust me in time." So not only did I have to be good with Andrew, I had to be super-good, because they were not for trusting anybody else.'

But in the end, partly because the alternatives were even grimmer, they agreed to Alex. In June 1992 she took Andrew home to Manchester, her fifth adoptive placement of a Down's syndrome boy, to join Matthew, Simon, Adrian and Nathan.

Alex soon discovered that life with Andrew was a medical endurance test. Within five weeks, at a routine examination, the doctor found a huge abdominal mass, thought it was a tumour and rushed him to hospital.

'They wouldn't even let me home to pick up pyjamas. The consultant was waiting on the ward.'

In fact, they discovered that Andrew's bladder was in the wrong place. As Alex said, 'His ears and heart were fine – just everything else was a bit dickie.'

So, over the last fifteen exhausting years, hospital visit followed hospital stay followed operation after operation – but he has continued to survive, even if he will never grow fully or have free movement or free will.

On the one hand, there are parts of Andrew that developed well. For instance, affection, the instinctive need for company and

Five Bells at Bristol Zoo, 1992. From left: Andrew (2), Adrian (14),
Simon (8), Matthew (10) and Nathan (3).

friendship and resilience, which he has beyond the norm. On the
other, there are things to do with his being a 'person' that didn't
survive or, more accurately, never developed in the first place,
crucial, huge things – like *thinking*.

Andrew's thinking processes don't appear to have developed
much, if at all – at least in any sense that we can understand. So
he lies there, in his cot, listening to music, apparently unable to
think, unable to feed himself or pull himself up, unable to see,
unable to control his body. His life seems dreadful, a nightmare
and, well, pointless.

And then – he giggles. A throaty, tinkling, happy sound of joyful contentment.

Who knows what wave of pleasure has washed through
Andrew to produce his joy – but it's infectious and moving. You

want to hold him, hug him, for being happy in spite of his twisted limbs and unseeing eyes. Joy at being alive? Joy at being?

If only he could tell us. It doesn't seem to come from any particular stimulus, though he likes company, so long as you're sensitive and he knows who and what and where. He especially loves his family, but only for a while, because he gets so exhausted, fighting the wheelchair all day, and fighting just to survive, takes so much energy. By teatime he's fidgeting once more – aware, and giggling – with a spontaneous, guttural outpouring of pleasure that comes almost randomly from within.

It's sometimes not easy to understand the point of all this. That question, again. What's the point of Andrew? What's the point of 'a lump' – he's no longer what Alex once called 'a blob' – who can only sit up when strapped into a wheelchair, who seems only to 'exist' within an insulated cocoon?

The answer turns out to be the greatest surprise of this book. Andrew is *the* point – personified – at the apex of why Alex gets such a buzz out of her children. He is her purpose distilled, without bells and whistles, without the usual frills and frolics of family, he is the purest form of what makes her tick. Seemingly a lump just lying there, he's all and everything, connecting to her by some kind of spiritual broadband – an extension of the maternal instinct between mother and baby, perhaps.

The best way to explain this is to imagine that he couldn't even hear, that he had no form of communication or movement at all. Even then, Alex and Andrew would still feel a joy in each other's presence. You can just stand in Andrew's room, quietly, and yet you feel he knows you are there.

The obvious explanation would be that they were together soul-to-soul, and that is what it can feel like with Andrew if you focus hard enough when standing over his cot. He touches your soul and, hopefully, you touch his. It is the touching of souls that elevates him above just being alive; it is what makes him human; it is what switches Alex on; love is touching souls.

These are things that Alex knows but cannot always articulate, or chooses not to. Her cleverness, her depth, is to do with that soulfulness, an instinct of awareness, and goes beyond verbal skills or emotional intelligence. It's a regular theme that people who see Alex meet a baby for the first time say that she has instant empathy, especially with children who don't immediately communicate verbally or visually, as if 'through the ether'. She'd probably say we get too hung up on words and meaning, and that the truth of a person is innate, and instinctive, that you don't need to observe them, or ask them, to know. But it's very clear that Alex can interpret Andrew in a special way – as can Louise, who has had a particular rapport with him since she first joined Alex to look after him.

When I described Andrew as having twisted limbs and lying limp in a cot, Louise was so incensed that she didn't say anything – she obviously saw it as an attack on both Andrew and herself, and Louise goes quiet when she's most hurt and angry. Eventually Alex told me, 'Oh, you've right offended Louise,' so I raised it next time they had a moment to spare.

Louise didn't disagree with my observations, but still thought I was terribly unfair.

'He's so rewarding, just smiles at you all the time, really happy, and yes he is quite disabled but I've seen … well, what I was saying when I complained about what you were describing – I can't see him like "twisted limbs and lying limp in a cot", it's a negative picture of Andrew. It made me angry. I thought, How dare somebody call Andrew that? There's a lot more to Andrew, more than three words – I was jumping on the defensive for him because

Andrew can't jump on the defensive for himself. I've seen him change a lot. I've seen new words come. OK, I'm not talking sentences, but Andrew *has* got more than three words in his vocabulary. He'll say, "I like it," he'll say, "apple pie, horrible, mama, hiya, yeah". He's started to say "no". That's one of his new words, "no".'

As Louise told me off, I could see Alex smirking in the playroom, a smirk that meant, 'Well said, Louise.'

And Angela Kearns – a kind of part-time Louise, who helps Alex three or four evenings a week and often looks after Andrew – would say the same.

Three out of three, not accepting the evidence of their own eyes. Why? Because they don't *see* the twisted limbs; they look past his physical shape into a deeper being that comes from holding and touching and feeding him, of 'being' with him – the connection of flesh and souls that one-to-one caring brings.

Having said her bit, Louise became conciliatory, almost apologetic.

'OK, I agree there is no thought process with him. I'm sure he recognises people's voices and he enjoys interaction with everybody, but that's probably about it. He doesn't think, "Oh, it's Monday morning and Louise is going to come and give me a bath." But he's happy to hear your voice and he normally thinks, "Oh, it's bath time if I hear Louise's voice," so I'm sure that there is a little bit of thought there. But not a lot.'

Broken promises

When Andrew turned 16, Alex decided she didn't want him to continue at Chatsworth School. In her view, he spent far too long sitting upright, strapped to his chair, and there was an alternative she preferred for him. The notion of Andrew being at school was questionable anyway. For instance, because of absurdities with the National Curriculum, Andrew had to learn French. Yes, really. Apart from being preposterous, it's an example of making a person fit the system, and wasteful of everyone's time and energy. Simon had to learn French, too, which was so ridiculous it brings out a snort in Alex that could be heard in Paris.

'The Director of Education says all kids must have access to a foreign language. So up to now Simon goes "urr-urr-urr-urr ..." what's he going to do, go "unn-unn-unn-unn"? I said to Janet Pardoe, the headmistress, "You can expect my kid to tackle French when he can blow his nose."'

The special teachers try hard to make the best of such bureaucratic nonsense, which requires them to teach history and geography to 'pupils' with below nursery-level intelligence. For instance, when the school covers topics like Ancient Egypt, the teachers come to school dressed as pharaohs. Or on the Mayan Indians, they serve meals on clay pottery. Or with geography, they teach the geography of the school, the layout of classrooms and what the weather might be like in Swinton. Though it's hard to believe that Andrew or Simon understand any of this, particularly Andrew who can only make out sounds, the alternative, giving up, is on nobody's agenda – but only to a point.

When it becomes painful or cruel or unnecessarily delays more positive options, mothers like Alex put away their sense of humour and pick up a cudgel. Which is what happened when Salford Social Services refused to allow Andrew to leave school at 16 and go on to the Waterside Resource Centre, a special facility for high-needs adults that already had Simon.

Alex's view was simple: the legal school-leaving age was 16 and Andrew had suffered more than enough 'containment' disguised as education. From 'school-leaving' onwards, the Waterside caters for the real requirements of its clients, rather than prolonging the educational fantasies of a system that force-feeds pretend 'learning' for its own purposes without sufficient regard for the individuals concerned.

'With Simon and Andrew, so much of their energies are taken up by surviving, there isn't any left of them for learning. They're knackered by just living. Fighting infections constantly, in and out of hospital, battling their bodies, illness, surgery – they can't concentrate on learning as well. So the Waterside is far better for them.'

However, Salford refused to deal with Alex's many requests for Andrew to go there, suggesting he was too young, even after she withdrew him from school on his 16th birthday. The problem for Salford was that even if they weren't breaking the rules, Alex and Andrew would be setting a precedent, and a difficult one for Salford to deal with, so it appeared that they didn't really know how to answer her.

But after a year of Andrew remaining at home in his cot, Alex could stand it no more. She took him in his special chair to Salford Social Services head office, with drinks and sandwiches and a change of nappy for Andrew, sat down in reception and said she wasn't leaving until someone senior agreed to deal with Andrew's case. They sat there for three-and-a-half hours and promised a decision by 'the next Tuesday'. Only then did Alex wheel Andrew out of the office and home.

Eventually, after battling for 16 months, Alex did get Andrew into the Waterside a couple of weeks before his 17th birthday – a year late, but a year earlier than if she hadn't fought. And for Andrew, an extra year at Waterside was worth all the effort.

Waterside

Whatever the delay with Andrew, Salford Council should be whole-heartedly congratulated for developing and supporting such an extraordinary facility. About a mile up the road from Swinton, Waterside is a collection of low, interlinked buildings on the edge of a concrete estate. It caters for high-needs adults from leaving school up to the age of 70 – people who are often misshapen or physically deformed, and others who, like Simon and Andrew, have little or no communication ability, mobility or bodily control.

On the face of it, such a place should be disheartening, austere and on the scary side of imagination, providing day care for about thirty people with the most severe disabilities that treacherous chromosomes and cerebral blitzkriegs can create. People who are bent almost beyond human recognition, crooked, curved, bowed, deformed, unformed; people who cannot move any limb or muscle; people who cannot see or hear or touch or move. People who are shocking. From the outside.

But picture this:

It is after lunchtime, they are lying there, or sitting in wheelchairs, or crumpled on tarpaulins on the grass, under an awning, in the garden, in the summer sun. A rock band is playing, because it is Simon's 21st birthday and this is his party. Simon is in his wheelchair, giggling and shouting and 'ya-ya-ya'-ing, waving his arms, vaguely to the music, but now, at the Waterside, in high-needsville, he's one of the smartest people, one of the most able.

To his left is a young lady, Miss Half-a-Finger, who is lying on her face, with one wide eye staring open, moving the top half of a single finger, sometimes to the rhythm, sometimes to herself. To Simon's right, a man in his 40s, Mr Living-in-a-World-of-His-Own, both eyes shut, lolling over the side of his wheelchair, muttering and spluttering. Just behind him, an impossibly thin woman in her mid-30s, Miss Never-Stop-Crying, silently sobbing, her whole narrow face a wail. And everywhere are tongues. Tongues protruding, tongues hanging out, tongues flapping and dribbling. From the outside.

Then you get in amongst them, close up.

Simon sees me, waves and yelps and shouts 'ya-ya-ya-ya', and demands, and gets, a cuddle. And that's it. You're there, on the inside. They're not a group any more; it's not a scene from hell, but a number of individual people listening to music in the sun. It's my 'Billy' moment, accessed through Simon, through his 'happy-to-see-you' beam. So, these are thirty Simons and Andrews, thirty people who are loved from the top of their spiky hair to the bottom of their oddly shaped toes.

A care worker tugs at my sleeve. 'This is Nicola. She's very bright – understands every word.' Nicola is maybe 35, with shoulders and hips and legs at war with each other so that she is forever crumpled upside down in a cot-like contraption, but still able to look up out of the corner of one eye, and still able to smile and snigger. The tip of her right thumb is held high, slotted between the first two fingers of her hand. If she wiggles the thumb, it means 'yes'. If she doesn't, that's 'no'.

We talk – I ask yes–no questions, way more communicative than expected – about TV, what she likes to eat, about her family. But, actually, she mainly wants to listen, to hear about me and my world, but now my world seems so banal compared with hers. If only she could actually talk, use words. Being one-to-one with her is like being with a foreigner who understands, but can't speak, your language. In time Nicola could tell me so much, her bright, bubbly brain could tell me what it's like being trapped …

But there's another tug on my sleeve, to be introduced to Miss Never-Stop-Crying. 'This is a good day for her. She's crying because that's how she communicates, isn't it …?

In every direction a person, a story, a 'living-despite-the-odds' epic tale, an angle no able body could imagine, as if trapped within a flesh and blood machine that doesn't function. But are they trapped? No more than the rest of us – and anyway, Simon's 'ya-ya-ya-yaing' again because the music's stopped while one of the carers tells the band that the audience prefers 'softer, slower ballads'. They begin again, an instrumental – 'Summertime'. Simon tries to clap but misses as usual, and there's another tug on my sleeve. Time to see the boss, Angela Johnson, time for the tour.

Like everyone who works at Waterside, Angela is deceptive, easy to underrate. Curly, blonde and 30–40-something, she touches a lot and calls you 'dearie', but this hides the wily determination of a social services veteran who knows how to get her way. To work for her is to adore her – unless you are a bovver-boy skiver, or intellectually lazy. Then she'd be a killer.

She appears self-taught, like one of those secretaries who 'seem' to be chief executive by accident, until you work out the obstacles she must have overcome along the way. And then, by and by, she mentions that she 'sort of', well, designed the place. Well, part of the team.

'Lucky, we were. You know, time and place. We told them, at the right time, that the place was wrong. So they let us loose, start afresh, back to basics, and Salford rustled up some money, dear.'

Angela is the kind of person who could pick your pockets for the right cause, and you wouldn't notice the money had gone.

A decade ago the extra-special needs crowd were looked after in day centres, draughty and echoey, half clinics-half school halls, with lots of wheelchair ramps and 'Willie's-having-an-epileptic-fit-in-the-toilet-again' intercoms. They were designed with the cleaners in mind, and the efficient feeding, treating and processing of complex people with significant parts missing. Then Angela was asked by Salford Social Services to re-examine the function of high-needs-ville.

'We rethought everything. Everything. What are we for, and how to do it? For instance – carpets. They didn't have carpets in day centres because of cleaning and dirty marks, and we thought, "Why not?" Banks have them, so why not us? Because we need them more – if somebody's taken by a seizure, or sat on the floor having "a behaviour", or banging their head with autism, or just wants to slide around the floor like Simon does – why should they get bruised or have a cold bum? So let's have carpets, big thick ones. Makes a huge difference.'

Angela floats off to the dining room, which is more like a hotel restaurant than a canteen, taking the time to talk with a couple of clients on her way, and clear up a table.

'Our people need the best chance they can get to feed themselves. OK, most can't, but this is where everyone can meet up and there are lots of different needs, so the tables are different heights – some diners are lying down, others sitting down, even some have to sort of stand. And the manufacturers who make the chairs have designed a special fabric that's waterproof with an anti-bacterial coating, so it doesn't feel like plastic or cold and hard, but leathery and soft. It matters.'

Off she goes again, still excited about the building, still remembering what it used to be like before she arranged to have the internal walls knocked down. Angela has the original drawings, the brief she drew up for the builders, the architect's plans, but just as you're stopping for a moment to take in the bright decoration and signs and lighting, she whisks you along the corridor, through a door, into a razzle-dazzle kitchen that's a bit like a school's domestic science lab.

'This is our sensory bakery. It's to simulate everything in a kitchen at home, gas, electric, different kinds of taps, sockets – see, the tables rise and fall for wheelchairs – so they can learn how to use ordinary appliances. And that *is* important. For assessing people, how to position them, and to help build up their self-esteem. So for some people it's rehab, for others it's teaching. For instance …'

Angela is definitely a 'for instance' woman. She has, it's clear, learnt from experience, in social work parlance, at the coalface, the hard way, she's not a college kind of gal.

'… for instance, they had one lady in here this morning, very complex difficulties, speaks through a Liberator, and it can take her ten minutes to open the microwave door because of involuntary hand movements and stuff, but she wants to do it herself. She's in a wheelchair and wants to cook, which could be dangerous, but she wants to make her own dinner because she gets way more than just food from that. She can connect with smells, tastes, cooking sounds, feeling food – it's good for them to handle food, to touch it, that's sensory baking – cooking in a tactile way. Simon likes to do bits of baking, too, he likes to get involved, put his hands in, feel the food, sniff at it. Oh, yes, did I tell you? The whole of Waterside is about "Smell, Taste, Touch, Sound". That's our foundation. So you must let me show you the Relaxation Room.'

And off we go again. Don't forget, the Waterside is for profoundly disabled adults, like Simon and Andrew. People to whom smell, taste, touch, sound are all there is. People who can't move unless moved. People who can't think, can't really do anything, who seem to be hopeless.

And the question this place has to answer is – what do we do with them all day?

Containment? That 'they' are simply slumped at wooden desks, in classrooms, catatonically watching TV? That 'they' are pushed in a line from a gym, to a bathroom, to a canteen, to a minibus waiting outside? That 'they' are prisoners of their minds and bodies and therefore of our systems?

To help me think again, Angela took me to the Relaxation Room.

'Take a breath. Sniff. Go on. Special scents, perfumes, and music, always some music. Different lighting, different textures. Go on, feel, feel this chair …'

And she's off again …

'This is a Stress Room. Somewhere for the individuals or staff to wind down. See, this room is designed to have no stimulus, very calm, low lights, neutral colours …'

And off again …

'My favourite, the Body-Relaxation Room …

'And the Communications Room …

'And come and see the special toilets – for people who have never been able to go on their own before …

'Oh, and Simon's favourite – our Multi-Sensory Room …'

The *what*?

'The Multi-Sensory Room. It brings out people's feelings.'

Enough. Well, maybe not enough, but a stunning testimony to an energetic woman with a highly motivated team, working for a well-enough funded local authority.

But all the time that wayward thought. This boundless energy and care is going nowhere except to ease the existence of people who, metaphorically and sometimes literally, can only move half a finger. How did that happen? How did a part of our society become so generous-hearted without most of us knowing? It's as if someone dreamt up a therapeutic fairground somewhere over the rainbow, yet it really does exist in a concrete backyard. If you tell Angela this, she brushes it aside.

'This kind of therapy is about getting into *their* world and when you're in there you know what to do. These things aren't expensive. The perfume costs virtually nothing. The multi-sensation tables are three-a-penny in health spas, but you should see how they work here. Our people love sensations, it's how they connect with us and themselves, not through talking. So we have hand massages and foot massages, we put gloves on, on their hands or using gloves on them.'

By now I am sitting on the vibrating sensory bed, listening to a specially edited music and effects track ('The caretaker at the Royal School for the Deaf put in the sound systems, dearie. He's a treasure and so imaginative'), I've got my feet on the heated water mat, I'm being pummelled by massage pads, I'm watching the disco-style light show projected onto the ceiling, while playing with an interactive computer screen – and the whole lot is on a platform moving like waves on the ocean, which is apt because the air is full of the smell of the sea.

'We do "intensive interaction", where a speech therapist mimics them. Remember when you were little and you used to copy people – if they put their tongue out, you'd put yours out, or if they said something, you'd repeat it, and really annoy other people. Well, we do that because it's a way of getting into another person's world, so instead of getting them to communicate the way we want them to, we make the same noises as them, same expressions. And often by doing that you discover that a noise they make that seemed nothing is actually a response, has meaning, and we can use that to communicate with them. The results can be breathtaking …'

A steely voice begins murmuring on the audio track, drowning out Angela. 'No one would have believed, in the last years of the nineteenth century, that human affairs were being watched from the timeless worlds of space, keenly and closely by intelligences greater than man's …'

What? H.G. Wells's *War of the Worlds*? How surreal is that? On the speakers in the Multi-Sensory Room, while the bed continues to vibrate, the disco lights flash – and then the Angela track fades back up with another 'for instance …'

'For instance, we've got one young man with virtually nil mobility, who recently came to us from school, has been quite badly behaved, had to be on medication, couldn't sleep, all the rest of it, came here, and within four weeks, Leslie, who was working with him one to one, picked up on an eye movement. And she worked out his little flick of the eyebrow was him responding "yes". The minute he realised that we knew what he was saying, his world turned inside out, literally, he could be understood for the first time ever, his medication was unnecessary, he slept through, and the whole quality of his life changed. Wonderful.

'But this was extremely stressful for the parents because they keep asking themselves, "Why didn't we notice? He must have felt so frustrated, cut off." But we tell them it's about looking at things a bit differently, which is what we can do. We're experts. Don't blame yourselves, it's just the way things move forward.'

The tour begins to wind down, Angela becomes more philosophical about high needs in general, the way you never meet an unhappy high-needs employee because 'they don't have to ask why they come to work, don't have to wonder if they make a difference'.

We pass through the Physio area – like a well-equipped executive gym – and walk across the car park, towards the garden where Simon's 21st birthday party is reaching its climax with the arrival of his cake. The band plugs in and starts up again. Only the staff can actually sing happy birthday, the rest of the crowd are slumped and snoozing and out for the count anyway – it's been a long day.

A knife is squeezed into Simon's limp hand and his key worker helps him push down to slice the cake, to a smattering of cheerful applause. 'Happy birthday, dear Simon, happy birthday to you …'

The scene is the same as before, bodies misshapen and twisted on tarpaulins on the grass, men in wheelchairs drooping and drooling, Miss Never-Stop-Crying is … crying. Simon, the baby who they said wouldn't see his fourth birthday, is 21 today. An adult. But what of his future? And what of the future of Andrew, his even more profoundly disabled brother?

Angela could have reads my thoughts.

'It gets worse for people with complex needs when they get older. When they're little and they've got disabilities it's "Oh, aren't they gorgeous, aren't they adorable, how do you cope, you're a marvel, you're a saint." People don't say that when they're 50, lost their teeth, gone bald, and they're still dribbling and have epileptic fits. People don't say, "Oh, what a shame, how cute." It's like, "I paid to have a quiet dinner, would you mind leaving 'cos you're making people nervous." It's a totally different attitude, and with people living longer and new medical techniques, we're now beginning to hit a situation where a lot of Down's syndrome people are getting to middle and old age.'

That concern – what happens when her children get older – occupies a lot of Alex's thoughts. Andrew, who is still 5-year-old size, may never grow big enough to be 50 and balding, but the need to provide him with a meaningful life is close to her heart. The problem is, how? Although the Waterside can take him five days a week, what will he do the rest of the time? And what kind of life can Andrew hope for anyway?

The great thing about the Waterside is the noise and the bustle and routine activity – most of it one to one, carer to client. Even if this sometimes seems to be filling time, that's enough of a purpose if the recipient would otherwise just be lying there, as a lump. For Andrew that's especially true when he's at home with his family, whether organised by Alex and Louise, or just the natural commotion of eight boisterous brothers and sisters.

Andrew at 17

Andrew can't see beyond a vague sense of light or dark. He can't feed himself, he has very limited understanding of the world around him, and he can't move without assistance. Not only does he have cerebral palsy, but with his digestive system at war with itself and his bladder the wrong way round, it is a miracle that Andrew has lived to the age of 17. And not just live, but thrive. If he senses someone is in his room, he'll splutter, 'Hi-ya. Mum-ma. Bye.' And beam, with his red, rubbery lips, knowing he's secure and loved in his cot. There's a value-added magic at work here, the magic of the family. Especially for Nathan, Andrew's best friend in the world. Andrew gives Nathan a purpose, to protect his brother, and Nathan gives Andrew a purpose, too, the purpose to survive.

So he does still breathe, as he listens to the sound of his family – he breathes and breathes. Life is noise if you can't see, can't move on your own. Every bang, every yell, every laugh, every cry is confirmation that you're not alone, not abandoned within a body that doesn't work. Without knowing it, the deafening, booming, crashing Bell family are Andrew's lifeline, his reason to cling on, to be alive. To Andrew, noise is life.

As David Coxon says, 'Andrew's content because he doesn't know any different, that's his life, the way it's always been and always will be. Fed, watered, looked after, loved – it's that simple, but he is simple, like a baby, but a baby who won't develop. If you think of him like that, his life has a point, being loved and being happy.'

Dot says much the same: 'Like having an adult with a baby inside. You don't know what's happening in there, but there's something.'

Yet he does have ways of communicating, a simple language that clearly gives him the satisfaction of being acknowledged, of being noticed. Andrew may only have a couple of working fingers, but when he pinches Alex's thigh every evening while he's being fed, and Alex pushes his hand back and calls out, 'Stop it, Andrew,' he laughs. It's a gurgling laugh, mischievous and happy, the highlight of his day. And a highlight of Alex's day, too, because she knows it means so much to him, and that the pinch is a sign that Andrew is reaching out to the world around him.

'He can do things. He can spit food out which is highly manipulative, and he can pinch and he can bite and he can cry and he can laugh, and he enjoys music and he knows when people are around him. He's very sociable, likes people. A family where he was the only child would be very isolating, he'd be too cut-off, too cosseted, he wouldn't have survived. He likes a lot going on, likes familiar people, familiar places. He gets anxious on his own or in places he doesn't know. He'll call out, "Ell-o ...? Ell-o ...? Ell-o ...?" waiting for a response. He talks a lot at night, when it's quiet. Andrew needs life around him, just to survive.'

Alex has said, on more than one occasion, that if she could live her life again, she wouldn't take on Andrew. Not because she doesn't love him, or that he's worn her out, but because having two wheelchair kids is five times more difficult than one, and that has a knock-on effect on the rest of the family. The problems with Andrew, with his mobility and high needs, have an impact on their spirit of adventure, and make expeditions that might be challenging seem irresponsible – and as the Bell family become older and more ambitious, they are slowed down by having a 'for-ever-baby' along. Not that this changes Alex's commitment to him. It doesn't. But she is able to talk candidly about the things she has learnt from experience. Her tone is loving, but matter-of-fact:

'I love Andrew, we all do, but I wouldn't take him again,' she says without the slightest hint of betrayal, self-pity or regret, while feeding and cuddling him, so the extraordinary detachment of her words is only shocking afterwards.

Alex is the embodiment, both physically and spiritually, of a new kind of earth mother. She can change an adult nappy while totting up the household budget, and write a letter to her Member of Parliament as nit lotion is purging the family's hair. These contradictions are the stuff of modern motherhood; the well-known multitasking has morphed into less understood multi-attitudes, in which emotional certainty does not exist. This may be because she has to be both father and mother, but it leads to analytical mothering, rather than 'my child right or wrong'. The end result is total support and total honesty, and a decision-making process that combines heart and head. The outcome is not academic, or like the pass-the-parcel responsibility of social workers. It is about making judgements that hugely affect her family's well-being, sometimes life and death – literally.

Take Andrew. Would he have survived without the bustle of the Bell family? Almost certainly no, his life would have been devoid of any interest, of any reason to fight. His already wracked body would have given up shortly after his mind had switched off. So, the love of Alex and family keep him alive – end of story?

From Alex's point of view it isn't that simple. There's still a decision to be made, from the other side, the analytical side, of her brain.

What if Andrew begins to suffer, or a new illness causes him pain? For most people the answer is easy – they should be treated until they recover, even if the treatment is onerous, perhaps even traumatic; life itself is reward enough. For Andrew the equation is more complex, the decision less easy, and one he can't take part in himself. So Alex must answer what is a very difficult philosophical question – when is life worth living, when should the fight be given up? 'I think, therefore I am' – but if you don't think, how does that throw the equation of life and death?

These are not peripheral points; they are what Alex has to deal with as a mother. Her answer, probably the only one that can make sense, is to balance joy and pain, although it has to be subjective within Andrew's world of limited communication. It is not absurd to say that the significance of Andrew's life is that he is alive, and any other meaning is a bonus. Therefore, so long as he is comfortable and not in pain, every effort should be made on his behalf, but Alex doesn't think he should suffer just to stay alive.

'Andrew has had a "no resuscitation" order on him since 1999. I felt that if ever he was in a life-and-death situation, I wouldn't want us arguing over a very sick child – I wanted everybody concerned to be in agreement now about what the treatment would or would not be. I'm proud I did that because it was a positive step, not to say I want Andrew to die – but there are certain medical procedures I would not want Andrew to suffer with. So he's got a "no resuscitation" order in his medical notes.

'People needed a lot of persuading to do that, and it's right that it's not just my decision. First, I approached the paediatrician and said we should look into this while Andrew was well – that is the time to make that decision. Then I spent a day with his social worker, then a day with his mum and dad. I said, "Look, I realise this is really hard but I need to know that we're all working towards the same end here," and they immediately said that's exactly what we should do, never flinched, agreed straight away.

'I went to speak to Janet Pardoe, his head teacher at the time, saying, "It's not that I'm giving up on Andrew, not at all, but I want us to be happy with the decision if it ever came to it."

'She said, "Yes, absolutely yes, but get a document."

'The paediatrician drew it up, it's in his medical notes, signed, dated. So Andrew will be given antibiotics and things like that, but if he ever needed to go on a ventilator, for example, I wouldn't give consent and I know that the other people agree with this – because we wouldn't actually be improving his quality of life, we'd just be increasing his suffering.'

Both Alex and Louise take huge pride in Andrew, that the 'blob' has become a 'lump', continuing to grow, if not very much in size, then in contentment. As Louise says, 'He goes to the

Waterside, he comes home, he lies in a cot, he gets fed, and he goes to sleep – well that's what Andrew likes to do, that's Andrew at his best, a good life. A very good life.'

And while it lasts, that's good enough for Alex, too.

Chapter Ten

Dealing with Down's

Dealing with Down's

The impact of Down's syndrome on the lives of people it touches has common themes, common visions and common experiences; some of them unrealistic, though none the less powerful for that. For instance, the vision of the 40-year-old man-child holding hands with his mother while shopping during the day, which birth parents often mention, takes on major significance when a couple are still coming to terms with having a baby with Down's syndrome.

Likewise, the impact on other siblings of having a brother with Down's syndrome, or a history of disability in the family, or odd notions like them having clumpy shoes, all these are repeated in different forms by different parents when they recollect the early days and weeks of 'coming to terms' with such a shocking, and unknown, trauma. That is the point when help, advice and simple facts are needed most, but often in the shortest supply.

When some parents look back to that time, they recall vivid memories, strange dreams and sometimes nightmares. One mother remembered lying in the hospital bed dreaming that she was surrounded by a squad of Down's syndrome men with flat caps and polo-neck jumpers, who were marching around the shops. Another recalls, 'If I could go through every cell in my baby's body, even if it took me twenty years, and take that extra chromosome out, I'd do it. But there's this helplessness. You've just been dealt this huge blow and you can't do anything about it. Nothing.'

Even objects take on huge significance. One father, who was interviewed some time ago, told an eloquent story about how Down's syndrome came to be symbolised by a tiny woollen hat.

'I bought it that day, the day my wife went into labour, into hospital, early. We hadn't bought any baby things, so the next thing I did after leaving my wife sitting in bed, exhausted but happily holding a beautiful little baby, was to race around the shops – we had no nappies, no cot, no pram, no clothes, and I came back with loads of stuff, including a little white baby's hat. This was literally ten minutes before the paediatrician came into the room to do the check. Our baby was so tiny that the hat didn't fit, even though it was the smallest in the shop. We had to roll the hat up, in folds.

'Anyway, I had gone through the whole birth thing thinking, "Oh, isn't our baby beautiful, just lovely features." I'd done the phone calls to the family; at this point flowers had started to arrive, people were coming in with presents, we were in the throes of euphoria, the fantasy had come true, we're all floating around …'

The mother continued: 'The midwife brings the paediatrician – a very young woman with long blonde hair parted in the middle, not long out of medical school, doing those incredibly harrowing tests, which have to be done.

'Then she turned around to me and asked, "You don't think there's anything wrong with this baby, do you?"

'And I just thought, "Ah-ahh-ahhh, worst nightmare time," and I said, "I dunno."

'"You don't think it's got Down's, do you?" – that's what she said, that's what she said.

'I muttered, "It has crossed my mind, yes." And at that point I just said, "*Take the baby out*." It's my belief, to this day, that had I been told in a different way, maybe things wouldn't have turned out the way they did. Not at any point during the whole process did anybody say, "Actually, it's not so bad." Everywhere I turned, people were negative.'

The father nodded. 'So we went through eight hours of "Wow, fantastic, we've got a little one, a bit early but it's fine." Then this devastation. Brutal. Then the chromosome test which takes two days for the results, so we stayed in the hospital, waiting. And it was up and down: one minute, "Can't be, baby's fine," then "No, it's not," then, "Yes, it's OK." The mind plays tricks.

'Because, looking at our baby, in that hospital, there were none of the obvious markers of Down's, but when you looked close, back and forth, yes and no, always on tenterhooks – really you know. You do know. Awful – it was awful. And basically that little white hat represents our baby as our dream, our dream child that wasn't Down's, because it was the last thing I did, putting the white hat on its tiny head, before we were told.'

Stories like that pepper the experience of being a Down's syndrome parent, the sense of being alone with only each other while having to deal with the greatest crisis of your life. And while the baby is given a social worker to look after its interests, the parents are expected to muddle along on their own, or with the help of extended families who are often just as bewildered. And they all have one thing in common. Isolation. Isolation from help and, more importantly, isolation from hope.

Parents with Down's syndrome babies say the same things: 'You're completely deserted.' 'No one says it's all right, you can deal with this, it's not so bad.'

So for weeks they may be rebounding from unexpected feelings. One day on a high, the next they might plunge into the lowest of lows, bouncing from torment to hope, then back to the blackest gloom. Some of what they do might be intuitive, other actions very calculated. In the morning they might be glacier-minded, analytical, but by the evening human bewilderment could take over again, leaving them wondering how to cope with despair and pain.

All the time wondering if they should build a life with their baby, or – or what? Couples can look down at their little, vulnerable, helpless baby and think the unthinkable: that they may not be able to provide the most supportive or suitable life for their child, that adoption may be a better way.

They will have bonded with their baby and want the best, but instinctively realise that they may not be the best parents, even though they can't just walk away.

Such was the case with Nathan's parents and Thomas's parents who Alex was already in contact with, and looking after informally. However, by then she had also set her heart on another, new addition to her family – Alex's first daughter, Chloe.

Little Miss Dynamite: Chloe

Initially, Chloe's mother contacted Nathan's mother, Sue, with a very tentative enquiry. Sue remembers explaining Alex's family, how she'd worked wonders with Nathan.

Sue got another call a few hours later asking to meet. But before the meeting, it was cancelled. Then another call to meet.

Meanwhile, Alex was intrigued as much as excited. She had thought, for a while, that a girl would complement her by now five boys – indeed, she'd been approved to adopt a girl when along came Andrew – but it was also the prospect of dealing so directly with the parents that fascinated her, the sense of starting off by sharing. But when Sue phoned Alex to say they would like to meet her, Chloe's birth mother became hesitant again. Everyone thought they understood why. It must be difficult for any maternal woman to willingly give up her daughter. Alex was so obviously the right solution that, once they met, there might be no turning back.

Three months after Chloe's birth, her mother took the plunge.

Alex was taking all five children to Chippenham for a few days for Nathan's seventh birthday party and Chloe's parents asked if they could go. And that was that.

The 'extended family' were there, Sue and her mum, Matthew's foster parents, they were all there. Everyone clicked. It just felt right. Everyone was really excited for Chloe.

The adoption of Down's syndrome children had come a long way from Alex's early days when they were talked of in whispers and handed over through proxies at arm's length. Chloe was Alex's easiest adoption, with most of the work being done by Chloe's birth mother. The paperwork sped through on the common sense and goodwill of a handful of different agencies, until the day that Alex took Chloe off to her new home, an increasingly large house in Swinton.

Chloe was demanding, but as she grew and blossomed she became the most active, the most energetic of all Alex's children. Now there were six – five lively boys and, at last, a girl.

Before collecting her from the temporary foster home in June 1996, Alex hadn't met Chloe. 'I knew virtually nothing about her except that she was part Portuguese and had a birthmark on her face. If I had walked into a roomful of babies, I couldn't have picked her out.'

When Alex arrived home with Chloe late on that summer afternoon, she soon discovered that the problems would not be about fostering or adoption, they would be of a different kind. Chloe's temporary foster mother had told Alex that she was a quiet baby, that she slept all night and most of the day, that she was a typical girl, perfect complement to Alex's all-male family. But nothing could be further from the truth.

From the beginning, Chloe hardly slept, and to this day she doesn't seem to have the normal rhythms or cycles of most people; if Alex puts her in bed, she just lies there awake, more or less all

Now we are six: (left to right) Andrew, Alex, Chloe, Nathan, Adrian (behind), Matthew and Simon at Nathan's eighth birthday party.

night talking to herself, disrupting the rest of the gang. So Chloe stays up after everyone else has gone to bed, and falls asleep in the play-lounge watching television. Alex's last act each night is to carry Chloe to her bedroom in the hope that she will at least sleep for a few hours.

Alex calls Chloe 'Little Miss Dynamite' because she never stops rushing around, chattering, poking every object, or grabbing at your sleeve. During tea she will stand up a dozen times, switch the taps on and off, press the microwave buttons, move her chair, sit back down; then up again, open a drawer, fiddle with some-one's pen, pick up a magazine, then sit down, up again, back to the taps, rearrange the cutlery, open a cupboard, squeeze the wash-ing-up liquid, move her chair, then sit down again. And that's during tea at home. If she goes out to eat, it's all the above times ten. Alex and Louise have a mantra, which they call out, hardly looking: 'Sit down, Chloe.'

'I was really looking forward to having a girl. A pleasant, demure little girl who liked to wear dresses, make-up, do girlie things. Instead, I got Chloe, who's more like a boy than any of the boys. She's a ruffian, a tearaway, a complete tomboy. Pink isn't her colour, she always wears trousers, she won't do her hair – she definitely does not want to look pretty. She wears jeans, climbs trees, and gets mud everywhere. You could never send her to ballet – you could never get her in a ballet dress anyway.'

For all her tomboy qualities, as if to confound expectation, Chloe is especially pretty and photogenic, dominating family photographs.

'She has no sense of danger, so she goes running off the whole time, it's just a big game to her. "There's space, I'm off." Play areas are very hard, or any building with several doors. I always find out if they're alarmed; if not, I ask them for a guard. Chloe doesn't understand that if she goes through a door she can't be seen. To her it's part of playing, looking for an escape route so we have to find her, but she'll run for miles, and I do mean miles. Most kids keep an eye on their parents, they're terrified of losing me – Emily for instance is constantly watching me – but Chloe doesn't give a damn, she doesn't have that mechanism at all.'

At school, Chloe is actually referred to as 'a runner', which means she is on a 'red behaviour plan', based on traffic lights. Some kids, the ones who never stray or experiment, like Emily, are on a 'green plan'; those, like Chloe, who constantly put them-selves in danger, are 'red plan'; then there are 'amber' kids, who are either coming off the red and getting safer, or have been green and are getting worse.

All staff at every facility are told, and deal with each child according to their colour plan; teachers, dinner ladies, coach driv-ers, even taxi drivers know that because Chloe is 'red plan' she cannot be left on her own for a single moment. For instance, when the bus comes she has to wait in her seat belt until an adult comes onto the bus to get her, and then holding her hand bring her into the school. And later, when coming home, Chloe can't be left to wait on the pavement; she must wait inside the building, and be the last on board, walked on the bus by a member of staff, belted up, and the driver will close the door immediately Chloe is on board. Emily just gets on and off the bus on her own.

Even so, Chloe has disappeared several times, once for fifteen minutes, because the supervisor put her on the bus then went back for someone else, leaving enough time, perhaps only a couple of seconds, for Chloe to race off.

These sudden disappearances are not planned. Chloe is an opportunist, but once free she will stop at nothing, racing over busy roads, climbing walls, leaping over ditches, fences, whatever is in her way. She loves water and would jump in the canal if she had the chance, even though she can't swim, because Alex knows that water is fun to her, not dangerous.

'Once she almost climbed off the end of Weston pier. I had to grab her from the railings. So now she's either in a buggy, which she hates, or we're holding her hand. Firmly.'

Eventually – by the time she's, say, 15 – Chloe will outgrow 'running off', not because she will discover a sense of danger, she's never likely to develop anxiety or fear, but because the game will stop being such fun, and because Alex has been working on her sense of shame relentlessly, telling her that only little girls run away, or never stop fidgeting.

'She's definitely improving. The first time I took her to the pictures she couldn't sit still for more than half an hour. She had to go to the toilet, have a lolly, buy sweets – but she will now sit and concentrate on a film for two and a half hours. OK, she doesn't understand it all, but she does try to concentrate, so that is a big improvement.'

Chloe aged 10

Chloe at 10 is still learning language, and can understand about three words in a row; any more than that will confuse her so that she can't pick any of them out – in the way a person trying to understand a foreign language, in which they have a limited vocabulary, is confused when more than a few words run together. For instance, if Alex says, 'It's teatime, go and wash your hands. Dry them. Then come and sit down,' she'll do that, because it's a routine and she knows what she's doing.

But if Alex said, 'Go to your bedroom, put your doll to bed, then get your slippers and come back to Mummy,' Chloe could not understand how to do that.

'It would be too much for her to follow. Or if I took her to the window and asked, "What's it like outside?" there's a possibility she might say, "Rainy," or "There's a rainbow," but if I asked, "What's the weather like?" she couldn't answer. I doubt if she would understand the word "weather".'

Likewise, Chloe can talk, but can't quite put a sentence together. But, there again, she's getting better. According to Alex, in the last twelve months she's learnt, if not sentences, simple phrases.

'She can describe specific things like "Callum's poohed his nappy" or "Nathan smacked me" or "Adrian's not put the video on." That's an advance, believe me. But she couldn't describe her day at school. Perhaps she could answer specific questions like, "What did you do at school today?" – she might say if there was something significant like "theatre group" or "went to donkeys", so she can keep events in her mind. But she can't write. One day maybe, a bit – she's a typical Down's kid in a class of moderate to severe learning difficulties.'

Within Alex's family, Chloe is normal. Anywhere else, she'd be slow or different – it seems to suit Chloe to live with people who have problems with the simplicities of living. She races around, grabbing at everyone and everything, playing physically like a boy. In all probability she may not understand that girls are different.

For Alex, that's the key to Chloe – that's she's a girl.

'The difference with girls is they're hell. I find girls really hard to bring up, maybe because I've just had more boys, but with girls it's all banging doors and screaming. You can't get round a girl, they've got their own mind made up, and stick to it. Boys, you can always get round a boy – usually through his stomach, like, "Do you really not want tea tonight?" That works without fail. Girls will stamp their foot and no means no, there's no way on earth you can persuade a girl. Their minds are set.

'And that's the point. She's a girl first and foremost. And then she's a girl with Down's syndrome. Definitely a girl. I always say that if Chloe had been my first, she'd have been an only child. She's very challenging, and she's everything to me. She's gorgeous, superb, everything I ever wanted, but very hard work. I'm just very grateful that I've got two girls and seven boys and not the other way around.'

Chloe probably does not have the awareness that she's a girl – in the sense that there are boys, and that girls are different from them – and it's possible she will never grasp the meaning of gender or sexuality. Down's syndrome adolescents of both sexes understand sex at about the level of the average 5 or 6 year old, so they are physically more developed than their moral or social skills can handle.

In boys this can lead to problems, which are dealt with by discouraging inappropriate behaviour, especially if it's carried out in public. Mostly, it's triggered by curiosity. Saying 'no', and reinforcing this consistently, usually stops such behaviour very quickly in people who by and large are eager to please. In girls, adolescence is more about what's actually happening inside, and it can be difficult to explain the physical changes to a teenager with an intellectual age of 5. And especially difficult if they act like a boy and don't understand the difference.

Alex treats this with a robust sense of humour, as just another part of the rough and tumble of having teenagers who mature mentally at a much slower rate than their bodies. To her, it's just physical; it's not about Chloe's behaviour.

'I'm not worried about her flirting – she'd get any boy who came near in a headlock. They asked me at the hospital, "How old do you think she'll be when she's ready for puberty?"

'I said, "About 35."'

Unlike most Down's syndrome men, Down's syndrome women can have children, though they have a 50 per cent chance of the child being Down's syndrome, but Alex will ensure that Chloe takes precautions as she grows up.

'Because, for a start, she's a very pretty little girl and she'll be a very attractive young lady, and I'm not having people taking advantage of her – not that she'd let them. At the hospital a doctor had to examine her and she shouted, "Get off me, you rude man!" So maybe she'll be OK, able to hold her own.'

It's doubtful that Chloe will ever be able to look after herself. The notion that she will get married, establish her own home and walk into the sunset with a husband, perhaps a Down's syndrome man, is a romantic fantasy; she's extremely unlikely to develop that kind of practical independence. She might fall in love, though, and knowing Chloe she probably will, and men will fall in love with her, but it will be more like 'puppy love' than dependent adult love, because Chloe will never be an adult in emotional terms. Lucky Chloe, lots of people may feel, she can look forward to a joyful life without the responsibilities and disillusionments that most of us endure.

The upside of Down's

More than any of Alex's children, Chloe embodies the upside of Down's, the beauty and the simplicity of an innocent life, where love is pure, and every day has a beginning, a middle and an end in the correct, predictable, satisfying order. She is healthy and happy, surrounded by an engaging and friendly bunch of characters, and loved – loved beyond measure. The irony of Chloe having Down's syndrome, and therefore being disadvantaged – disabled – in society's eyes, but, in fact, having the very best of lives, and being loved for what she really is – that irony is at the heart of the rush-along, make-every-second-count world we live in, and is at the heart of this book.

Chloe will be happy and loved *because* she's simple, not in spite of it. She will have, naturally, what most of us crave, and she won't have to try, because the interferences and dismays of modern life will not cling to her cells – that extra chromosome 21, while denying her normal development, also denies her disappointed aspiration.

And part of that is the love of two families – both of them large and lively, full of personality and joy and fun. When her birth family come up to Swinton with their other children for the weekend – and they do so frequently – there can be no less than sixteen people in Alex's house, linked to and through Chloe. As she races around, overwhelmed by choices of who to play with, there doesn't appear to be a divide where one family stops and the other begins. Her birth family, smaller, a shade quieter, dissolve into the shrieking, boisterous Bells without a join, with Chloe's father in the garden organising a game or taking pictures, and Alex and her birth mother working their way through a pot of tea in the kitchen.

As Chloe rushes in and out squealing with delight it's impossible to imagine the pain and uncertainty of ten years ago. It seems like a miracle. But it isn't. It's the product of good people doing their best, of using their intellect, their self-knowledge, and making tough, brave decisions; people who did not *know* –

Chloe emerging.

there is no knowing at those times – people who made the best guess, gritted their teeth, and stuck by it. That's not to say that it is easy – it is not.

Legally, Alex is Chloe's mother. But this has never mattered because all parties have just 'got on with it' and put Chloe's interests at the centre of everything. Chloe now calls her birth parents 'Mummy' and 'Dad'. That's not because Chloe has worked it out for herself – she hasn't. It's because Alex has told her, 'Your mummy and daddy are coming to see you today'. That takes self-confidence and great generosity on the part of Alex, and is typical of the way that Alex has always tried to put her children first, however hard this can be – and with open adoption it can sometimes be very hard.

Open adoption

As experience of it grows, it's becoming clear that open adoption is often heart-achingly difficult, especially for the birth parents, even when there's total commitment and goodwill on all sides.

For any birth mother, adoption is almost always appallingly painful; every natural feeling, every emotion is engaged in wanting to keep the baby, even though common sense or circumstances clearly dictate otherwise. Over the centuries, the kindest advice has been to make a clean break, to try to move forward without looking back, to accept that the child, while eternally in your heart, will build an independent life with its new mother. Although it is not that easy because the emotional umbilical of the maternal instinct continues forever, the child being out of sight does mean that there are not constant reminders for the loss and guilt to be reawakened by. To put it another way, 'in sight, in mind' brings with it the cruellest challenge to the heart, and that's the everyday reality of open adoption.

With open adoption, there's no closing the door as you leave, it's like a love affair where the other party never lets you go, never lets you grieve and move on. On each meeting, the feelings explode as the yearned-for presence is re-established as if it had never left. And that's just on the emotional surface. Underneath, where duty and self-examination hide, every encounter brings the eternal question: Did I need to have her adopted? Could I have coped?

A particular issue has been Chloe's habit of running off, which has become especially apparent – on one occasion she somehow managed to get free at school, and ran straight over a busy road and was found inside a private house putting on the householder's make-up. Given that her birth parents have other young children, and Chloe is such a handful, Alex has insisted on Angela being with them when they visit as an extra pair of hands.

An outside observer might think this is trivial, but it is not. It goes directly to the core of the process of care and control that is open adoption. When birth parents give up their baby for adoption, they relinquish their rights over that person. So far so good. But if they continue to stay in touch, especially to the degree that her birth parents have with Chloe, the powerlessness must be palpable, and it is easy to see why a relatively small issue can take on enormous significance.

The story of Chloe is actually a stunning success, as is apparent when you see her rushing around at the centre of a world that seems to suit her so well. While there are many challenges, when all things are considered – especially for Chloe – though it might not be a fairytale ending, it is pretty close.

Chapter Eleven

Mr Nowhere: Thomas

When Adrian totters off for a week to a respite home it costs £750. This includes his food and lodging – but not entertainment, clothes or his pottery classes. For Chloe, who needs two-to-one supervision, the bill would be greater – perhaps £1,250 per week. And Callum, with high-needs autism, would cost his local authority over £2,000 per week. If the state, or social services, had to meet the expense of the Bell family, all nine children, it would cost around £10,000 per week. But Alex is happy to get a fraction of that, without a thought or murmur of complaint.

Depending on the disability, Alex receives an allowance of about £100 per week for each person, and help with transport and equipment. However, the various benefit systems are so complex, and often so illogical, that it's hard for her to keep track. She has seventeen benefit books from a variety of different places: the Disabled Living Allowance comes from Blackpool, the carer's allowance from Preston, family allowance from Newcastle; some are weekly books, some are fortnightly and some are monthly books, so there isn't a regular amount of money that comes in every week. Alex's answer to this is to deal in cash – until recently she had never had a bank account.

This works because it's simple and direct. Alex is wary of credit, so if she needs a new cooker she saves up for it: ditto, the family holiday. She does have a mortgage on the house but drives over to Bolton every month to pay the instalment in cash. Partly, this is because it helps her to budget, but the main explanation is that Alex doesn't trust banks or, indeed, any organisation where she can't look the person in charge in the face.

Over the years she has learnt that big companies and bureaucracies have little or no understanding of families like hers, and are often hostile, unintentionally or otherwise. Such organisations are more comfortable dealing with 'the norm', and Alex's family are anything but normal, so there's a standoffish sense of corporate cynicism from most of the outside bodies she deals with, an unspoken 'What's she about, then?' as if it's inconceivable that a rational person could really be interested in the waifs and strays she has adopted. Alex treats this with resigned good humour, and tries to avoid dependency if at all possible.

At the apex of this glowering, paternal, 'We know what's best' culture is the biggest brute of all – government, national and local, along with its quangos, committees and authorities. In the face of their target-oriented structures, Alex ticks none of the boxes, and worse, she confounds their orthodoxy by being successful. It doesn't matter to them that Alex saves the public purse hundreds of thousands of pounds a year – it isn't their money. And, likewise, it doesn't matter that Alex's family is happy and healthy – they aren't their children.

The actual social workers, teachers and medical staff who deal with Alex on a day-to-day basis are often excellent, although it usually takes them a while to understand how her family works. The trouble comes from the team leaders, the consultants or assistant directors who seldom meet Alex and are rarely respectful enough to deal with her on an equal footing. Their assumption of superiority from a distance, often comically confounded by events, would be hilarious if the effects weren't so distressing.

Too often the authorities, the law, social work practice, and particularly the bosses, simply lack humility or the ability to listen. They absolutely *know* better, especially if the person they're dealing with is a mother. And nowhere was this more apparent than in the case of Thomas Johnson, Alex's seventh child – and especially in the way the authorities dealt with his mother Patricia.

Patricia is a freethinking, trusting woman, the sort of person who would make a robust but kindly deputy headmistress. Forthright yet caring, she has a knack of describing the absurdities of her situation as if the people in command were inadvertently less than understanding, rather than baddies. She shakes her bewildered head and condemns with a knowing glance rather than harsh words, the rebuke all the more devastating because of her mild, offhand manner. Patricia was the first person to explain that doctors and social workers 'act as if mothers don't have a brain, that having a disabled child must make a person simple and incapable of judgement. I mean, don't they have mothers themselves?' Once said, though innocently and without malice, that remark has stuck – still by far the best explanation for the social services' highhandedness that seems to follow Alex and her family around.

Tom was born on 11 October 1983 at Grimsby Maternity Hospital. Patricia's pregnancy had been routine for a mum aged 30, Tom's two elder brothers were normal, and his parents had no inkling that he would be Down's syndrome. Patricia had been working with special needs babies and knew the paediatrician well, which meant that when Patricia was informed about Tom having Down's syndrome at least it was handled with sensitivity.

'It never crossed my mind that I would have a handicapped child of my own. I moved to Grimsby when I got married and worked with the mentally and physically handicapped, covering all aspects of special needs for a paediatrician called Dr Hunter. Tom was born exactly to the day; he wasn't delayed in any way. He was a healthy 9 pounds, and I remember Dr Hunter walking through the unit, and she rubbed the back of my hand and said, "Hiya Pat, I'm just going to have a look at him for you." Then she came back and she said, "Erm, I'm really sorry, Patricia, but I think he's Down's."

'I'm lying there, this can't be true, no, she's got this wrong.

'Apparently Down's have the line right across the palm and splayed fingers and toes and flat head, which she had spotted.

'My life changed in an instant. I remember dreaming that night so clearly. All I saw was Down's men with flat caps and polo-neck jumpers trundling around the shops, and I remember thinking, "Gosh I've got all this ahead of me." Anyway, Tom was diagnosed Trisomy 21, but he'd got no hole in the heart, no physical problems, so I brought him home. I thought, "I'll take him home. It will all work out."'

The Johnsons learnt the hard way that the authorities, particularly North East Lincolnshire Council (Grimsby), had a budget and an agenda that usually didn't suit their purpose. This sense of isolation, of simply having to get on with it on their own, because the support available was not what they needed, was set from the first few days, and over the years became alienation because of Pat's frustrations in dealing with a nebulous authority.

'All through having Thomas nobody came to me and said, "Do you know this is available?" He was a toddler before I knew I could get free nappies, and I didn't know anything about attendance allowances or special support. And it made me stronger – I started to ask questions because nobody was telling me anything. You felt as though you were asking for something you were not entitled to and people did treat you differently because you had a Down's syndrome child. They seemed to suggest there must be something not quite right with the mother, she's not a round shilling, because she's had a Down's child.

'But there's nobody to blame for this, there's nobody you can kick on the shin and say, "Why have you done this to me?" so I was left feeling numbed, the future I'd hoped for would never now be possible. I don't class myself as religious, though I am a Christian, but there's nobody to kick and say, "Here, what are you messing about at?" And I couldn't understand what had gone wrong, and their attitudes. But once I'd got my head round it, and there was quite a battle, everything that Tom was entitled to I went for.'

Patricia became fed up with people talking down to her; likewise Tom's father Paul, who was a shift worker then, couldn't believe the 'amateur' attitudes of a £300 million a year council, attitudes that were being imposed, 'like it or not', on his family, and underpinning it all was their strong instinct that Tom's problems were not confined to Down's syndrome. Although he walked at 13 months and was physically developing well, he was behind average Down's children mentally, but whenever Patricia raised her concerns, their advice was patronising or twee: she got metaphorically patted on the head and told, 'The experts know best.'

'I remember taking him to a clinical psychologist and saying that I thought Tom was going backwards rather than forwards, and stagnating. I knew Tom had to be reaching certain goals and he wasn't getting close. We got no eye contact with Tom, he was insular in whatever he did, he didn't mix very well, I used to take him to playschools but he wouldn't interact, he played on his own. But they wouldn't accept that there was autism spectrum there – I think the psychologist just put me down as a neurotic mother.'

Grimsby was almost in the dark ages when it came to facilities for special needs children. Tom was saved because, like Chloe, he kept trying to escape from school, but in the case of Tom, he succeeded – running like the wind and for miles. Perhaps out of embarrassment Grimsby arranged for Tom to go to a part-residential school, St Anne's in Hull, across the other side of the Humber Bridge. As Paul points out, this was only the first of several examples of how public money gets squandered if reasonable facilities are not built locally, because Tom would travel there by an expensive taxi every morning and back every evening – until the Friday, when he would stay for the weekend to give the Johnson family much-needed respite.

Tom had become a nightmare to take care of: he was constantly agitated, hammering on walls and shouting out. Patricia and Paul found it impossible to look after him at home – not least because of the disruption he caused to their other two sons. Patricia used to weep because she was so tired.

'Thomas would only sleep, at most, four hours, so we gave him medication to make him sleep and to try and calm him down, but it stopped his learning process.'

With Paul's employment now calling for him to be away from home regularly, sometimes for weeks at a time, it was obvious that the Johnson family would have to do something to prevent a complete family breakdown. But the local council had little to offer, and wouldn't even acknowledge that Tom was autistic as well as suffering from Down's. All Grimsby ever said was, 'Give it time,' while Patricia felt constantly guilty at not being able to 'cope perfectly' with a situation that was relentless in its demands. As any mother would, she wanted a solution for all her children, but in the real world where Patricia lived a decision had to be made for the health of everyone, and in desperation Patricia agreed to let Tom spend longer and longer periods at the residential school, although she knew it wasn't a permanent solution, which is what the Johnsons wanted – but with the lack of facilities in Grimsby there was no other option.

Then Patricia's mother-in-law bought a magazine 'with a story in it about a lady who had several Down's children'. The article is still in a box in Patricia's keepsake drawer.

'I took the magazine and it laid in a drawer in my dressing table, but every now and again it would pop to my mind and I'd think I must contact that lady, Alex Bell. So one evening I wrote and said, "Look, I'm not coping too well finding somewhere for Tom. Have you got any ideas or hints?"'

In the same way Patricia still has the 1993 article, Alex still has Patricia's letter.

'Her letter was nothing to do with "Will you adopt my kid?" It was simply, "He runs off, so I can't go shopping with him," or "How do you go on holiday?" Just questions, that's all it was.

'I answered and then she phoned and said, "Can I bring Tom over to meet you?"

'So she came over with him and dad Paul. I remember, Tom had a green T-shirt and green and white striped shorts, and he was 10. And Paul sat on the step at my back door and smoked the whole time and never said *anything* to us at all. I mean it was dead obvious to me from the first meeting that Tom was autistic, but Patricia just kept saying, "He's not like the rest of them, is he?" And then we phoned each other for a while.'

It's not surprising that Paul sat on the step outside. Two resourceful, energetic women had discovered a kindred spirit in each other, and their mutual admiration has not faded to this day. Patricia, because she thinks Alex is that rarity – an exceptional person who worked out what she wanted to do in life, and then went on and did it; Alex, because she knows that Patricia, for all the difficulties she had coping with Tom as a mother, fought and fought and fought to get the problems acknowledged – and then bullied and battled to get the solution.

The first time Patricia left Tom with Alex, it was only for a few hours, but Patricia already knew from Alex's house and the other six children that it would be perfect for Tom. So Patricia spoke to Sue, Nathan's mum, about how Sue had got Nathan there and asked, 'Do you think she'll take Tom on?'

Sue said, 'Ask Alex yourself, see how things go,' so Patricia did.

'Yes,' Alex said, 'if you can get everything in place I will have him.'

And so he started staying with the Bell family for weekends and holidays, but it had to be a private arrangement, because Grimsby Council didn't want to acknowledge it.

On Monday 2 April 1996 Alex moved into her present large house, so having Tom didn't cause too many difficulties, except making sure outside doors were always locked, that the keys were hidden, and that Tom's bedroom was far enough away from the other children so that they could sleep. In fact, he was so noisy that was almost impossible, but the Bell family took Tom in their stride, although Alex knew that he was a terribly disturbed young man who needed to settle down long-term.

'He was damaged by his past treatment, the fact that everybody just thought this is a weird kid, this is a really badly behaved lad, nobody ever understood him until he came here. He was an opportunist runner, you could not let him free anywhere, he had to be held onto at all times. He was a self-harmer, he used to head-butt brick walls, he used to strip off and run round naked, he used to make himself vomit, he was constantly soiling, he didn't sleep, he had terrible fears and phobias that were not recognised – the school said this was just Thomas being weird, but it's not, those were very rational fears to Tom.

'He had this mad fear about birds, he had a terrible fear about stairs going down, not with stairs going up, but going down he was terrible. He was obsessed with ghosts when he first came here, absolutely obsessed. He was terrified of needles, but he has no problems with them now. All those things we began to work through with Tom, so many things it's beyond belief.'

The obvious question to ask Alex is: why did you want him?

Alex's reply – 'Well, nobody else did, and Patricia couldn't manage' – doesn't seem adequate, it seems too altruistic, but Alex could see the progress in Tom when he was with her family, and that was enough for her. Alex is motivated by a challenge, especially when she can make a difference, and though Andrew was physically demanding, and Adrian a challenge to her heart, Tom was so overwhelmingly difficult in so many ways – but also so rewarding as he improved – that Alex was bound to say, 'Yes, I'll have him.'

Like many autistic people, Tom did not like change. Adrian, who is far less autistic than Tom, will become moody if a slipper is out of place, but with Tom a tiny alteration in routine caused him enormous distress. This wasn't Tom being difficult or self-ish, it's a recognised symptom of autism, and was exacerbated with the constant changes of personnel at his residential school. Again, this wasn't the fault of the school, just the way boarding facilities have to be organised, but each shift-change caused a trauma for Tom, with different people getting him dressed or feeding him. Patricia had worked in special needs schools and she knew that however much they try to have a routine and set regime for a child, it just couldn't be made to happen.

'Tom didn't like the slightest difference at all, down to incredible detail. I don't know if you've noticed how Tom eats at home now with Alex; he'll eat one portion first and then the next and the next, then he turns his plate round, his glass has to be at a particular position before he sits down and starts his meal. Everything has to be perfect, and if you change his routine it upsets him tremendously.'

And to make matters worse, because Grimsby did not have an adequate local facility, and his family couldn't manage him at home, Tom was forever going backwards and forwards, between a residential school in Humberside and Alex's house, forever moving. This was especially harrowing for Tom when he had settled down to a routine with the Bell family during the school holidays. A pattern evolved – of a highly disturbed boy, cheerful and amenable in one environment, but distressed and disruptive in any other. Tom was beginning to find that Alex's routines, her set of regular characters, provided stability – when he was there – so in 1994 Patricia asked Alex to take Tom permanently. Alex agreed.

'After a year of having him – most weekends, all the school holidays, six weeks, the whole time – we decided to get hold of the social worker and see if we could actually get some funding for it. Instead, social services said they wanted me to adopt him and I said, "OK, we'll see what happens."'

Alex already had a sense of foreboding: she'd seen the way bureaucracies behaved when faced with non-standard procedures; she knew how quickly the paperwork, the reviews and assessments could pile up. So the two women agreed to split the responsibilities. Alex would continue with the caring, while Patricia dealt with Grimsby, went to the meetings, and wrote the letters.

However, in attempting to regularise Tom's relationship with Alex, several legal issues came to the surface, many of them financial – or worse, social work policy – although irrelevant as far as Patricia was concerned. 'I knew that Tom would be happy with Alex and she would give him a place for life. It was as simple as that.' Unfortunately for Patricia, and ultimately for Tom, when three councils and an adoption agency collide, nothing is simple. In fact, virtually every aspect becomes infuriatingly complicated – while Tom continued to shuttle backwards and forwards.

First, in spite of not having the appropriate local facilities, Grimsby wanted their child to stay in their area, perhaps because they didn't want to pay an outside council, so Patricia wrote several letters, making them realise that money should not be the issue.

Meanwhile, Tom continued to shuttle backwards and forwards.

Their next objection was that Alex was not based in Lincolnshire and therefore she wasn't on their list as a registered carer. A few more letters and that objection was kicked into touch.

Meanwhile, Tom continued to shuttle backwards and forwards.

Then yet another cause for concern – the one that would come to be decisive: Alex had too many children already. To Patricia it was always one thing or another.

'Now it was that Alex has got six others. Everything was negative, everything. But I knew Alex could cope. I knew she had people to help, and if she couldn't have coped Alex would be the first to tell you.'

Though Patricia understood this, the authorities stood by their interpretation of the rules and regulations and shook their heads. While Tom continued to shuttle backwards and forwards, Patricia wrote more letters and spent countless hours waiting outside austere offices, until Grimsby Council finally agreed to commission an 'independent' assessment of Alex's abilities to care for Tom – essentially an adoption report.

The only problem was the organisation they paid to carry out the assessment – the Manchester Adoption Society – had a track record with the Bell family, and might find it hard to be independent. Alex was certain she knew their answer from the beginning.

'Some years earlier the Manchester Adoption Society had said that they would only ever place four children with me. At the time that was fine, I was actually on their management committee and we all got on very well. Then they started to assess me for Thomas. I asked them many times, "Why are you assessing me for Thomas when you told me you won't place more than four children with me?" And the only answer I ever got was, "Grimsby Council have asked us to do the approval and we don't know the outcome until the end of the process." That's all I got from them for virtually a year, while that assessment was going on. But I didn't believe them.'

And, meanwhile, poor Tom continued to shuttle backwards and forwards.

Looking back on this period, it is interesting to see the way that bureaucracies support, or refuse to censure, each other. This issue, that the Manchester Adoption Society had a duty to declare a past appraisal of Alex, is not in the subsequent paperwork, which in itself is a questionable omission. Perhaps inevitably, their conclusion was that Alex should not be approved: Thomas would place additional pressure on an already overstretched carer.

However, they had not appreciated how much of a bureaucratic street fighter Alex can be in defence of herself and her children.

'A couple of days before the adoption panel meets you get your report through. You can read it and comment on it before the report goes to panel, that's how it's done. Of course mine for Thomas said, "We do not approve this placement," which I had expected all along. I thought, "Right, this is my adoption report, I have a right to withdraw."

'But if I withdrew it immediately, the report would not have gone to the panel members – I wanted them to read it and know why I was withdrawing. So I waited until the day before the panel meeting, and then withdrew it. I was saying, "I am not going to a panel and being disapproved because of a procedure that was wrong and should never have been done in the first place."

'I remember phoning up and saying, "I'm withdrawing this application," and it was panic stations then, like "Why?" and I said, "Because it's not the right solution for this child, and I'm not allowing something so wrong to go through."'

The Manchester Adoption Society went ballistic. In fact, that very night Alex had the Director of the Agency on her doorstep along with the deputy.

'They came around pleading with me not to do this because they'd never had a complaint before. And I said, "Well, you should have told Grimsby at the start that you had put a block on me after four children. But you didn't – so you've got a complaint now."'

For a while after the adoption application was withdrawn, nothing changed. Tom continued to stay with the Bell family in

Swinton – ironically, he was spending more and more time with Alex, and thriving, a point accepted by every assessment, and there were many of them. He responded well to the consistency – that he was part of a stable family – and that he had such a close and disciplined relationship with Alex.

She was the first carer to set Tom specifics limits, the first to create a concept of acceptable or unacceptable behaviour in a boy with severe learning difficulties. As Alex saw it, Tom might be at the bottom end of the ability scale, but everyone could be taught what was right or wrong if you tried hard enough. However, though the various authorities could see this, praise it even, they then embarked on their own statutory equivalent of unacceptable behaviour – allied to Catch 22. It was the moment farce became tragedy, when the actions of an English local authority were tantamount to cruel and inhuman treatment.

When Alex recalls the episode now, in her kitchen over a late evening cup of tea, she appears to be philosophical, a distant half-smile on her calm face. She doesn't raise her voice, or thump the table but you know she is still angry, thirteen years later. The mother, eternally protective of her children, wary and alert – even if only at a memory. An organisation she was required to trust by law betrayed her duty of care to a child, and Alex does not forgive that.

She does understand that there will always be pressures within social caring. Authorities have to balance out the wider issues versus the individual case, but Alex has no respect if the process is needlessly cruel or illogical. In those cases, somewhere deep within, Alex becomes Henry V's Agincourt soldier, imitating the actions of a bureaucratic tiger. And extraordinarily for a lone mother, she has sharp teeth and knows how to use their rules and appeals against them, when necessary. And in the case of Tom, it was definitely necessary.

As we talked, the house had gone to bed. Alex paused for another sip of tea, shook her head and rubbed her eyes, searching for the right words, burned by the past, by a story that damaged a helpless and confused 12-year-old boy.

Then there it was, a tiny outward sign of internal fury – the tensing of her usually limp right fist on that heavy wooden kitchen table.

'After the adoption report, I was still having Tom. It was completely unofficial between Patricia and me. Then social services in Grimsby decided that because it had not been recommended by my own agency in Manchester, they didn't feel that they would get it through their own adoption panel. They felt the best option was to put it to their fostering panel, so that's why it went there. And, of course, they turned it down. For the same reasons, "Hands full." So it was still "no".'

No. Thomas Johnson could not continue to live with Alex Bell.

Crucially, this was no longer an academic matter. With the Grimsby Panel's decision, Tom could no longer stay with Alex, he must be taken away. The very next day, a social worker would have to drive to Alex's home in Swinton and remove Tom on behalf of his outraged and very reluctant parents – if necessary, by force.

When you study the documents, a dozen or so pages of badly written standard forms, this was a 'Jobsworth' decision of breathtaking cowardice, and a disgrace. From 100 miles away, the Grimsby fostering panel took the line 'nanny knows best', even though it was clear that the social worker and mothers involved – who all had special needs experience and knew Tom well – had the ability and above all the proximity to weigh up the issues and make an informed decision that he should stay.

While talking about this, Alex needed to stop for a while. She finished her tea, got up, rinsed our cups in the sink, stood for a moment in the hushed house, and then realised that Chloe had finally fallen asleep in front of the television in the playroom and still had to be put to bed.

'Come on, love,' she whispered, while picking her up and carrying Chloe in her arms down the corridor, past the specially equipped disabled bedroom that Andrew shared with Simon, past the nine anoraks and woollen hats drying by the front door, past Adrian's pottery beside the birthday cards on the dresser, past Callum's room with his zipped up safe-bed, past Matthew's football photos, past Nathan's room, with three Dr Who Cybermen painted on the wall and a sound of wheezing and snoring, past Emily's Snow White and the Seven Dwarfs bedroom, and through into Chloe's own room, decorated as a lilac boudoir.

Alex leant down and tucked her into bed, with Chloe muttering 'What?' as Alex nestled her head on the pillow. She gave Chloe a kiss, checked that the curtains were open – 'Chloe would sleep in a field if she could' – and walked out, gesturing to the room at the end.

'Tom's,' she said, 'a yellow and orange sunset, with a surfer on a wave.'

Then it was back to the kitchen table to talk about a rare but distressing time when she was unable to protect her family.

'Yes, there was a day when Tom was taken away. Up until then, they hadn't moved him in case it went my way, but when it went the opposite way the social worker was ordered to take him back. This was Liz [Donaghue].

'She said, "It doesn't matter what I want to do, I have to take him away," and she came and took him.

'Patricia was mortified, I was mortified, one of the few times I ever actually cried – and I don't cry, me, very rare – for half an hour on his bed. Not because I was missing him, not because I felt bad about me, but because I thought, "There's nothing else left for this kid after this." Remember, at that time I didn't believe they would ever bring him back. And, worse, they returned him to the residential school.

'As I walked out to the car with Liz, I said, "You're taking one of my babies."

'She said, "I've got to," and they went and that was it.

'She was always lovely, Liz, and I don't think for one minute she wanted to take him. He had been with us for a couple of years on and off and then became so disorientated. How do you tell someone like Thomas why. You can't.'

It didn't seem to matter to Grimsby Council that Thomas had been doing well with Alex, that his parents wanted him to stay with her, that she wanted him, or that there was nowhere else for him to go. A committee who had never met any of the principals sniffed through the paperwork and rules, and pontificated, so that an innocent, settled boy would be escorted from a happy home to an impersonal institution. No wonder Alex cried – most of us would have cried along with her.

Patricia was so scandalised that she began to campaign, writing to the local paper about how ridiculous the Council had been.

'All the time Grimsby are advertising, "If you want to foster, just ring up, we need foster parents." Meanwhile, I've found this woman that's wanting Tom and they're not letting him go. And they never give you a straight answer. Every time I went to one person and said, "Can you tell me what is happening?" they didn't know. "You need to be talking to somebody else."

'Liz was very good – but if you wanted to go above Liz you had to make an appointment, and they had to go through the facts all over again. It was endless, so frustrating, letter after letter after letter after letter – phone calls, "We'll call you back," but they don't get back to you, and it went on and on and on. I think they got sick of me. I think they expected me to give in, they just thought, "This is now four years, she's bound to give up," but I didn't. At the end of the day I knew where I wanted Tom to be. I'd found a perfect place but they wouldn't let him go.'

The official reason was that, with six other children, Alex couldn't cope. The fact that she'd been coping perfectly well for a couple of years didn't seem to matter. But then, resourceful and persistent to the marrow in her bones, and thinking about Tom every day, Alex decided to attack Grimsby at its most vulnerable spot. On paper, legally, below its bureaucratic belt.

She submitted a formal appeal.

The Authority, used to having things its own way, howled and shuddered. An appeal against a panel decision is both rare and administratively traumatic. It has to be investigated by the Director of Social Services, who must scrupulously inspect and re-evaluate every stage of each decision and come to a transparent, and supposedly independent, adjudication. That's in theory. But in reality the majority of appeals are turned down, not least because the Director is essentially judging his own panel members.

While Thomas continued to shuttle disconsolately between residential school and the Johnsons' home, Peter Hay, acting Director of Social Services, began his inquiry by visiting Patricia Johnson, who, as expected, didn't mince words.

'Peter Hay came to our house and he said, "Thomas's case is unique. We've never placed a child with a woman that's got so many children. The problem is ordinary people cannot manage."

'I said, "Well, Alex is not an ordinary person, and the fact that extraordinary people might be rare doesn't mean that we have to take them out of every equation. If we do encounter one like Alex it should be factored in, because it's part of the situation."

'So then he said, "What would you like me to do?" And I said, "I would like you to go and visit Alex and actually meet her. Everyone is making these comments and these decisions, but nobody is getting off their backsides and going and meeting her. People in Grimsby say you can't do this, but they've never met the woman." And Mr Hay said, "OK, I'll go and have tea with Alex." So he went.'

Alex remembers it well, showing him around the house, explaining how her systems work.

'It was in the school holidays, so pretty horrendous in this house, but I'd sorted out all the children to go to various places. Chloe was in nursery, and the rest went off with various friends to do activities, so I could actually talk to this person. He was here a couple of hours, didn't say much, asked a lot of questions, then left. I liked him, but couldn't guess what he would decide. Then a month later he overturned the panel's decision, which was pretty unique – it's very rare that a Director would overturn his panel's decision.'

Patricia couldn't believe it, she just didn't think a bureaucrat really would be independent. 'Peter Hay came back and said, "You're right, Alex is fantastic." So he changed the decision. He turned it round.'

Peter Hay's Foster Carer Appeal Report is an interesting document. On the one hand he has nothing but praise for Alex, but on the other he goes out of his way to suggest that 'Miss Bell' had changed her stance on certain issues – for instance, whether she would ever take on further children – although there's little specific evidence of any change. Perhaps he does this to spare the Foster Panel's blushes, not least because his document taken as a whole is a stunning slap in the face for the Mr Nannies and Mrs Jobsworths of the Grimsby fostering panel. Hay wrote:

There is no evidence that Miss Bell cannot cope with the demands upon her. [...] There has never been a placement breakdown for a child in the care of Miss Bell. [...] There is no evidence that Miss Bell's care of Thomas [was] not working. [...] Thomas requires the stability and long term care that Miss Bell is offering and has provided successfully to other children. [...] It is clear that Thomas's needs and best interests can be best met by Miss Bell.

Some people would murmur, 'All's well that ends well,' and watch Tom wander off into the sunset. However, that might not be his point of view, if he could tell us. But Tom can't. So we can only wonder at the trauma of endless shuttling between different bedrooms for an additional year and a half, for a disturbed Down's-cum-autistic 14-year-old who was desperate for stability, and for his family, whose agony was heightened and extended. Paul, Tom's dad adds, 'People will never see the tears Patricia sheds to this day. As parents we made very hard decisions to provide the stability Tom needed, to give one of your small children away because the situation has become untenable and something breaks inside. But, throughout, Patricia never lost sight of what was best for Tom.'

And if there is a happy ending – it only came after 100 letters and because two tough women fought like ferrets. After all, happy endings do not absolve eighteen months of unnecessary pain – yes, a year and a half.

The moral outcome of this episode should be the utter condemnation of an inflexible and unfeeling fostering committee – precisely because Thomas's inner agony so easily came to an end from almost the very day the panel were roundly humiliated and he went permanently to Alex. This only serves to underline the harm they had caused to a person they were charged to protect. As

Alex went to pick up the pieces she couldn't help thinking that her job had been made more difficult than necessary.

'Tom had so much stacked against him: he didn't have a correct diagnosis; he had medical problems that no one discovered; he had behavioural problems – I had reports to say that this kid "could not be managed within a family". He had terrible decisions made about him early on in life, about going to residential school at 6 – for God's sake, they don't even put you in Eton till 7. Everything was against that lad.

'I think he was definitely on the way to secure accommodation, a sort of prison, for his own safety. He would have been sectioned as an adult, drugged up to the eyeballs, kept in an institution somewhere. That would have cost Grimsby an arm and a leg, and been a terrible life for him.'

The overriding lesson with individuals like Tom who don't have the speech to express what is causing them pain is: 'Listen to the mothers.' Although all the experts were saying, 'This child cannot be managed in a family,' that was largely because he had become institutionalised. He didn't sleep at night because he was used to waking staff being on duty, so if he wanted a video at two o'clock in the morning they put a video on. It took Alex and family ages to sort this out, but they managed it.

The first night Tom went to Alex permanently in 1997 when he was 14 he got up forty-five times, and Alex can remember thinking, 'Oh, what have I done? I shouldn't have had him. They were right all along.' She had to lock his bedroom door and Tom would scream and shout because he wasn't used to being in bed at night, but gradually he settled in.

'I took terrible risks with Tom. He was on a toddler strap when he arrived – he was 14, remember, and I said, "I can't put him on that, it's like a dog lead." And I never did. I would stand at the front door and say, "Thomas, go and sit in the car," knowing that he could easily shoot off and I wouldn't catch him because he was Linford Christie fast.

'I thought, "I am the one who has got to give this child some kind of responsibility." I used to hold his hand for a long time, then we progressed to where he would push the trolley with me and my hand would be next to his on the trolley; now he will go and help me with the shopping and he never runs off. He is totally happy about his life, that's the difference.'

Thomas at 24

Tom is now 24, healthy and getting on with a simple life, a gentle and lovely person. He's not a bright lad, but he's slotted within the Bell family perfectly – because he's accepted as he is, for who he is. He's Tom, everything he does is appropriate to him, and nobody attempts to make him into something that he isn't.

During the day, Louise usually looks after him. She has a special role and special relationship with Tom, attempting to give him a rounded, satisfying life. Louise is partly paid for by Grimsby, though for how long no one knows, because Tom is caught in a bizarre administrative labyrinth. Since the manoeuvring in his early teens, no one knows who is responsible for him. Tom's legal status is … anybody's guess. Because by the time Grimsby Council had moved him backwards and forwards and changed their minds, he was approaching 16, past the age when a person can be adopted. So Alex can't be his 'legal' parent. Nor can the local authority, without the consent of Tom's parents.

Tom is also beyond the usual fostering age, and though he's living with Alex, and Grimsby help out with Louise, Alex has no legal power to make decisions for him. Likewise, his parents, the Johnsons: they passed his welfare and control over to Alex many years ago, and though they keep in touch, and have been actively trying to find a 'best for Tom' solution, they see Tom as part of Alex's adopted family. However, though he is officially an adult, Tom cannot give 'informed consent' to that, because he would have no idea what a question meant, let alone know the answer.

Put all that together and, according to Alex, Tom is in legal nowhere's-ville.

'He doesn't actually belong to anyone or anything. I don't foster him because he's an adult – that's only for children. I'm not a registered care home and Lincolnshire only place their adults with registered care homes, so therefore he's not legally placed with me. He just lives here, because there's nowhere else for him to go, but he doesn't exist in actual fact. He is on the electoral register, I put him on that simply because I had to prove that he was a resident in Salford, but Salford won't acknowledge he's a resident, because then they've got a legal responsibility and would have to pay for him. So he's Mr Nowhere. In limbo land, and he will be forever now.'

Although it's obviously a shame, Tom's lack of legal status doesn't make Alex angry. To her it's one of those petty little things that mean pretty well next to nothing until something goes wrong, and she can worry about that when it happens. Far more important to Alex is the progress he's made in the last ten years as part of a caring family.

'When he came here, he was not used to consistent handling, which is bad for any kid, but with Thomas it's much more complicated. For instance, he can only follow one instruction at a time, and in the right order, so you learn to split everything down, like when he's going to bed, it's "Thomas, go to the toilet, sit on the toilet, now we're going to wash our face and our hands, clean teeth, Thomas." Then it's "Go and get your pyjamas on, Thomas, put your clothes in the laundry, get in bed, now go to sleep."

'And everything is split up like that, whereas Matthew you can just say go and get ready for bed, but not Thomas. For example, this was something that Matthew did recently. I said to Tom, "Right, go to the toilet, get ready, we're going out."

'Now because somebody else was on the toilet Tom couldn't go straight away and Matthew said to him, "Well, get your shoes on then."

'Now that jumped the ritual – it wasn't the same, Tom couldn't do it, he could not put his shoes on before he'd gone to the toilet, and he got very agitated.

'Matthew said to me, "What's up with him?"

'And I said, "You've changed the routine. He's got to do it in a certain order for it to work."

'But a lot of the other children, if the toilet's occupied they'll go on to a different part of the routine and go back to the toilet because they're able to do that, but Thomas can't.'

In the life of Thomas Johnson – he can't properly be referred to as Thomas Bell – only three words matter. Tom is happy. He's found a slot in one of the strangest families in Britain and gets along just fine. He's the most anonymous of Alex's 'babies', and quite handsome in a regular-guy kind of way, with deep-set dark eyes and clear features, slim, dapper, physically very un-Down's. Nor does he have any of the medical complications. With Tom, the Down's is mostly in the mind, along with the too-long-ignored autism.

He will never be able to read and write and doesn't easily learn, which is probably just as well, because he can't use any of the special needs educational services in Salford who rather meanly say that he is the responsibility of Grimsby and so won't let him use facilities like day centres.

But Alex and Louise make up for that, teaching him life skills, like how to shave and shower himself, and they have a diary with so many activities that his weekly schedule is at bursting point.

Tom loves pottery, he loves swimming and water aerobics, which he thinks is hilarious. He goes to the gym, he does target golf, he goes to the pictures, and for meals out to the pub. He goes hiking, he loves trains and trams and buses, so he has a bus pass. They take him to the theatre; Alex pays a fortune for theatre tickets, but she doesn't mind because Tom has made so much progress. The first time Tom went to see *Lord of the Dance* he was terrified of the dark, and cowered in the corner of their box for the entire first half. For the second half, he sat on Alex's knee and fell asleep – that's when he was 14. Now he loves it, because Alex persisted, a gradual process that she worked through with him.

He also has a weekly paper round, delivering the *Salford Advertiser*. Louise stands at the gate of every house and gives him a paper. It takes Tom twice as long as it would take an ordinary person, because Tom has to tickle every dog and stop and talk to every child, and he goes at a slower pace than most people anyway, but it's helped him to meet almost everyone on a local estate. When Thomas rams the papers through the door he often bangs the letterbox so the householders open the door, see it's him and say, 'Oh hiya Tom, hiya.' But it's something Tom has to do himself, it's his work.

Alex tells him every Thursday, the day before so he's prepared, 'Tomorrow's Friday, papers day,' so he's knows when he gets up in the morning.

When you ask Alex about Tom's future, she says, 'He will stay here as long as I can keep him, and just grow old, staying busy.'

At that moment it's hard to remember that he was once a wreck, the victim of a ping-pong childhood and unwieldy care system, which rewards conformity and penalises deviation.

'The ones that nobody else would have'

Alex often says that it takes a brave, or desperate, care worker to recommend a placement with her family, even when they see it works, because they get worn down by laws that are too 'risk averse'. So Alex's greatest allies have invariably been independent, strong-minded social workers who are mothers themselves, and are less convinced by the dogma or current thinking that spews out of postgraduate social services courses.

'Louise comes out with some absolutely corking comments, and she said, "Social services get upset with us because this is a therapeutic community within a family, which their books say isn't a possibility."

'A therapeutic community must have social workers, psychotherapists, thousands of pounds a week, and then they say, "You can't possibly have a one-carer-to-nine ratio, these people should all be one-to-one." That is why they can't get their heads round it.

'Sometimes I do think, "God, I wish I could go somewhere on my own," but the children aren't paperwork that I can file away for the evening or have a weekend off. And I accept that, because I was interested in the most difficult children, the ones that nobody else would have, because there are kids out there that social workers are condemning to the care system forever and that is not right, and if I can kick up a bloody fuss and get them to change their decisions and therefore improve a child's life,

Seven Bells. From left: Tom, Nathan, Chloe, Matthew,
Simon, Adrian and Andrew.

even the odd few that I can help, that's what I want to do with
my life.

'That's why I fought so hard for Tom. Because otherwise he
was condemned – and by the very people who were meant to help
him.'

Chapter Twelve

To love and to lose: Emily and Callum

As Alex's family grew, so did her confidence. A beguiling group of helpers joined her, self-selected like an ad hoc repertory company: Dan, who packed shoppers' bags at Tesco in Swinton, was gradually working his way around the house, painting increasingly lurid murals on every available wall. Apart from a huge Elvis by the fridge, Dan's *pièce de résistance* is a vibrant wild animal jungle and underwater scene that extends all the way around the playroom and even across the ceiling. With Alex's mischievous encouragement Dan is feverishly finishing the corridor before realising that no wall space is left. Perhaps he's hoping Alex will move house, and he can start all over again.

Next, there's Anne, who ambles down the lane once a week to relieve Alex of a couple of baskets of laundry, and bring them back 'ironed as an art form'. She used to do it with her husband Bill, but sadly he has recently died.

'Chloe is very upset about it still. She keeps coming up and saying, "Bill's died … oh, Bill's died." He actually came to pick the washing up on a Monday night, as he always did, while the kids were having their tea, and on Wednesday morning he went to the hospital because he had a bad head, and had a brain haemorrhage at the hospital and just died, just like that.

'But Anne's still doing the ironing. I'm very lucky. She actually phoned me the day after he died and said, "I still want to do your ironing."

'I said, "I think you should have a few weeks off," and she said, "No, no, I won't have anything to do if I don't do your ironing."'

Then there's Neil, part-time odd-job man, gardener, builder and comedian, who is never happier than when trying to convince Alex that she should commission some ambitious artefact; for instance, a fountain in the garden or a 'hanging conservatory' – a scheme turned down by Alex, so far.

Along with her children, Alex conducts this ensemble like a small chamber orchestra. On occasion there can be fifteen people in the house, every person with their own line of banter, their own opinion. The Bell house is unusual because it's private and public at the same time, a close-knit family with half the neighbourhood coming and going – and often staying.

If you say to Alex, 'You're like one of those jugglers with plates on a stick that stay up because they're spinning,' she'll reply, 'But they don't keep spinning on their own, you know. We do that,' and she'll gesture to the half dozen people who have 'popped in' – one of whom happens to be a taxi driver who's come to fetch someone and who's talking to Neil about golf. A car toots outside – someone is blocking in someone else, but Neil just waves out the window. It's the man who's delivering Thomas's supplements; he can wait until Neil has reached the golf story punchline, or carry the supplements in himself.

At such times Alex is in her element, usually laying the kitchen table or talking to a helper about one of the kids, who are making their own din in the playroom. It adds up to the kind of organised chaos of a busy newsroom, or the school gates at going-home time, or the pub five minutes after the match has ended. But, for all the mayhem, there are rules, there is order, and the key to that, unseen, unheralded, is that the Chief Executive, the Bell family boss, knows how to communicate and make decisions – and knows how to manage.

A year or two after Tom came to stay permanently, Alex moved into the rest of her rambling house. Until then, she had occupied only the top part; now Alex took over the garden level with a TV room, pool room, a small flat, and two extra bedrooms – it was already large, but now her home was enormous.

'I thought, "What on earth can I do with all this extra space?" but it was obvious – you put children in it. What else would you do?'

After her experiences with the Manchester Adoption Society and Grimsby Council, Alex didn't want to take chances, so she went to the best, approaching Nottinghamshire Social Services, thought to be among the finest local authorities on adoption, in June 1999 and they agreed to assess her for two more children. Although by then Alex already had seven dependants, at their first interview the senior executive didn't ask even once if she was biting off more than she could chew, or questions like, 'What on earth do you want two more children for?'

At the end of the meeting they said, 'Fine, Nottinghamshire will assess you for two additional children.'

By the early 2000s the process of adopting disabled or special needs children had come a long way from the pioneering days of a decade earlier, when Alex seemed to be a single-mother eccentric and was treated with suspicion if not hostility. Now the executives at Nottingham worked with her as professional to professional, a process that took two and a half years, while Alex began to look more and more closely at her old friend, 'The Book' – *Adoption Today*.

The content of the magazine had also become more businesslike. Gone were the photocopied, typewritten pages in smudged black and white: *Adoption Today* was now in two colours, computer-designed and edited to appeal to parents who had space in their hearts, and in their houses, for a difficult but rewarding child. It was by and for people who knew what they were doing – although it was never stated, every page seemed to be headed 'No time-wasters, please'.

In spring 2003, a few months after Alex had been approved by Nottingham for two more children, two adverts appeared. The first, on page 10, was for a 5-year-old girl called Emily (name changed).

In the same issue, when Alex turned to page 11, there was another advert, by the same care team, with the same phone number – this time for a 4-year-old boy called Callum (name changed).

There was no linkage between the adverts: the magazine promoted them as two separate children, with hugely different problems, but to the expert eye of Alex Bell the clues were there. So she called Emily's social worker to ask why the kids were being advertised separately. To her, although it did not say so, they were quite obviously sister and brother. The social worker replied that it had not occurred to them that anyone would be able to take them both.

Emily's mother, a young woman who found parenthood difficult anyway, could not cope with the ordeal of two such challenging children. Almost from birth she had recognised her daughter's hereditary condition from large brown freckles on her

(Original advertisement for Emily, aged 5, in *Adoption Today*.)

EMILY is a cheerful, responsive child. She is strong-willed and loves to be the centre of attention. She has global development delay and her speech in particular is delayed. She is beginning to interact well with other children. Emily has been Looked After since April 2001 and has been with her current carers since November 2001. She has Neurofibromatosis and, as a result, developed tumours of the optic nerve in November 2000. She has had a twelve-month course of chemotherapy and her health will now need to be regularly monitored. Emily has a Statement of Special Educational Needs and attends a special school.

Ethnic/racial origins: white English

Family needed: ideally, an adoptive family who can provide firm boundaries and have an understanding of special needs children. Long-term foster carers will also be considered.

Contact: direct contact with her birth parents and grandmother is planned.

is a happy, contented child but is very much 'in his own world'. He has autism and severe learning difficulties. He has no speech as yet but does make babbling noises. ▮▮▮▮ has developed an attachment to his foster carers with whom he has been with since April 2001. He has a family history of Neurofibromatosis although he does not have this condition. He has a Statement of Special Educational Needs and is due to start at a special school in April 2002.

Ethnic/racial origins: white English
Family needed: ideally, an energetic, resilient adoptive family with an understanding of autism, although long term foster carers will also be considered
Contact: direct contact with his birth parents and paternal grandmother is planned

(Original advertisement for Callum, aged 4, in *Adoption Today*.)

CALLUM is a happy, contented child but is very much 'in his own world'. He has autism and severe learning difficulties. He has no speech as yet but does make babbling noises. Callum has developed an attachment to his foster carers with whom he has been with since April 2001. He has a family history of Neurofibromatosis although he does not have this condition. He has a Statement of Special Educational Needs and is due to start at a special school in April 2002.

Ethnic/racial origins: white English family needed: ideally, an energetic, resilient adoptive family with an understanding of autism, although long-term foster carers will also be considered.

Contact: direct contact with his birth parents and paternal grandmother is planned.

body – called café au lait spots: she had them too. And then when Callum was autistic, their mother virtually gave up.

Social services provided home-based support to keep the family together, with cleaners and childminders, but eventually both children were taken into care. It was clear that sister and brother would have to be separated because no foster home could be found to cater for them both. Emily was 3 and Callum 2 – born exactly one year apart.

While in foster care, Emily's illness became more serious than at first thought. Tumours developed, and though they could have been anywhere in her body, cruelly the tumours were in the optic nerve of her left eye, and therefore inoperable. The only treatment was chemo and radiation therapy, especially traumatic on a girl so young, and harrowing for her carers. This led to Emily having three separate foster placements because people found her medical treatment difficult to live with. Given such specialist needs for such different children, the social worker and family finder told Alex that they did not believe the care that was needed could be found in one family.

'I said, "Well, you've found me now, haven't you?" And they looked at each other and said, "OK".'

Nottinghamshire had funded Alex's approval in the hope that they would be able to place two Nottinghamshire children with her, but to their credit, they simply sold Alex to Emily and Callum's local authority.

'Yes, they sold me. Nottinghamshire's assessment money was returned by the new lot. You're just a commodity, one that's bought and sold amongst agencies, which is fine by me.'

From the very beginning, Alex intended to adopt Emily, but only to foster Callum. Though she wanted to keep sister and brother together, she understood the strain of looking after a severely autistic child, the impact on the wider Bell family, the likely costs, and wasn't prepared to commit to a long-term burden on behalf of everyone else. But Callum was Emily's brother, and by fostering him Alex could bring them back together again.

'It would have been wrong of me not to – but it's the hardest placement I've ever had, because it was outside my experience in that they were not Down's kids, and they were on care orders, which was new to me as well. They were siblings – that was new to me – and in two different placements, with two separate families. And separate social workers, which meant everything took twice the time.'

So first the usual paperwork, the interviews, committees, matching panels – but now times two. And only then, only when everyone was satisfied, was Alex allowed to actually meet the kids for the first time.

'Its like, "Oh my God, I've committed myself to these two really difficult children, and now I've got to meet them." Emily was sweet but very demanding. She was 5, got on my knee and constantly had to have my attention. Just had to be the centre of everything – a dominating little kid.'

The plan was to assimilate Emily first. Then, when equilibrium had been re-established in the Bell family, perhaps after a few months, to take on Callum. Alex decided that the family's holiday near Stow-on-the-Wold would be the best time to introduce him to the others, so at the end of two weeks he could simply come home with them. But before that, they had to welcome Emily.

Alex prides herself on telling her children everything, so they knew in advance. For a few weeks she showed them photographs, saying, 'This is Emily. She's coming to live with us. This is going to be her bedroom and we're going to pick her up and bring her home.' The children weren't concerned, because that's how the Bell family live, with other children coming to stay. 'They just think that every family does this,' she says.

Emily arrived on 29 May 2003 – just two days before Alex's 48th birthday – and settled in quickly. She was bright and breezy, but she was also controlling – what Alex calls 'a girl with attitude'. It was how Emily had survived traumatic cancer treatment and several disruptions, by being bolshy and stroppy and dominating; she had learnt to cope by being her own boss. Alex was expecting it, though that didn't make it easier to deal with, but did allow her to forgive Emily her increasingly rare excesses.

'It was the world according to Emily, but because I put firm boundaries in she has to conform. She now understands that she is part of a family. I don't think she'd ever felt part of a family before, that she's not the only thing. So when she'd say to me, "Am I not special?" I'd say, "You're as special as everybody else here in this family." But Emily has got to be the centre, she's got to be super special, to be put on a pedestal, and that doesn't happen with us; we're all super special in our family, so it's been a hard lesson for her to learn.'

The advert in *Adoption Today* said that Callum 'is very much "in his own world"'. That was an understatement. Blond, blue-eyed and angelic – within a few of months he had destroyed his bed, chewed a carpet, and disrupted the household by calling out in the middle of the night, then diving off his bunk and breaking a collarbone. He wasn't being naughty or deliberately difficult, it's the way of severe autism, a terrible and painful hardship for a child to have, and all the more distressing because he was such a beautiful-looking boy.

Autism is a neurological condition in which the pathways in the brain aren't connected correctly, so what a normal human sees as stimulation an autistic child might see as bombardment. That's why Callum puts his fingers in his ears or covers his eyes – ordinary levels of activity can be too much for him. And where we would walk in a room and see a person sitting at a table, Callum might focus on a flickering light bulb, or a fly on the window – things we wouldn't notice will flash at him, which can be distressing, and often intensely frightening. Worse, the autism is heightened by learning difficulties, or by neglect as a baby, or being traumatised by going into care as a toddler.

But for all the difficulties, autistic children can be so confounding and complex that they are also fascinating, especially when under the observational microscope of Alex.

'Being autistic is not only awful, it's also very strange, because nothing makes sense to you. Conversation doesn't make sense, mood doesn't make sense, you don't understand people's body language, you don't understand anything that's going on around you, it's a buzz, it's annoying you. You only want to sit and twiddle this piece of cloth you've got in your hands but nobody wants you to do that.

'It's difficult because you're not on the same planet as the rest of humanity – that's how I explain it to the children. They don't understand why Callum is the way he is, so I say he's from planet Zod. For instance, he'll suddenly become hysterical with laughter for no reason, something has tickled him, it's hilarious and he's got to laugh and scream out loud, though nothing's happened.

'And the kids will say, "What's happened with him then?"

'I'll say, "Well, somebody on Zod's just told a joke." That's the way I explain it to them. And they can accept that quite easily.'

Many autistic people have no social niceties, because other people don't exist to them. Tom, who's got autistic tendencies, is like that. He will sneeze, and where normal people would put a hand up or get a tissue or turn away, Tom will just sneeze at everyone, because he doesn't appreciate the feelings of others, so why should he turn away? It would be a social nicety to get a handkerchief out or to move his head to one side, and that isn't natural with autism.

Likewise, other people don't exist emotionally, which is why autistic children have problems bonding, you can't get close to them. As Alex says, they don't do relationships.

'You only exist as a teapot exists, to serve a purpose, to give them a drink or whatever, simply as an object, and that's all you are going to be. I'm only there to give Callum food, to change his bum – that's why there's no reciprocal cuddling. Autistic people don't want that. When he wants something he will get hold of my hand and take me to it because I can meet his needs, which basically are warmth, clothes, food and somewhere to sleep.'

None of this a criticism of Callum – he is a victim rather than a villain – but it does underline that Down's syndrome and autism are often polar opposites. Down's people are outwardly emotional and adorably so, whereas with autism, if there is emotion it's inward and generally difficult to comprehend. Similarly with fear and pain: an autistic person can be terrified of the most banal sounds or objects, but might walk out into busy traffic without a thought.

And pain might actually be a pleasure. When he jumped off the bed and broke his collarbone, Callum did not cry. There was clearly something the matter with him, he was holding his arm, but at no stage did he show discomfort. You've got to be in touch with your body to understand pain, and autistic people are not in touch with their own bodies. For Alex this raises issues in supervising him.

'Callum can't maintain his own safety because he doesn't understand the consequences of his actions – he wouldn't understand if he ran in a road a car would get him. If he puts a hand into boiling water and burnt he would feel it but might not feel it the way we feel it. He wouldn't know how to pull out of the water – he wouldn't have that understanding. I am not saying he would find it pleasurable but he might not find it uncomfortable either.'

Unlike a child with Down's syndrome, Callum has no physical characteristics that mark him out as disabled. In fact, he appears normal in every way, except that he has child-model good looks, with neatly brushed short hair, a fair complexion, and usually wears a clean white shirt and open collar. At teatime he sits quietly at his place looking straight ahead, elbows on the table and hands holding his head, seemingly in a trance while waiting for food to arrive. As the boisterous Bell family gather around the table, chattering and yabbering, fiddling with plates, cup and spoons, Callum takes no notice, still staring silently into infinity. He seems like a patient, well-behaved boy in deep thought, innocently beautiful.

Then the food arrives.

Callum doesn't even look at his plate, he simply scoops the food up, as fast as possible, ramming into his mouth, hardly chewing, or noticing the taste, texture or colour – it is food, just food. And while he gulps it down, his expression hardly changes, he continues to stare straight ahead with huge, unblinking eyes.

From behind comes a mantra, Alex's voice saying, 'Chew, Callum, chew. Chew, Callum, chew. Callum, chew,' with Matthew joining in gruffly like an ineffectual father figure.

The first few times I saw this happen, Alex would have to reach forward and hold his hand, to physically stop him bolting the whole plateful in less than a minute, at which Callum would let out a little whine and frown, although he would slow down. But if Alex kept his hand from the plate for too long, he would start to regurgitate the food he had already eaten, heaving it up his throat so that he could chew it again, whooshing it around his mouth while alternatively swallowing and heaving. This causes Callum injury because the digestive acid that rises up leads to mouth ulcers. And worse, the stinging pain that accompanies the sore is a sensation he likes, even though, as Alex knows, it's harmful.

'As a baby, food was not always available to Callum. So it was like, get the food down before it disappears, it's not there to be enjoyed; it's there to be swallowed quickly before somebody takes the plate away. He can't stop himself eating, either; he will eat anything you put it on his plate no matter how much he's eaten, and he will carry on and eat and eat and eat. His appetite would not condition him to stop because being autistic he doesn't listen to his body and his body doesn't tell him "you've had enough" anyway. He would eventually throw up because his stomach is overloaded.'

Such abnormal table manners are quite common with autistic children, but after a few months of 'Chew, Callum, chew', he learnt to pace himself, to finish his plate mouthful by mouthful, and then wait for the next course. This may not seem like much progress but Callum doesn't have the urge to please, or understand misbehaviour, so even a small change needs patience and persistence beyond most of us.

Alex's main ally is her sense of humour. 'He gets great value out of a Christmas dinner, because he eats it about fifteen times.'

To the casual observer, none of this seems apparent: Callum is a lovely, easy-going, compliant young boy, end of story. But with familiarity comes a deeper understanding of the challenges and hidden anguish of living with an autistic individual who has little sense of good or bad behaviour, of joy or sorrow, of anger or love. Given Callum's almost poetic beauty, it's impossible to see him as an empty shell, devoid of human emotion or understanding. I could not do it anyway. I found myself ascribing to him all manner of traits and feelings that were simply my mind playing tricks. And this is a trap that wider society falls into, and which might not be in the best interests of Callum.

For instance, the law and social work practice do not have the flexibility to deal honestly with the different kind of reality that is Callum's world. As I did early on, they romanticise and flatter from appearance, and thereby don't provide the best support for either Callum or his carers. Alex once said something that troubled me greatly, because it seemed so unfair, so insensitive. She said, 'Callum is a little thug.' All I saw was the angelic boy who sat so serenely at the end of the tea table and I thought that it was Alex who was the thug for saying that.

However, the very next morning when I arrived after her family had gone off to school, Alex was in Callum's bedroom with Louise attempting to piece together the ruins of his heavy wooden bed. Neil had constructed it a few weeks earlier using three-inch screws and four-by-one planks, building a lattice of spars and hinges to somehow keep Callum in at night. As Alex tried to contact Callum's social worker, Louise showed me the splintered wood and how a very heavy force had bent the screws.

'Don't know about you, but I couldn't do that,' Louise said, shaking her head, 'and he is only 6. God knows what he'll be able to do when he's 26.'

I was shocked and astonished. Demure little Callum – capable of such powerful destruction?

Alex returned; his social worker was 'in a meeting'. Of course.

'We don't take it personally, that's just autism. It's not Callum's fault, but severe autism can be a wicked, isolating thing for a kid to have. Just awful. He wanted to get out and the wood was in the way.'

'Still think he's a little angel?' Louise asked me, with an ironic smile.

Alex had both arms across her chest, holding her elbows, eyebrows arched, letting my stunned silence provide an answer.

'I'm glad you've seen this because most people don't believe it. His social workers don't.'

Over the next couple of years I learnt that Alex's 'He's a little thug' statement was far more caring and helpful than the head-in-the-sand attitude of many professionals who were sometimes in denial about the reality of autism. Severe autism is an appalling affliction and those brave souls in the front line need worldly support, not platitudes. Callum can be a thug – OK? That's not his fault, but it is the truth. He doesn't mean it – he doesn't have a concept of what a thug is – but denial is not in his or anyone else's interests, and leads to social services being tempted to short-change him and his carers.

Typically, even though he'd previously broken his collarbone jumping off the side, it was only the destruction of his wooden bed that finally spurred Callum's social services department to commission a risk assessment report, which recommended a safe bed, also known as a safe space, so that Callum could be securely contained all night, for his own safety and so that the rest of the house and Alex could get some sleep.

'It cost £2,500 and is like a room within a room, like an Iraqi isolation cell, that's what I'd say it was. If it was on the front page of the *Daily Mirror*, there'd be an outcry, but it's an accepted piece of equipment for an autistic person so apparently it's fine. He can't get out because all the zips are on the outside. And once he's zipped in – he's in. For however long we decide. He accepts now that it's bed. It works.'

If that seems draconian, it does allow Callum to live in a house within a family – far better than being in an institution – and it's that kind of tough but realistic thinking that is the hallmark of Alex's philosophy. Don't blame, but don't pretend either. He shouldn't be blamed because there's no human dimension to what Callum does – because there's no human dimension to severe autism; but nor can there be sentimental wishful thinking about his behaviour, not least because Callum may get injured in the process.

A few decades ago he would have been drugged most of the time, perhaps in a padded cell, because he can be physically destructive – not to others, but to himself. And if he's made to do something he doesn't want to, he might head butt, bite or kick out, not to hurt, but in simple frustration; not too bad in an 8-year-old, but at 18 the effect might be hazardous. Other children improve with age; Callum won't. He'll just be a very big severely autistic man.

Nevertheless, we can still respect him for being human, only don't expect a smile, or a handshake, or love. He can't do love – any more than a car can do love. Alex summed this up one day after he had deliberately soiled the playroom.

'Does Callum annoy me? No, not at all. This is who Callum is. He can't help being the way he is.'

None of this is easy for Callum's home social services, Sambridge (not the real name). They are responsible for an individual with no clear life-path, who may become more difficult as he gets older, and this is all the more tricky because Sambridge are 200 miles away and failed to transfer oversight of Callum to Alex's local council, Salford, in spite of agreeing that they would do so. As Callum settled in, Alex became increasingly frustrated at Sambridge's lack of support. From my observation this appeared to be at least partly cynical, because Sambridge seem to act as if not responding to the phone would make a need for support disappear, that the carer would have to sort it out themselves, and Sambridge would save time and money.

Over a period of two years, Callum improved hugely. With well-directed drugs and the amiable stability of the Bell family, he began to sleep through and calm down – once he even walked over and held my hand, a touching moment for a boy so isolated within himself. His regurgitation decreased and although appearances can be deceptive in cases of severe autism, he seemed, if not happy, contented. But still Alex decided against adopting Callum.

Ironically, her main reason was not because of his behaviour, but because she had learnt not to trust the local authority and their wishful thinking.

'I don't think it's in his best interest to be adopted by me. I'm very committed to looking after Callum for as long as I can, but I'm not prepared to lose the financial back-up of his local authority. At present, if there's a big problem Callum's home social services have to respond, whereas Salford might say, "We'll put him on a waiting list and see what we can offer him." That would be no good for Callum because his needs are so complex – like incredibly expensive respite and equipment and safety issues. Those would stop if he was adopted and that would drag us all down financially.

'Anyway, it makes no difference to Callum whether he's adopted or fostered. It's the same placement, we treat him the same way, so that's how he'll stay.'

More recently, another issue arose that may have impacted on Alex's attitude to adopting Callum: the health problems of his sister, Emily, became a great deal more acute.

Alex had always been aware of Emily's illness and, of course, the treatment she had received, and though her social worker had said the tumour in her optic nerve was most likely in the past, Emily had a schedule of six-monthly MRI scans. The very first scan after moving in with Alex picked up that the tumour had started growing again. Worse still, it was moving towards the other eye. Alex realised this before the consultant had even spoken to her.

'You go to the hospital to have a follow-up scan, you wait two or three weeks, no results come through, no response, everything must be OK. And then suddenly you get a phone call from the hospital and one of the girls says, "Miss Bell, Dr E wants to talk to you."

'The blue light switches on – it really is as traumatic as that – because it's the consultant personally on the phone, saying, "There's something the matter with the last scan. Will you bring Emily in to see me next week?"

And I'll say, "But she's got an appointment in three months' time."

'"No, I want to see her next week."

'And you know damn well that they're going to tell you something terrible, otherwise they get their secretaries to ring. And then you go in and everything erupts, just erupts. You hope he might say, "Well, there's a bit of a problem here," but no, it's "The tumour has started moving again. We've got to act immediately."

'Then she's being referred to Christie's Hospital, and then it's more blue lights flashing. Like, she's got to have some more tests, like we're talking tomorrow, and your whole life is upside down.'

This is the time when the National Health Service shows its best side, from the highest consultant to the lowliest volunteer driver. This is the time when social services are not 'asked' to provide facilities – they're told – and they do so willingly. This is the time when the traffic lights of our bureaucratic corporate culture all turn green, when no expense is spared, no late-night hour begrudged, no reserve saved for another day. The time when a child is seriously ill and Alex Bell has to find another gear.

'I have to be Alex the professional, but Alex the mother too. I have to balance between both – never hysterical but never detached.'

As Alex expected, the prognosis was bad. Well, very bad. And the more the system piled on help and resources, the worse it seemed. The equilibrium of care changed: no longer was Alex writing letters, chasing, or waiting in line, now the assistance came to her unasked, every helpful phone call seeming like another harbinger of doom. On the one hand, a cold technological process begins – but it's allied to warm-hearted 'person-oriented' caring.

'When Emily went to Christie's it all happened very quickly. You get a Malcolm Sergeant social worker attached to you who is wonderful, who only treats cancer patients, that's all they do. You get a paediatric oncology nurse within days of the diagnosis because people can go to pieces. You get the Princess Diana team, the respite team comes in, the hospices start working with you – and in a way you think, "Oh my God, look at these people that are involved in our life," but they're there supporting your care of this child. And I know they're thinking, "Well, she's only had Emily a short time. Is she going to be like other people who have been with this child, who couldn't cope with it? Is she going to send her back?"'

But such a challenge to Alex had the opposite effect; it made her even more determined to see the problem through. With the possibilities of chemotherapy exhausted for the present, Emily would need one session of radiology every day for the next thirty days, sometimes harrowing, sometimes painful, and always exhausting. So exhausting.

'I told Emily that the inside of her brain was a little bit poorly and we had to get it mended so she'd have to lie on this machine every day for a while. It was very scary, a lot of people walking round with no hair, pulling tubes and drips, but she just said, "OK".'

Emily had a sixth sense that she must collaborate, unexpected in a rebellious child who would usually be asking 'Why?' a hundred times before breakfast, and who would exact a special price for any cooperation. In fact her cooperation went beyond compliance – she began actively to help, due in part to a remarkable scheme at Christie's called 'play therapy', which is touchingly pragmatic. The super-hi-tech radiology unit cost many millions of pounds to build, and many thousands every day to keep staffed and maintained, and yet the slightest movement by the patient renders the treatment useless, or conceivably harmful – especially with the kind of high-precision radiation that was needed on Emily. So the hospital used a play therapist to turn the treatment into a game – in Emily's case the game of staying absolutely still while the machine rumbles through its miraculous process.

Alex has been too close to too many X-ray machines for far too long, so she asked me to go along as Emily skipped down the corridors in her light-up shoes. The radiation unit looked like the inside of a spacecraft, with a central bed surrounded by the robot arms of a car assembly line and a clinical head restraint as if for a futuristic fighter pilot. The operators retreated behind heavy lead screens, the machine hummed, whined and rattled, and as the life-saving burst of radiation was delivered to the precise micrometer of the tumour in Emily's optic nerve, both of her shoes lit up, stimulated by the magnetic force field.

Emily didn't notice because she was concentrating so hard on staying as still as a frozen snowman. That was the moment when my anger at a child being so betrayed by fate tumble-turned into a prayer of thanks for the good of people – and society – that we can give so much for hope when even hope seems hopeless. The radiation unit took on the mood of a shrine as an unseeable power surged into Emily, as technology and medical science nudged God to provide deliverance from despair.

After a surprisingly brief time the lights in Emily's shoes went out, she lifted her head with a smile, and the treatment was over. For today. She had another twenty-nine days of radiation to come and then a month or two before we'd know if it had worked at all. And every day, while Emily skips down the orange and yellow corridor, a taxi waits patiently outside to take her and Alex home to an adopted family who could understand only that Emily had 'a poorly eye'.

The treatment was effective – to a point. It slowed the remorseless progress of the tumour, but it did not cure Emily, because no cure is possible. Emily is now 'in remission' and will need a major MRI check every six months for the rest of her life, a life that Alex has accepted may be cut short.

'This tumour will grow again. But they don't know when, which is why she's highly monitored. When I spoke to the head radiologist, a lovely Indian fella called Dr Rao – really lovely and very, very straight – I said, "I need to know what I am taking on. Whatever you tell me, I'm still going to adopt this little kid, but I need to know what I am adopting, I need to know what the future may hold for us because I've got many other kids as well."

'He said he's had children with the same tumour as Emily, but he's never had anyone live beyond 14. I was glad to know that because it made me realise what I was doing, but never ever in a million years would I have said, "Well, I can't cope with this." Never. I never considered it at all.

'Because that was why I'd got Emily – that was why. Not that I knew about it, but that was why fate brought Emily to me. She needed somebody strong enough to stand by her and support her through it. And I hope I am strong enough, I hope so but I don't know. And, so far, I've not cried about Emily because to me it's not a tragedy. It was before she found us, but now everything is OK, Emily will have a good life however long that is. She will always be loved and she will have somebody to cry at her grave, and that is the important thing, that she has now got something she didn't have before.

'I always think none of us know how long we've got to live any-way. We could all be dead tomorrow – who knows? – so the fact that Emily's life may be limited is more about what I say when Emily asks, "Can I go to college when I am 21?" She'll ask that all the time: "Can I go to Matthew's college when I'm a big girl?"

'And I'll say, "Course you can, Emily."

'Or she'll say things like, "I want a baby in my tummy. Am I ever going to have a baby in my tummy?"

'And I'll say, "If you want one, Emily, but they're hard work."

'I would never damage her dreams that she grows up and she goes to college and she has a baby. So I don't dwell on it – not like, "Oh, isn't it tragic, it's not fair." This is the only life that Emily's got, there's no alternative, especially when she's got gradual dete-rioration, because she *will* deteriorate, she will know that things are getting worse, she will notice that herself, and then she will say to me, "But why can't I do this? I used to be able to do this."

'And that will be the time that I have to explain to her that she's got a problem that means she's going to get worse. And worse.'

Commitment day

Though Alex understood the bumpy journey ahead, on 2 June 2005, a cheerless Thursday, she went with Emily to Manchester Crown Court for a routine gathering that was, in its way, remarkable.

Commitment day. The day of Emily's adoption.

An adoption ceremony is a cold legal process, the confirming by the courts that a young lost soul can henceforth be attached to a new parent or family, a family different from the one of their birth. That much is obvious. The actual handover, the conferring of that individual with a new name, new identity, new place in life, is frosty and forbidding, probably by design, to underline the seriousness of what's happening. The magistrates stare down from their high bench in front of a mighty magisterial crest as they pore over voluminous documents – while asking questions they already know the answer to, as if just to make sure.

'You understand the circumstances of Emily, Miss Bell? You are sure?'

Alex tried to hide her rebelliousness, replying, 'Very sure.'

'You must be very brave, then, Ms Bell.'

Alex shrugged. 'Brave would be one word. I could think of a few others.'

Gradually, the atmosphere changes as the focus moves towards the 7-year-old girl, dressed in pink, fiddling with her hair and giggling: lots and lots of giggles, mainly awkward – especially when a magistrate asks Emily questions. Not 'Do you agree to this adoption?' but 'How do you like school?'

On the subject of adoption, there was no discussion – none was needed: the outcome was predetermined. Like a marriage ceremony the proceedings seemed to be for appearances, although under the legal surface, in the world of feelings and emotions, it was all happening.

Trying to stay solemn, the senior magistrate managed to sniff and smile simultaneously while pronouncing the adoption complete, and inviting Emily to come forward and collect her certificate. But Emily had other ideas. She leapt up from her chair beside Alex, rushed forward and hugged the magistrate, even giving her a gentle kiss on the cheek.

There was a smattering of applause from the half dozen people present and, in spite of the stuffy surroundings, a couple of tears – though not from Alex. She affected the air of 'business as usual' while proclaiming 'there is not an ounce of sentimentality in me', but neither the adoption officer from Nottinghamshire nor the two social workers believed a word she said. Though Alex is not the kind to cry at weddings, everyone knew, just knew, that her heart was touched – and that she was, indeed, brave. Yes, brave. Because, for all the pretences, the disavowal of emotions, Alex lives in a field of feelings, whether sentimental or not, and she's got a lot of pain ahead.

Whatever Alex says, on that drizzly Thursday her heart was touched – though not because of the ceremony or the conferring by a court of what had already happened on the inside long ago.

But because a giggly 7-year-old girl, now officially adopted, now officially her daughter, was thrilled to have a certificate and a new name – which meant that from today she wouldn't have to wear a hospital bracelet that said 'Emily—' (surname omitted). Now the hospital staff and everyone else could know that she is Emily Bell. And she's got a certificate to prove it.

That hospital bracelet is likely to get a lot of use over the years ahead as the best medical care that Britain can provide does its utmost to make Emily's life as comfortable as possible. She's already been accepted at Francis House, a children's hospice in Manchester, a cheerfully sprawling jumble of buildings converted from a Catholic convent, which accepts children who are 'not expected to live into adulthood'. This is said matter-of-fact by staff who have long since worked out how to deal with the death of a child, sometimes to cry, sometimes to pray, but always to accept fate without anger or pity.

Francis House, a charity under the banner of the Family Rainbow Trust, is yet another enriching discovery I made while tagging along in the busy, peripatetic life of Alex Bell and her family. It's a chatty place, open and engaging, unafraid to discuss death in everyday, real terms, where jargon and diktat are left at the front door. They say that 'children come here to live, not die', and they mean it, with a breezy ordinariness that creates an aura of routine calm. 'We're here to guide a process,' they say, 'especially to care for the families, because their pain can be helped.'

The referral usually comes from a hospital – as in the case of Emily – that a life-limited child and her family will need support, probably for several years. Initially, sporadic respite care is arranged, in which the child goes for a weekend to become used to the surroundings in which their last weeks or months will be spent. Francis House have 300 clients on their books – that's 300 children who are not expected to reach 18 in the Manchester area alone – but only seven beds, with two kept for emergencies, so because of lack of space and funding they can only give each child respite for nine days a year.

As part of the preparation for the rocky road ahead, Emily went there for a long weekend, and told Alex she loved it.

'She'll go there whenever she needs to go. At the moment that's not very often because she's not deteriorating, she's stable. It was like, "Would Emily like to come and stay here for a little holiday?" making it a special place that only Emily goes to from my family, not for anybody else, none of the other children were invited.

'She didn't ask why at all, she just says it's where the poorly children go, that's what she knows, but we haven't got to the next step yet, which is: "Why do I go?"'

The bedrooms are different colours, so they've got an orange room and a yellow room and a red room, and then they show you a special room, a rainbow room – all the colours of the rainbow – which has a special significance at Francis House. Again, they don't shy away from the reality of its purpose, there are no euphemisms, they tell it how it is. The rainbow room is where the children go when they're dead.

At the end of a short corridor, before the room itself, is a small flat, with a bed-sitting room, kitchen, bathroom and phone, where the family can stay and gather, and meet relatives. Then through an internal door and into the rainbow room itself – just a simple child's bedroom, with a single bed, a couple of plain chairs, and a heart-rending poem on the wall:

To my dearest family, some things I'd like to say,
But first of all to let you know that I arrived OK.
I'm writing this from Heaven, where I dwell with God above,
Where there are no tears or sadness, there is just eternal love.
Please do not be unhappy, just because I'm out of sight,
Remember that I'm with you, every morning, noon and night.
That day I had to leave you, when my life on earth was through,
God picked me up and hugged me, and said, 'I welcome you.
It's good to have you back again.
You were missed while you were gone.

As for your dearest family, they'll be here later on.'
(Anon)

Just a child's bedroom. Welcoming, but cold.

Cold because a child may be lying there for a week after death, tucked up, as if asleep. Then you notice the french windows and the walkway to a parking area out the back, and you realise – with surprise, no matter how prepared you are – that this little child's bedroom, so neat and tidy is, in fact, a morgue.

The staff at Francis House learnt long ago that families, especially parents, have no idea how they will react to a child's death.

'A lot of families say, "We won't want to see our child afterwards, after they've died,"' says Margaret Hickey of Francis House. 'But they do. They want to say "goodbye". And here the child is in the bed, tucked in, looking lovely, and so they sit there for ages, taking turns with grandmothers and uncles, for hours and hours, holding their child's hand, "being" with them. It's a pleasant, often beautiful, way to embrace. And it helps closure, helps them move forward. That week, that week in the rainbow room, is worth a year of mourning.'

Then after that poignant week of saying a private cheerio like a bedtime story, the hearse backs up to the french windows and the public goodbye takes place in a church built for adults – a child to be buried among 70–80 year olds. It's a familiar process to the professionals at Francis House, but unimaginable to families, or the adoptive mothers of children who were never expected to be toddlers. Because that's a major part of Francis House, dealing with children who were life-limited from the moment they were born.

Such parents are matter-of-fact, they absorbed the shocking news, the pain, the 'it's so unfair'-ness long before, meaning that personal tragedies are not even thought about, let along spoken. At a get-together lunch for parents organised by Francis House, everything is a syndrome, they know encephalitis from leukaemia at first hand, or from the mother at the lunch plate beside them. They don't talk about death, they swap tips on a new kind of shower hoist, or oxygen cylinders that keep running out – a mother even jokes about being supplied incontinence pads for her elephantine 7-year-old who's the size of a 14-year-old.

'"They don't fit," I keep telling them, "they don't fit!" Then they just say, "It's regulation age what matters," not the size of his bottom.'

But as they sit around in smalltalksville, snorting and shrugging at social services – if you look very closely you can see a resigned sadness behind every hastily made up face; you can see the hearse coming soon; you can see the rainbow room in their eyes.

Alex had gone with a purpose – to see if Francis House could accommodate her whole family when Emily is there for respite, because the family suites only have two or three beds, whereas the Bell family need ten. So after lunch she asked the cheery administrator outright, waving her hand around the large luncheon room.

'Is there any chance we could stay here? We could bring in some camp beds, air mattresses …?'

At first he didn't take Alex seriously and shook his head at the madness of it, then surprised himself by nodding at the possibility. '… Well, we don't use our dining room at weekends …'

The door has inched open; Alex will do the rest. If the time finally comes Emily will have her family there.

Emily at 10: a perfect tree with too few seasons

When the adoption magistrate said, 'You must be very brave, Ms Bell,' she was talking for the rest of us. Alex may just reply, 'You're not brave if it's something you have to do, if there's no choice,' but it's the way a person deals with the inevitable that marks them out as brave or not. Alex doesn't hide under the covers or put her head in the sand, but nor does she wander around with a funereal gait. She seems to have found a way to fold Emily into nature, as if a perfect tree, though with too few seasons. A seed grew out of winter, budded in spring, blossomed into a blazing summer, then came a radiant autumn, and finally chilly winter. Always with the focus on Emily, only Emily, and what's best for her. Alex, and Alex's feelings, do not merit consideration – except in the context of how her family will deal with Emily's journey.

'She had something happen at 2, she had something happen at 6, you can work out the maths. The first thing that will go is her eyesight, she will become blind, and our lives will change – how we are going to cope with a dog, a guide dog, I'm not sure. Then she'll understand that she's deteriorating in some way. I mean she's had as much radiotherapy as she can ever have in her life now, so the next time it's got to be chemotherapy again, and that will upset everybody because she will lose her hair. They will do it one more time and that's it, because they can't use the same drugs again, then there's nothing else they can do.

'All I can do is make it as good as I can – Emily will never go through this alone – that's what I can give her. She'll have her family. It will affect them a lot, so I've not mentioned it to them yet. I don't think it's the right time. Matthew does know that she has got something in her brain that doesn't work right but that's all he knows. He will get very emotional … oh God, he'll be awful, he cried about our Joe and that was a cat, he still cries about the cat.

'Even if we've got to say "bye bye" to her and she's not with us any longer, she'll be part of our family. We'll have her pictures and we'll talk about her. We talk about my mum now and she's been dead about ten years and she's still part of their life.

'There are lots of things I don't know, but I can say at this stage that I will be able to deal with it. Who knows what I'll say when I'm sat in the rainbow room at Francis House, I don't know. But one thing's for sure – we'll all go to the funeral. Oh, and Matthew will cry.'

Last year Emily went to Lourdes, not for a miracle cure, but because it's an enriching experience, a spiritual week where children have a fantastic time on a quasi-religious tour with a hint of Disneyland. She came back to another bout of treatment and an operation to relieve pressure inside her head. Through all this Emily is accepting and uncomplaining, as if it's a personal, unstated destiny that she has to fulfil.

While the taxis come and go at the Bell family house, everyday life continues. The consultants send their reports, the family goes off to the theatre. Emily has yet another scan, it's Nathan's birthday. An 'irregularity' is found, they're going to Blackpool for the weekend. Emily has an operation, Simon's got a cold. That is the routine stuff of the saddest of all prognoses, but also a real miracle. Not a cure from God, but the coming together of Alex's family in a never-ending human hug.

'The miracle is that Emily found us, a family who will be able to cope with her for the rest of her days. It's a miracle that I saw Emily's picture at exactly the right time. And all the battles – because, God, it wasn't easy – and then, at the end of the day, you get "life-limited" plonked on top of you.

'But I have no regrets at all. This is Emily, part of Emily, this is Emily's life, she doesn't think it's unfair, why should I think it's unfair?

'To really love somebody, you've got to be prepared to lose them, that's part of loving; to love and to lose, they go together.'

Alex had no idea how prophetic her words would be, though not about Emily, but her 8-year-old brother, Callum.

'Breathe, Callum, breathe ...'

During the early autumn of 2006, Callum invented an ingenious, but lethal, new way to stimulate himself. He began to self-asphyxiate. This was first noticed when he was at school. Callum simply collapsed, crashing to the floor and injuring his head. Later, it was Alex who discovered the reason, that Callum was holding his breath until he became unconscious.

The textbooks were consulted but no one had encountered such a harrowing problem before, let alone developed a treatment. The bottom line? Callum's Social Services (Sambridge Council, not their real name) asked Alex to keep an extra watch, but otherwise were not prepared to help.

This did not satisfy Alex, especially after Callum 'suffered' several more bouts at school. She applied for an extra 30 hours a week 'assistant's' allowance – about £125 – enough for a junior carer to keep a constant eye on him between arriving home and going to bed. Without this, Alex believed that it would mean less attention to the rest of her family, and physical danger to Callum. But Sambridge refused to budge. There could be no more money.

To Alex, this was the final straw, especially as she believed that Sambridge had reneged on several agreements in the past, so she gave them an ultimatum. More supervision, or Callum would have to leave in the 28 days stipulated in her foster agreement.

On one occasion, in the entrance hall immediately after tea, I saw Callum *begin to* asphyxiate, swaying backwards and forwards, and watched Louise and Callum's helper Evette grab his shoulders while shouting, 'Breathe Callum, breathe …' until he blinked open his eyes, shook his head, quietly moaned – and began breathing again.

Harrowing isn't the word.

In the face of such obvious distress, Sambridge had severely let down both Alex and Callum. Leaving aside the caustic rudeness of their correspondence to Alex, they had undermined the unwritten contract between carer and social services, that their first duty is to 'the client', in this case Callum.

Though Callum has made stunning progress with the Bell family – and with adequate support Alex would have remained keen for him to stay – she had reached the end of her tether. On 6 November 2006 a social work manager came to take Callum away. Although Alex had looked after him for almost three years she was not officially told where he was going. And for several months Sambridge would not allow him to see Emily, in spite of a legal requirement that siblings must be kept in close contact.

Alex remains broken-hearted but adamant. Sambridge have not lived up to their responsibilities and she has asked for an official appeal not only to allow Callum to see Emily but to have Callum returned to Alex's care with assisted support from Sambridge.

In the meantime, Callum is somewhere in England and Alex had gradually lost contact with him – perhaps Sambridge's intention since he left. With absence, the heart heals over time, and in that Alex is like all of us. So now it seems extremely unlikely that Callum will ever be coming back.

Chapter Thirteen

Happy returns: more about Matthew

I'm sick and tired of people who moan and groan about Down's syndrome. I am not having it. Lots of my friends are DS; me, Jenny, Chris and Toby, and they are the best. I love being Down's. Down's syndrome means that if anyone wants to get up and help each other to do brilliant things, they can.

Matthew Bell

On 24 April 2007, Matthew was 25.

Alex arranged a special birthday lunch at Worsley Old Hall for the whole family – requiring almost military logistics and organisation. Altogether, twenty-two people and assorted equipment were loaded into four vehicles, convoyed across a bright sunny Manchester, to cram around a long, busy table, taking over what had until then been a haven for the quiet Sunday-eat-out crowd, mainly elderly couples and in-law gatherings.

When the Bell family arrived, the diners reacted in the usual way; they were fascinated – and appalled. Fascinated by the chattering tribe who descended on the luncheon room like a travelling circus act, with wheelchairs and balloons, changes of clothing and nappies. But appalled by the sudden gust of life in many varieties, all of them noisy. This was special needs on the borderline of public acceptance, where you could feel the unspoken regret from a dozen private diners that their cosy lunch had been so completely invaded, but who knew they couldn't justify a 'shush', let alone a complaint.

The kids were polite – Alex saw to that. But they are kids, even the 20-plus ones, and it's Matthew's birthday party, and it's Sunday, and there are lots of people, and waiters, and half a dozen helpers – like Louise and Angela and Debbie and Clare – and Simon's shrieking, and there's jelly, and everyone's talking at once – well, sort of talking, shouting really – and Chloe is sulking because she's strapped in, and Emily wants 'toilet', and Matthew is describing how to make the perfect Spaghetti Bolognaise, and Nathan knocks over his orange juice …

After half an hour, a grey-haired grandmother with extravagant spectacles and frown-lines passes by, stops, her arthritic fingers hovering over Simon's spiky head. 'How many have you got, love?'

'There were eight when we left home,' Louise answers, feeding a wriggling, pinching Andrew, who says 'Hi-ya' to the ceiling.

'Hi-ya,' the grandma answers, touching Simon at last, hands kneading his shoulders. 'From a special school?'

'All hers.' Louise shakes her head and points over at Alex, who has half an ear on this chat.

A younger couple drift over. 'Do you mind us asking – how do you manage …?'

Emily returns from the toilet with Angela. A family table intercepts, asking her name, with Emily twisting her hands in front of her frock, Miss Cutie.

'Oh, they're good today,' Alex is joking to the younger couple. 'This is best behaviour …'

'I think it's wonderful,' the young woman says, over Nathan growling 'Arggg' at Chloe and glaring, pirate-style, then smiling …

After an hour the whole dining room is rocking to the Bell family beat; most of the diners have visited their table. True, the 'just-us' intimacy has gone, but it's been replaced by an almost bawdy camaraderie because the unconscious simplicity of the Bells enjoying a party meal has swept reserve away – if these disabled kids don't care about boring old etiquette, why should we? And then Matthew gets to his feet, a speech in his head; the actor has memorised his lines. The chatter drops – but only a bit.

'I'd just like to say thank you for coming to my birthday, everyone is lovely. I am 25 years old and happy. I am going to be a famous actor and work at Manchester United. I'd like to say – there's another lad who's 25 today – Robert, my twin brother. I wish you was here, Robert. I love you. And my mother, Jane.'

Alex jabbed Matthew in the ribs with her elbow when he sat down. 'I hope Robert has said nice things about you too, on your birthday.'

Matthew's life has always been dominated by two things: by trying to meet up with his birth family, in particular his mother, Jane, and twin brother Robert; and by his dream, however hopeless it has seemed, of working for Manchester United in their headquarters at Old Trafford.

During the winter, Alex had been working her magic on them. Matthew was a full-time student at Eccles College and her aim was to wangle a term of one-day-a-week work experience – though the club had never taken on a Down's person before. At first sight, Alex's plan seemed reasonably straightforward.

'We went on the official Manchester United tour and talked to the guide who was leading us round and he gave us the name of the person we needed to get in touch with.'

And then, by coincidence …

'The guide went and told his boss about Matthew, so that when we called he was aware of what we were talking about. That man was Damian Preston and he went to Elaine Alexander …'

Damian Preston is the supervisor while Elaine Alexander is no less than the head supervisor of the tours and museum.

'… and between them they decided to let Matthew go on a work experience course, the first Down's they ever had.'

So simple, eh? But Alex doesn't explain that it was actually a carefully worked out strategy, that she had been on several tours and met the guide before, that she used Matthew's charm to create a friendly buzz, that she went to see Damian and Elaine in person, and that she had spent quite a while working in advance on the answers to their questions. In any case, her plan worked, and for eight Wednesdays, Matthew had his perfect work experience, and it *was* work.

Damian Preston and his team created that clever mix of making him do useful tasks, but keeping an eye on him, helped by Matthew's broad knowledge of Manchester United and his eagerness to please. There were highlights – polishing the cups in the trophy room, dozens of them, including Premier League medals and shields, and occasionally bumping into players or ex-players – but the brunt of his efforts were routine, working on computers, or sending out flyers, perhaps boring to some people, but not to Matthew.

'I did the tours, taking people around. After doing that I did the museum as well. In the office I was licking envelopes and folding paper inside. Then I took them around. I was an assistant. My job was to talk about the players. In the changing room I took the people to the places where there are pictures where they change, and I had to say the name of each player. That was easy for me. That is what I did do. And answer questions. I know the answers; I always know the answer. I did.'

Matthew was a big success, so Alex followed up with the second phase of her plan. In early July, Matthew officially left Eccles College forever, to begin a new existence as an adult, 'me own man' as he put it. In fact, he went further; after his last day at Eccles, Matthew announced, 'I've now retired,' although, perversely, he began getting up earlier each morning. This spurred Alex on to begin the complex process of building him a rounded, useful life.

First and foremost, Alex and Matthew's greatest success: after his work experience there, Manchester United were impressed enough to offer him long-term employment, to begin with, one day a week. Let's say that again.

Matthew has got a job at Manchester United.

The man himself, of course, takes it in his stride.

'It's the best for me because I like Manchester United, my club. I know the ground. Old Trafford. I won't miss Eccles. Some good friends I will miss. But I will have new friends at Manchester United – they know who I am, you know. My boss Elaine always says hello. It's a good job. I have a free lunch every day.'

Matthew will not be asked to take a tour around on his own. Old Trafford is huge, too vast for Matthew to memorise every corner, and he could get confused, so he will go round with an experienced tour guide. But Matthew is able to answer questions and give instructions for customers who pay to go on tours because he has such a fantastic knowledge of Manchester United. As Alex says, 'He can talk about football till the cows come home. And longer. Believe me.'

Manchester United has an impressive record on disablement. At every match 208 seats are reserved for disabled fans and their carers; there are 100 places for visually impaired, with plug-in audio description booths; special access has been built into the ground, with an 'Ability Suite', a plush hospitality area that has a lowered bar for supporters in wheelchairs. Most of this is organised by the Manchester United Disabled Supporters Club, set up by United and now a model for other Premiership clubs, and is another sign of the unique attitude in the North West, that the whole community, individuals and institutions, play a part together in encouraging people with disadvantages to be full members of society.

Of course, Alex Bell knew all this. So she probably wasn't as surprised as the rest of us when United offered Matthew his part-time, but long-term, job.

'He'll be attached to one of the guides and they've all taken to Matthew. He knows them by name and they call him "mate" and understand that he's got a big thing about United and they're big fans as well. So they talk to him as an equal, but they do realise he needs that extra eye kept on him. And also, there'll always be people, some members of the public, who think it's funny to take the mick and things like that. But I think the staff would come down on it, straight away, and say, "Look, you don't treat our people like that, please."'

So the sun shines on Mr Happy – a typically happy ending for Matthew. Except, it isn't an ending, it's a beginning, the beginning of a life-long love affair between an obedient, very talkative Down's syndrome man and the supporters of his own beloved club. Picture him, bright-faced, a bit jowly, forever a boy, wandering along with the tours, swapping statistics and incidents that the real fans love so much, of conquests and catastrophes that might not always … well, in Matthew's words – connect? For instance, he can get halfway through a sentence and then drift off, or not completely make sense. This is all part of his charm, but it can be slightly off-putting to the uninitiated.

And then in ten, twenty, thirty years' time he becomes a locker room legend at Old Trafford, to stand beside Bobby Charlton. Only this legend has never kicked a Premier League ball in anger, never been part of the 'playing' team; instead, he's become part of another team, the folk behind the scenes, the wider family that is Manchester United.

Fantasy? A dream? Oh, but football is about dreams, dreams thwarted and dreams come true. Without dreams there would be no football, and no Bell family. Alex is a dreamer, but practically so, demandingly so – every night there's a new dream as her head hits the pillow. But when she visited Old Trafford that chilly October day, Alex didn't mention her dream because she knew the backroom staff had already embraced the Matthews of this world, their collective minds made up years before when the world's most famous club decided it had the space to do a bit more for all its people. Matthew was probably in before Alex picked up the phone.

After all the penalties and yellow cards against him, Alex has helped Matthew score the winner in extra time, and even the other side are cheering. The twin who was left behind at Watford hospital – for nine long and lonely weeks in the bleached-out laundry area, because the maternity hospital never get babies left and had nowhere else to put him – that Down's twin now works for Manchester United.

Hoorah! go the crowd, as they turn to clap themselves, because that's what we should all do. We've moved so far from those days of thirty years ago, when guys like Matthew were teased and mocked and feared and shunned, of crossing the street, of locking them in 'hospitals in the hills' – and we all did our bit, by being tolerant, encouraging, befriending. It wasn't 'them', it was all of 'us'.

Hoorah! The Down's twin does the tours at Old Trafford. The ball's in the corner of the net.

But like her namesake in the manager's dugout, that doesn't stop Alex wanting more.

'I'm hoping that Manchester United, over time, will take him on for two days a week. There's also the training ground, which is not open to the public, at Carrington, which Matthew would love to do as well. So, hopefully, when he's doing well, maybe they'll find him something to do at the training ground, one day a week, which would be great because then he could meet players. Even if it was something like taking the drinks round, cleaning the boots, collecting kit, that kind of thing, he'd be happy.'

So that's him sorted, maybe two days a week. What about the other three days? While many people might sit back, satisfied with a task completed, Alex has hardly begun.

'He's going to, hopefully, get a direct payment from social services for twenty hours a week, that's what we've applied for. So, he'll have a worker to help him do things that interest him, like going to a college to do a cookery course – because he loves cookery – one day a week. He's also going to join Thomas and Louise for ten-pin bowling, and pottery, he loves pottery, too. Then the theatre – he'd like to work backstage at the Octagon Theatre in Bolton, he had workshops there, so they know him quite well – that's maybe one day a week. And he's been helping at the donkey sanctuary in Manchester, another day a week – though he's refused to muck out the stables, doesn't like, you know, the dung – oh, and …'

Alex hadn't noticed that she had filled his time for seven days a week. So much for 'retiring' when he leaves college – Matthew won't know what's hit him, which is exactly how Alex wants it. Her job as mother continues, indeed intensifies, when her kids leave full-time education. No empty-nest syndrome for her, no wondering what to do when they leave home, because they won't be leaving and her biggest challenge as a mother – that of keeping them fulfilled and busy – is just beginning.

Ironically, the very thing Nathan's Sue, and Tom's Patricia feared most – that image of a Down's adult-child in their 30s, holding hands with their mother while shuffling round a supermarket, is one of Alex's greatest joys, that her family will stay at home forever – though they'll be too busy for the supermarket. Maybe the Chinese are right, that to have a Down's baby is to be blessed. But, of course, there are people out there, many people, who don't see it that way. Matthew's birth father, for instance.

'He ain't heavy ...'

When we left Matthew earlier in the book, at the age of 18, he had asked After Adoption to search for his birth family, in particular his twin brother. They had found and contacted the family, Matthew's birth mother had called the organisation back enthusiastically, but when a possible meeting was in the offing – silence. And for Matthew, heartbreak. The general view was that his father, who was thought to be uncomfortable with the idea of having a Down's son, had stopped the contact. This had worked as a veto because After Adoption have a rule that they can only arrange a meeting if all parties are in favour; if not, they are not allowed to provide information, in particular addresses. Hence, an impasse. Though Matthew may be desperate to meet his birth mother or twin brother, without their address he could not do so.

However, as part of the research for this book, I located his birth family – after discovering a single letter written about, of all things, a new deodorant to a men's health magazine, from a person who just happened to be Matthew's twin brother – and then chasing up that lead through local council documents.

Having reached that point, earlier last year, with Alex's encouragement, I decided to approach Matthew's family, to discreetly discover if they would – after all – be keen on a meeting.

Apart from Matthew and Alex, four people are involved, and their names have been changed to protect their privacy. First there is Jane, Matthew's birth mother; next, Lawrence, his father; Robert, his twin brother; and Martin, an elder brother, who was 2 when Matthew was born.

There are lots of ways to approach people – you can write a letter, phone, or contact them through an intermediary – but usually the best way is to be 'up-front' and simply knock on their door. The family live on a private estate of modern, brick-built, detached houses in the Home Counties, with a dark blue, company-style car outside, and on the second visit, a Saturday lunchtime, Matthew's mother, a gentle-looking woman in her 50s, came to the door wiping her hands on a cloth.

Standing on the doorstep I told her, 'I'm writing a book about Alex Bell, who's adopted nine Down's or disabled children. I think you know—'

'Yes, I know Alex,' Jane replied, 'know of her.'

Then I mentioned Matthew, what a fine person he is …

She interrupted. 'Why are you telling me this?' she asked, as if it didn't concern her.

'Well, you know,' I replied, 'he's your son.'

Jane appeared to glance furtively over her shoulder, back inside the house. 'How did you find us?'

I explained that it wasn't difficult. Her family were in the electoral register, not trying to hide.

For a while she seemed uncertain, undecided, saying this had come 'out of the blue', but she did smile when I told her of Matthew, how he talked about her a lot. Finally, she asked for my phone number, saying that she 'might be in touch. We'll have to see.' With that she nodded 'goodbye' and retreated back inside the house, closing the smart front door without looking around.

I left with the impression of a friendly, wary woman, unsure whether to be alarmed or excited by my approach, but who would certainly want to phone.

The days passed – no call. A week, still no call. A month – nothing. Jane was not going to call back.

Alex was disappointed but understanding. 'It's him. Dad. Maybe he said "no", maybe she was too scared to ask, it's probably what happened before. I feel so sorry for her, poor woman.'

But Alex did not think we should give up, though this now raised a further question, perhaps *the* question. Presuming he could be found, should an approach be made to Matthew's twin brother, Robert, or should the family now be left alone?

For a long time that question never left my mind because it was not only about Matthew – I knew he was desperate to meet his twin brother and mother – or about Alex, who wanted a happy ending. I didn't want to give up because it seemed such a negative, a disavowal of the good side of humankind.

So I continued to monitor the movements – if any – of Robert, to see if he surfaced anywhere away from his family home. Then, in April 2007, I discovered an advertising flyer that included his name in a company handout some distance from his parents' house, and I surmised that he had left home and might now be able to act independently. After a discussion with Alex, I travelled to Robert's office to see if he would meet me. At that time I had no idea if he even knew about Matthew; there was even a possibility that his parents had never mentioned he had a twin brother.

By now 25, Robert worked for a small technology company in a charming market town outside London, and he met me in the staff car park, talking as we wandered around the cars on a hot and humid afternoon. I could immediately tell that he was Matthew's twin – they had a similar nature. A round face, friendly, kind and gentle, with an open, honest smile, Robert listened attentively, then invited me into his office. Yes, he did know about Matthew – his parents had sat him down when he was 15 with his brother and explained. And, yes, he always wondered, always wondered about him.

From listening to Robert the story became clear.

His mother would love to meet Matthew. Indeed, she's not the only one. Robert wanted to meet him, too, and thought about him often. Especially when his birthday came around. The problem was the impact it would have on Matthew's birth family, particularly his dad. Lawrence had never been able to accept a Down's child, and probably never could. Robert had thought about it very hard, but up to now his decision had been that it would not be suitable to get in touch with Matthew because he believed it would actually drive his family apart. By that he seemed to mean his parents.

'It's got to be one of the hardest things to do, to give up your son – would send you nuts, and it just doesn't go away, does it? I realise my brother would like to see us, I want to see him … but I'm just not sure. If it was something I'd never thought about, then probably I'd say "yes". But it's something I've thought about a lot and I'm not sure it's the right time because of the impact it would have on other people.'

Sitting in that office with Robert was both uplifting and sad. Uplifting because he was a generous and sensitive young man who cared deeply about every individual, and instinctively respected the eternal responsibility that family has for family; yet sad, because he seemed to be trapped into feeling that there was no choice but to appease the darker forces that swirled around, to accept that fear and prejudice were in control, and with them, hurt and bitterness. It felt like good intentions, good love, was being swept away by bad.

We swapped phone numbers, agreed to stay in touch, then Robert went back to work

When I told Alex, she wasn't surprised.

'It must be very difficult for Robert. He probably would love to see Matthew but Dad still rules the roost and he hasn't got far enough away from Dad yet. I mean, his mother's never been able to get away from him, not after half a lifetime – what chance has a young lad, still making his way in the world?'

Alex's world-weary, patient sigh was born of her many other struggles, over so many years – most of which turned out fine in the end. That's the impression she gives, that it's only a matter of time before a happy outcome is inevitable. Well, perhaps, but not if Matthew's birth father has his way.

While travelling back from meeting Robert, my mobile phone rang. It was Lawrence.

As I pulled over to listen, it became clear that Lawrence was furious and had no intention of hiding the fact. I began to explain, to suggest a meeting, but he was shouting, cutting across any explanation or discussion. Then strangely, for no apparent reason, he calmed down to an icy cold tone, as if, belatedly, he cared what I thought of him.

'You see, Mr Clark, I ask myself what has it got to do with me? This has nothing to do with me or my family.'

'Well, you're Matthew's father.'

'That has nothing to do with me.' This was not said as a complaint, but as an accusation; he was accusing me of unnecessarily involving him, of bringing him grief.

I told him that Matthew was a terrific person and that so much of his life had worked out really well, but he cut across me for a final time.

'I want you to stop interfering with my son, my family. Is that understood?'

With that, he hung up.

That conversation – although it was perhaps a little too one-sided to really be a conversation – leaves all of us in something of a dilemma. It's pretty clear that Jane would like to meet her son Matthew, and he's desperate to meet her, his birth mother; equally, Robert and Matthew want to meet and in the way of twins could perhaps build a long-term friendship. Alex, too, is very keen to introduce Matthew's family into the wider 'Family Bell' – like the other birth parents of her children. However, one man keeps all these people apart, possibly because he wants to protect them or protect himself. That's not only sad, it seems unfair.

Alex sees the heartbreak in human terms. Though disappointed at an opportunity missed, to her it's confirmation that she is blessed, and has the best and happiest family in the universe.

'Poor mother. She must be devastated by everything. Poor twin brother. Poor other son. Poor Matthew. And all because of one man, and his unhappy family. Yet we're so happy. From their point of view it's even sadder that Matthew's come to such a happy family. And the really bad thing is that he might see Matthew as the cause of their unhappiness, whereas it isn't Matthew at all.'

The leading man is oblivious to all this, his full and happy life keeping him too busy to dwell on matters that are beyond his control. As the years open out before him, Matthew Bell has a great deal to look forward to and some modest goals to achieve. Working at Manchester United is a dream come true and there will be other thrills, and a spill or two, as Matthew's alumni become the first Down's generation to grow up free of restraint and bigotry. One thing is certain: Mr Happy will continue to be happy, because it's the way he was designed, with an easy-going, friendly nature – that he shares, like so many other qualities, with a kind young man in the South who was designed the same way.

Though not identical, they have the bond of twins that developed side-by-side in the same womb, and often they think of each other. True, they have a tiny, minor difference, which comes from Matthew having an extra chromosome 21 in every single cell, but the similarities far outweigh the disparities. Instinctively, Robert knows that, as he knows that in time they will get together.

Because it's not a chromosome that keeps them apart.

Chapter Fourteen

Battling on

There are those who see the rain.
And those who see the rainbow.
But only lovers see the pots of gold.

This is not a story about disability or adoption, therapeutic communities or social work – it is a book about love. In Alex's case, revulsion followed by love, with dribbling Billy in his long-stay hospital ward when she was 13. Then later, ever-increasing love for the kids whom nobody else would take, whom she saw in adoption magazines.

It is also about the love of an idea: that a small community can radiate sunshine through the rain, that a seemingly disadvantaged group of people can be so happy, positive, so adored and affectionate. Perhaps this happens because they appear to be in a perpetual childhood, a place from which the rest of us are exiled far too early.

We look on, mildly embarrassed to be gawping, but get swept along by their simple lives, and that just being together makes them happy. For a moment we catch a glimpse inside their world of innocence. These are special people, pure, glowing, golden.

And then it's gone, that fleeting glimpse of Eden. The playroom is a playroom once again, the angels morph back into fleshy adults with unexpected – disabled – features. Rapture then reality, in two blinks.

Love's flipside is also at the heart of this book – all the mothers or fathers of Alex's children, who at some point couldn't deal with their own 'Billy moment' as they were left emotionally stranded by fate. One moment, total commitment to a gorgeous vulnerable baby; the next, an ugly bundle and a shudder at the image of a 40-year-old hulking child. But later, as we have seen, that revulsion turned back to love, as they embraced and celebrated their increasingly cherubic offspring.

That's the 'love-me, love-me-not, love-me' rollercoaster world of Down's syndrome.

But with Alex it doesn't begin with 'love-me'. She commits first, and grows to love later. To her, the gushy notion of being motivated by instinctive love is 'sickly' – it's about being needed, a sense of duty, that there's a job to be done, an unwanted life to be improved. Love comes later, usually quickly, but love is not the initial point. On hearing about how Alex adopts Down's children, a religious friend remarked about her thus: 'God presents mankind with a problem, but provides the answer,' and that's as close to the truth of Alex as anyone has got, that it was born into her. To Alex, of course, it's even more basic.

'It's not a mystery at all. This is what I do. It's as simple as that. And I get as much out of it as the kids and that's why it works. Because nobody could do this twenty-four hours a day, seven days a week forever, without some kind of comeback, reward. Not money, that's not important – no, it's me, it's everything, my whole existence is the children, and there's nothing wrong with that. And I deliberately go after the most difficult children imaginable. All my children are quite daunting for different reasons, aren't they? That's the challenge. But they're great, absolutely superb – I'd have another nine tomorrow if I felt we were right for the kids.'

Alex is not pretending. She *would* have more. In fact, she recently applied for 8-year-old identical twin boys, both with Down's syndrome, who were advertised in 'The Book', now provocatively retitled *Children Who Wait*.

For Alex, the story of Jack and Charlie (not their real names) goes back eight years, when she received a phone call from a married woman then in her early 50s. Mavis and Ted Brown (again, not their real names) had agreed to adopt the twins in 1997 while they were tiny, not long after they were born, and Mavis phoned Alex for advice.

'My first thought was "You lucky beggar",' says Alex. 'I had always wanted to adopt twin Down's boys. These were babies and I could imagine how beautiful they were. But I had just agreed to take Chloe, and anyway, this woman and her husband were looking after them, and she sounded lovely, though a bit inexperienced – there again, who isn't? Of course I was dead jealous, and even more so when she said she was 47 and her husband 52. I thought that's very old to be adopting Down's babies, but good luck to you. She called me several times. I think she wanted reassurance.'

Eight years later, in 2005, Alex read the advert and realised the coincidence was too great. Jack and Charlie must be Mavis and Ted Brown's twins. She wondered what had happened for the adoption to break down. She also realised that few families would apply to adopt two disabled 8-year-old boys, one with asthma and one with no speech. So she contacted Cheshire Social Services

are twin brothers who have formed a close relationship. They have Down's Syndrome. ▮▮▮ is an affectionate and loving boy. He loves Bob the Builder and thrives on attention from adults. ▮▮▮ is a lively and affectionate child who loves 'rough and tumble play'. ▮▮▮ particularly likes Teletubbies, swimming amd walks. Like his brother, he enjoys one-to-one attention. ▮▮▮ behaviour has improved and his overall health is good, although he has Asthma. ▮▮▮ has no speech, although he is making efforts to use sounds and words.

Ethnic/racial origins: white English

Family needed: a white adoptive family or permanent foster family who could offer consistency, affection and clear boundaries

Contact plans: annual Letterbox contact with their birth parents, direct contact with their present foster carers to be discussed

(Original advertisement for Jack and Charlie in *Children Who Wait*.)

JACK and CHARLIE are twin brothers who have formed a close relationship. They have Down's Syndrome. Jack is an affectionate and loving boy. He loves Bob the Builder and thrives on attention from adults. Charlie is a lively and affectionate child who loves 'rough and tumble play'. Charlie particularly likes Teletubbies, swimming and walks. Like his brother, he enjoys one-to-one attention. Charlie's behaviour has improved and his overall health is good, although he has Asthma. Charlie has no speech, although he is making efforts to use sounds and words.

Ethnic/racial origins: white English Family needed: a white adoptive family or permanent foster family who could offer consistency, affection and clear boundaries

Contact: annual Letterbox contact with their birth parents, direct contact with their present foster carers to be discussed.

Department and said the Bell family would be interested in adopting the twins.

'If they've got others who are interested in Jack and Charlie – great. But if not, if they can't find a family to adopt them, they would be destined to stay in the care system for the rest of their lives. Moving, always moving, from foster home to foster home – that's if they can find decent foster homes in the future. It's not so easy when it's two of them, and when they're pushing 20.'

The immediate response to Alex was doubtful, a cool 'Don't call us, we'll call you.' The Social Services Family Finder, Fiona Taylor, meant, 'You've already got nine kids, difficult kids at that. You are not exactly what we're looking for,' which was what Alex expected and she got ready for a long wait. However, to her surprise, Fiona Taylor came back quite quickly, to say they would prepare an assessment on paper. A few weeks later, Alex was surprised again. Social services wanted to come for a home visit. They couldn't make a 'paper' decision because people in the Department had such strong views.

'Too many passionate "no"s, too many fervent "yes"s,' Fiona Taylor told Alex. 'We will have to come and see you.'

'The chances went from a 90 per cent "no" to a 70 per cent "no".' It was at least progress, Alex thought.

The social workers arrived, sniffed the air, poked through Alex's cupboards, if not her soul, supped her tea, and met the Family Bell. In spite of the chaos and the noise and the heaving mass of nine busy bundles of humanity, they decided that the twins should take their places around Alex's broad-shouldered kitchen table.

But, of course, they didn't say that.

They said, 'We'll let you know.' Privately, though, there were hints and nudges and little asides like, 'The managers have said

"Go for it," and "All we need is for the money to be approved, and that's a formality."'

'I think it might be Bell United,' Alex said, with excitement. 'Eleven – my own football team. Then I really will stop. I'll cancel the Book.'

After that, nothing. Time passed, as it always must when dealing with social services. The future of the twins would have to wait.

Then, after Alex had made half a dozen chase-up calls, Fiona Taylor phoned very apologetically to say 'no'. The reasons given were superficial and silly: the twins needed to be with normal children for proper development; they needed to ride bikes in the garden, but they couldn't at her house; they liked a bath every night and Alex had too many children to do that.

Her hopes having been raised, Alex was downhearted, though not so much for herself as for the twins. She didn't use the word cowardice – that's my word – because it seemed to me that yet another of those remote managers, who may not have taken the trouble to meet with Alex in person, had vetoed from a distance. But Alex understood – her life has been understanding this kind of thing – and would put it another way, more charitably than my suggestion of cowardice. She'd just say that the collective courage required in dealing with really difficult and vulnerable children was not there.

'It's so much easier to say "no". As usual, social services are taking the safe option – safe for them – leave the twins where they are, in foster care, with a couple who are 56 and 62. Before long they will retire, but the boys will still need to be cared for, will still need a secure home, will still need a family – forever. That decision, like loads of other decisions, was "Don't rock the boat", but easier for social services. The hard option is to say, "Fostering is not going to meet their long-term needs. At 18 they're not going to be getting jobs, they're never going to be able to look after themselves, they'll never be independent. Let's get them adopted, let's get it sorted now." Which is what the advert in the Book was saying, too. Otherwise, it's foster home to foster home to foster home.'

The social services department accept that 'no' was a reversal of an earlier internal decision in Alex's favour. It seems that some-one, somewhere – one person, it is believed – came down against the Bell family, even though Alex was actually recommended by the Family Placement Team. However, the twins had been advertised in *Children Who Wait* for *adoption*, for a permanent home. If Alex's was the only application to adopt the twins, a request would have to be made to what is called 'the Permanency Panel' to have the twins' interests changed from needing adop-tion to fostering, in order to turn her down. Streetfighter Alex knew this and wrote a point-by-point letter, addressed to the Panel's chairperson, explaining that the twins were heading for foster limboland.

For a layperson, it's a moderate, clever letter; it ends with a request by Alex to be able to address the Panel in person – in a sense, to be Jack and Charlie's advocate for adoption.

Alex checked that the letter had been received by the twins' Barnardo's social worker, then sat back and waited. And waited. But, scandalously, her letter was not passed on. Alex's points were never put before the Panel, so a decision was made with-out important information being available to the members. Apart from serious bureaucratic mismanagement or devious-ness, there can be no explanation for ignoring a polite and per-fectly proper letter, and the request it contained to address the Panel.

The Chair of that Panel, Sue Fergusson, did not even know the letter existed, even though Alex subsequently raised it with senior managers, and had been told it was being dealt with.

Cheshire Social Services are embarrassed by the implied maladministration of not dealing fairly – or even at all – with Alex's submission, although they still have not offered a credible explanation. Meanwhile, a smashing pair of identical Down's twins languish in the kind of bureaucratic fug that caused Thomas so much unnecessary anguish a decade before. It is that vision, that honest persistence can win in the face of bureaucratic incompetence and intransigence and transform innocent lives for the good, it is that vision that makes Alex so doggedly determined to force a proper, fair-minded hearing.

But then that has always been so in the life of Alex Bell. From the matron in charge at Swinton Hospital telling a helpful 13-year-old girl to go away, onto the empty chairs of 1982 and 'You've got no chance, love,' through being sincerely rebuffed over Simon, then the social services' disgrace of Tom, followed by the outrage of Callum disappearing at the very last minute one evening in early November 2006. Until, finally, Cheshire Social Services, where the Chair had no idea what was going on, while her authority pronounced an impenetrable 'no' – as usual, from a distance.

'Who are these people?' you may ask. 'Why do they turn away enthusiastic, informed help?'

Indeed why? Perhaps, because according to the law 'they' know better. 'They' are the people we – society – pay to nurture and protect the most vulnerable members of our community, 'they' are the committees and panels that judge without proximity or pity – they are the people Alex has had to battle and outmanoeuvre every step of the way.

Thankfully, it does seem that twins Jack and Charlie are doing well for the moment, so perhaps it is right that they should stay at their current foster home until that is no longer possible, and Alex accepts that. Her point is that the Family Bell could be assessed in the meantime, so that there would be no need for a distressing and drawn-out hiatus when they finally have to be moved – a move that is sure to happen one day. And maybe another day, and another, as two innocent boys remain on the social services' fostering roundabout in perpetuity.

Privately, the social workers with the most intimate knowledge of the twins concur, but it seems the 'system', that impersonal and convenient whipping boy for so many unbending pronouncements, is in command. With no one else to speak up for the boys and no right of appeal, Alex submitted an official complaint. The only problem – the Chairperson of the Permanency Committee hadn't seen that either.

Chair Sue Fergusson now feels 'it would be inappropriate to comment'. And that's it. No further explanation. Presumably, they want everyone to assume that their actions are in the best interests of those two poor boys, although with no further explanation it's reasonable to wonder if Cheshire Social Services have put their own welfare first.

In social work, the name for the breakdown of an adoptive placement is 'disruption', a nicely chosen euphemism for adoptive parents dumping back to the nomadic care system children they had vowed to look after for life. One can have sympathy for the Browns, who were, after all, in their 50s when they adopted the baby twins with Down's, but the Social Services Department don't deserve to get off so lightly. Though hindsight is a wonderful thing, to some it would have seemed likely that the adoption might become disrupted.

An example of this may be found in point 12 of Alex's letter to the Chair of the Permanency Committee.

The final point I would like to make is this – Jack and Charlie are in this situation now because a previous social worker made an incorrect decision when they were younger – they both deserve this not to happen again.

Partly, Alex means that they were given to parents who were a bit old to adopt, but the obvious question then arises – what about Alex? She was 52 in 2007; she won't retire, everyone knows that, but what happens when she's no longer around?

'I will do this until I die but, as with all parents, I worry about what will happen to my family after that. So I've formed a trust, called the Woodland Care Trust, which will keep them together under a board of trustees. Then they can stay here, looked after in the house as a family, and social services won't come in and split them up. That's their future. Even without me. And I'm sure it will work.'

A few years ago, after she adopted Andrew – child number five – Alex worked out the problem at her kitchen table. Though Down's syndrome people have a shorter life-expectancy than most of us, these days they often live well into their 60s. She was a single mother, and with no other heirs, what would happen after she was gone? None of her children would be able to look after themselves, let alone the other seven, and she did not want to see them simply taken over by the state.

'There's too many of them for one person to care for, and I wanted them to be able to stay together as a family. If they lost me, at least they could keep each other.'

That was where the idea of the Woodland Care Trust came in. Alex asked around; a friend suggested a lawyer – Philip Laidlow, a tax partner with the Manchester firm of Leightons – and Philip came up with the idea of a trust.

On one level the principle is simple: All Alex's assets – money, possessions, cars and, crucially, her house – would be pulled together into a single fund and left in trust for the children, administered by an accountant or lawyer. Otherwise the children would have to pay a huge sum in estate tax (death duty) on Alex's death. But that wouldn't resolve how they would be cared for. For that Alex would need a further idea.

Philip, who agreed to work for Alex pro bono – i.e. for free – explained that financial assets are one thing, but human beings – especially youngsters, many of whom were physically incapable of signing their names – are quite another. There would need to be a transparent and permanent agreement, perhaps like the articles of association that companies have, overseen by what amounts to a board of trustees, again a bit like company directors. Alex loved the idea.

'Philip told me, "You need to get some trustees together." So I thought about the people who know my children very well and would like our family to carry on as long as possible. I asked all the parents. Andrew's mum and dad were "too nervous", which was a pity because they would've been great. Sue immediately said yes, and Thomas's mum said yes without thinking about it.

'Then I approached other people. Janet Pardoe, she's the ex-headmistress of my special needs school and Nathan's godmother. I've known her for over twenty-five years and she's got a lot of connections. Then my friend Alison, she's a foster carer for Manchester and she used to be Matthew's nursery carer. Then Jane, my cousin, who's a social worker – Jane will be the legal guardian of any children under 18, that's already been decided. Finally, to keep the minutes when we have a meeting, there's Jill, who is not a trustee. She's PA to a top person at Manchester University and she volunteered to do all the paperwork.'

They meet once a year – around the wooden kitchen table, of course – seven capable women with the purpose of ensuring and protecting a family of eight, with Jill keeping the minutes. It has the character of a parish council meeting, with a printed agenda, and the discussion is well informed and professional. It ranges from the banal, the redecoration of the playroom, to the sophisticated details of Emily's treatment, and to the downright ambitious – the launching of a half million pound charity to build a new respite home for Down's adults. Alex had found a piece of land, and the members of the trust were to go off and inspect it for a respite home.

'Respite' is very much an Alex word – Sue once said, 'The letters R-E-S-P-I-T-E are etched on Alex's heart' – certainly she is highly committed to raising the funds to build a respite home.

For families who look after the long-term disabled, respite is a crucial breathing space. It allows family carers to go on holiday, have a relaxing weekend on their own, or just take a day off. Remarkably, many parents or brothers and sisters who valiantly care for Down's syndrome or autistic relatives have virtually no support. Perhaps a social worker will pop by from time to time, but families are usually expected to just get on with disrupted lives on their own, 365 days a year.

Hence, respite is very low on the government's list of priorities, partly because they know that caring families are trapped. Trapped by their sense of duty towards those who they love. The government understands that families, once they've accepted responsibility, rarely walk away, no matter how exhausted or disillusioned they become. We might call that scandalous – the government would call it pragmatic in the face of scarce resources – but everyone agrees that there's a desperate, and increasing, shortage of quality respite care available.

The Director of Social Services for Salford, Anne Williams, was delighted when Alex and the Woodland Trust announced their plan to launch an appeal for a respite home in the borough. The vision is a bold one, because it has to be. Up to now, the respite care that has been available is dowdy and institutionalised, often converted town houses with draconian rules and fire regulations, that are dominated by a big square sitting room with high ceilings, where the heating is tropical, and the residents are expected only to eat and watch television, before being shunted off to regimented bedrooms as early as decently possible. Nevertheless, they are full – such is the need for respite, although according to Anne Williams families often return prematurely and distressed.

'If the place is miserable, they can't enjoy their own holidays because of feeling guilty about leaving their disabled son or whatever behind. They care too much, how could they have a good time? Some will, literally, come back after two days. So apart from needing much more respite, we need exciting, enjoyable, happy places, and we need them now.'

So that is Alex's plan. Initially to begin raising money and locating a small parcel of land, big enough for a large eight-bedroom house, ideally near a park or green space in Salford, perhaps even a farm. Once underway, a scheme can be designed to build and maintain a respite home for 'medium needs' adults, people like Adrian, Thomas, Nathan or Chloe. It should have all the latest high-tech equipment and entertainment systems – it should truly be a place of fun, so that parent carers can go on holiday feeling happy.

Alex is not daunted by the challenge, or the endless forms to fill in, or the meetings, or the prospect of raising £500,000. It's urgently needed for families who deserve to be supported – that's the end of the argument to her.

'My mum used to say, "You'll get enough rest in your coffin." As long as the kids are all right, this is the kind of thing to live for. I'll tell you something else. We can do it. Because we have to.'

As she looks ahead at the next ten years, then beyond that, heading towards 70, and beyond that, Alex knows that she can never rest – not that she would ever want to – because she will never be able to stop being a parent to her family, no matter how old her 'children' are. Though she pretends to take life day by day, booklets and application forms gather on the far end of her kitchen surface – Alex's adult parenting survival pile.

At present, special needs adults are abandoned by our institutions when they leave college in their early 20s; they plunge into a void of meaningless tasks, at the mercy of whatever their parents can 'grub up' on their behalf, or hear about while hanging around the local library. These are usually 'courses' in things like artwork, dance and music, though the emphasis is not on learning, it's on passing time in a day centre, so that their parents – who are not accustomed to having them at home all day – can continue to function.

Having found Matthew three part-time jobs through persistence and contacts, Alex knows that the parents of special needs children get very little help, and being Alex she wants to put that right. This is not only about information, it's about creating possibilities that will help provide fulfilling and useful roles in life for those who are not able to find them on their own.

So another Alex plan is to create a special needs training unit, which would start by teaching Down's people how to carry out various routine, learnable tasks, and then gradually begin to provide those tasks – as proper useful work – to organisations and customers who would pay modestly for it. She'd like to establish a training unit with up to five groups of young people with disabilities, in little gangs for various things.

A gardening gang, a DIY gang, a shopping crew and a pet care gang, looked after by a mentor who has the skill in an area that they want to pass on to these young people.

The shopping gang could go shopping for old people who are housebound, with pictures on the shopping list if they couldn't read. The DIY gang could do house repairs for OAPs. The gardening gang could mow the grass for people who are housebound. And the pet gang could walk dogs for people who can't walk them.

Alex has got it all worked out in her head – including their outfits.

'I can see it now, in different colours – the gardening gang in green boiler suits, with their names on so that they know that that's their uniform. The DIY crew in blue. The shopping crew in maroon red. And the dog-walking gang in yellow. And, when they're all together they will form a rainbow, which brings in our corporate image. A rainbow.'

This kind of scheme works well in other countries, with social services helping local groups organise the work gangs, who are also giving something back to the community while they're being trained, so the community will pay, usually only small amounts of money, for their services. Adrian and Matthew and Thomas would all be candidates, Nathan, too, with Chloe in the shopping gang or the dog-walking gang.

Alex sees the day when the scheme could be training twenty to twenty-five young people with learning disabilities on a permanent basis.

'At the moment there's nothing else out there except meaningless stuff and hanging around in day centres; it will give them focus, that feeling of work, a sense of purpose – and that's something we all need.'

Which is probably what Alex needed, too, all those years ago, when she began to assemble one of Britain's strangest but most inspiring families – a sense of purpose. It's what families provide, and these days it's hard to see them any other way, except as the Family Bell. An oddball collection of interdependent characters who move as a family, who think as a family, and who play and bicker and love as a family. A family that, for all its obvious physical and psychological problems, works very well, better than most. Indeed, a family that should be dysfunctional, functions perfectly.

Epilogue:
The Bells are ringing ...

During the twenty-something years since Matthew arrived and the family began, a huge number of people have believed, have given a part of themselves, have taken risks, stayed up all night, helped, or simply smiled with encouragement – which is what it takes. Alex could not have done it alone, and in that multitude of mostly anonymous people who have provided their time, or just their faith, none is more important than Louise.

Louise isn't just Alex's right-hand helper, she's part of the family, an oldest, biggest, grown-up daughter-cum-sister. Alex and Louise know how each other thinks, and though the relationship is also professional, Louise has invested her heart in the family. No surprise, then, that they were top of the invitation list to her party to celebrate the wedding to her long-term partner Nick on 9 September 2006.

The Bell family had been excited all day, even the big kids like Matthew and Adrian. Most had special outfits, some bought for the evening. Thomas had a new shirt and tie that his birth mum, Pat, had sent. The girls swirled around the playroom like Julie Andrews, in apricot dresses purchased specially from Marks & Spencer. Nathan had a blue and grey sweatshirt from Asda.

Adrian and Matthew wore matching black-and-white shirts. And Andrew shone in a brand new blue-and-white striped top, with 'Funky little dude' printed on it.

At half past seven they were ready, and on a warm September evening, Alex and Angela packed them in the larger of her minibuses and trundled off to the seventeenth-century Smithill Coaching House, a glooming black-and-white country mansion on the edge of Bolton.

When the family Bell arrived, the guests were mingling in tuxedos and ball gowns, politely waiting for the festivities to start – but the kids are nothing if not forward, wandering in, hearing the music, heading straight to the dance floor before finding a table, and starting the party on their own. The small talk stopped, the room turned to watch, the disc jockey raised his eyebrows – as the dancing began.

There was not a smidgen of self-consciousness or restraint as the Bell family gave it everything they'd got, dancing with each other, and with anyone who passed by, especially Louise. Nathan was a surprisingly cool mover; he jerked to the music like Michael Jackson on steroids, fortunately without pointing to his groin. Adrian only moved from the waist up, dancing with his lips and eyebrows while facing the wall. Chloe hadn't quite worked it out and rushed round and round in circles, as Matthew sort of groaned from his abdomen, occasionally shifting weight from one foot to the other along with the even more occasional wave of a hand.

Meanwhile, Simon clapped and clapped and clapped from his spinning wheelchair, as Emily flirted from person to person, holding them close, even to heavy-beating rock music, men and women alike. Tom is a swayer, more backwards and forwards than side to side, and hadn't worked out that you stop when the music stops. But the star of the show was Andrew. Strapped into his chair, his unseeing eyes came alive while his mobile face moved with every beat and harmony; he seemed to be swallowing the sounds, devouring the music deep inside, in a way that his wrecked and wracked digestive system can't manage with food.

For a minute or two, the other guests gaped with affectionate amazement, but then they left their drinks and took to the floor: such is their capacity to get a joint jumping, Alex has considered hiring the Bell family out as a party-starting ensemble.

Later, Matthew read a poem and led a toast to Louise and Nick 'who we love the most', while Alex gathered up sweaters, a handbag and a strangely discarded shoe, because it was time to leave, Chloe clingy as she said 'Bye-ya' to Louise for two whole weeks, Louise replying, 'Just go, yer daft beggar.'

Alex Bell – 'just this person who mends children'

Driving the family home, over the screeches and cackles and even someone snoring, Alex was talkative, it was that time of night, and that kind of day, a day for looking forward and looking back, a realising that Louise will start her own family soon, of taking stock of the sacrifices Alex has chosen to make.

'This is year 21, and I still *love* it. I couldn't have got married and been ordinary, not that I'm saying Louise is ordinary, but I always thought adoption is a bit like a marriage because you have to put in a lot of hard work and commitment – which is why I can't get married, I've committed myself in other ways. When you do, you get so much back, even though it's draining. I mean Louise getting married is a bit like me taking on another child – don't tell Nick I said that …'

Getting her children out of the minibus and into the house is a routine operation. With Angela to help it only took ten minutes, and then via extensive tooth-brushing into bed. Each has their own colour toothbrush, otherwise they get lost. Simon is yellow, because he's Alex's sunshine boy, Matthew black, because he's moody, Adrian red, because he makes her angry, Nathan is green, because he's the green monster …

Alex put on the kettle, paid Angela, and took her usual position, leaning against the work-surface, letting the day, another long day, wind out of her.

'Maybe I am getting more tired the older I get, but I'm thriving on what I do – I mean most people of my age are into grand-children. That could never be me.'

Grandchildren. One thing Alex can't have, says she wouldn't want them anyway, but when Louise brings a baby to work, we'll see. Another of the many contradictions of Alex, that go right back to the beginning, to Billy, the hulking Down's syndrome man-child who lunged at her forty years ago.

The kettle boils, she makes tea, always her moment to become philosophical.

'I think this book should be dedicated to Billy, whether he's alive or not. I think it should be, "To Billy, who touched my soul". Because without meeting him I'd have been married to a busi-nessman with 2.4 children and a nanny, or some awful thing like that. It wouldn't have made me happy. I think I'm really fortu-nate.

'The day I met Billy was my pathway to a different world. I was taken away from the world of private schools and bankers and au pairs and swimming pools and all that horri-ble stuff, and headed into the road of nit lotion and Disability Living Allowances and nappies. I do about a hundred nappies a week – there are probably houses built on our nappies, some-where.

'But it's fine for me, proving myself constantly to people, and fighting to get out of bed at five o'clock in the morning. That was much better, a much better pathway.

'I'm poor but I've got focus, and I've achieved wonderful things. I've changed society's viewpoints. I've made life better for nine individual people and countless other people. I've changed minds – including yours. I've saved Sue, and Jill, and Patricia. I've pushed boundaries, I've challenged authority, and I still carry on doing that and I love it. And I don't care that there will never be a statue to me. I'm not doing it to be remembered. I do it because it needs doing. It's just that some people sit back and think, "Well, if I can't change anything, I won't bother trying." But nothing is changed until one little person does something. In my little bit of the world, that's what I do and that's a wonderful thing to be able to do. I love it. Every second of it.'

Louise was off to Egypt for her honeymoon, Angela had gone home, Alex was alone at her kitchen table, the house was quiet.

'Mum-ee.'

A muted cry carried in from one of the bedrooms.

'Mum-ee.'

Alex stood up, began rinsing our cups in the sink. 'Social services say it cannot work. But it does – because I'm a mum. As a mum I can manage nine very difficult children, because I do everything. I'm a therapist, I'm a teacher, I'm a nurse, I'm a social worker – I'm all those things, but first of all, I'm a mum. So I can give twenty-four hours, which social workers can't do. And it's all-consuming, you are giving everything, there is no me. I don't mean that in a ter-rible way, but what I'm doing is total care, there is no room for me any more, there is just this person who mends children.'

'Mum-ee …'

Enough of talking. She was needed. Which is how she likes it.

'Coming, love.'

And with that, she was off.